Litigating Psychiatric Injury Claims

Litigating Psychiatric Injury Claims

Editors
David Marshall
Anthony Gold, Solicitors

Jenny Kennedy
LLB (Hons)
Anthony Gold, Solicitors

Rehana Azib
Barrister

Bloomsbury Professional

Bloomsbury Professional Ltd, Maxwelton House, 41–43 Boltro Road, Haywards Heath, West Sussex, RH16 1BJ

© Bloomsbury Professional Ltd 2012

Bloomsbury Professional Ltd is an imprint of Bloomsbury Publishing plc

All rights reserved. No part of this publication may be reproduced in any material form (including photocopying or storing it in any medium by electronic means and whether or not transiently or incidentally to some other use of this publication) without the written permission of the copyright owner except in accordance with the provisions of the Copyright, Designs and Patents Act 1988 or under the terms of a licence issued by the Copyright Licensing Agency Ltd, Saffron House, 6–10 Kirby St, London, England EC1N 8TS. Applications for the copyright owner's written permission to reproduce any part of this publication should be addressed to the publisher.

Warning: The doing of an unauthorised act in relation to a copyright work may result in both a civil claim for damages and criminal prosecution.

Crown copyright material is reproduced with the permission of the Controller of HMSO and the Queen's Printer for Scotland. Any European material in this work which has been reproduced from EUR-lex, the official European Communities legislation website, is European Communities copyright.

A CIP Catalogue record for this book is available from the British Library.

ISBN   978 1 84592 113 2

Typeset by Phoenix Photosetting, Chatham, Kent
Printed and bound in Great Britain by CPI Group (UK) Ltd, Croydon CR0 4YY

Foreword

A book that helps in the litigation of psychiatric injury claims has long been necessary. This book fulfils that need with its successful alignment of learning, experience and utility.

This area of personal injury claims has developed significantly in modern times. This work covers all legal aspects of such claims including the future outlook.

The essential principles of liability and compensation provide the framework within which lawyers must consider the merits of a claim. From *McLoughlin v O'Brian* to *Hatton v Sutherland* the House of Lords have reviewed and developed the judicial exposition of the law on psychiatric injury. This is dealt with succinctly and helpfully.

The differences between primary and secondary victims and the right of recovery are often difficult to resolve particularly as the factors affecting them are based on policy rather than principle. This rightly receives considerable and careful attention.

It has to be remembered that the law does allow recovery for all victims who have suffered mental injury from intentional torts because foreseeability is not required. So such liability deserves its place in the overall analysis.

Litigators have to understand the basic medicine of psychiatric injury. Knowledge of the standard works of definition and categories is indispensable. Therefore DVM IV and ICD 10 and their application are considered along with the medical background and problems of diagnosis.

The well known decision of *Hinz v Berry* in 1970 set a humane and sensible path for compensation in these cases—humane through the remarkable judgement of Lord Denning, and sensible in treating such injury as properly deserving reasonable compensation just as with physical injury. Thus the section on compensation is so important.

Being equipped with the legal foundations is the right approach but experience of the practical steps in assessing and pursuing these claims is vital and is well dealt with.

What of the future? The government consultation and response following the Law Commission Report on psychiatric injury leaves this area in the hands of the courts and lawyers for its further development.

In such circumstances this book will be part of the thinking and preparation of all involved—lawyers, judges and those involved in diagnosing and treating cases of psychiatric injury.

All the contributors to this work are very experienced and competent. Let us be grateful to them for this excellent work.

Lord Brennan QC

Preface

We aim in this book to provide practitioners with an essential practical guide to handling the complex issues arising from psychiatric injury claims.

Such cases are technically challenging with regard to establishing liability and causation. They are also demanding, with often difficult clients who may lack insight into the nature of their injury. Claims are often controversial, with many people seeing psychiatric injury as in some way qualitatively different to physical injury and less deserving of compensation. They are, however, also very rewarding when successfully concluded for clients who had often lost all hope that anyone would listen, let alone enable them to recover compensation for what has happened to them.

We look at the problematic history of compensation for psychiatric injury and aim to provide an essential route map through the 'patchwork quilt' of the current law. Chapters on liability deal with primary victims in 'shock' cases and in 'non-shock' cases (including stress at work), secondary victims and the victims of intentional acts, including statutory discrimination. We also look at compensation recoverable for the injury, including the complex issues of causation that often arise. We also set out the practical steps that need to be taken when handling instructions in such claims.

Specialist chapters have also been contributed by Dr Martin Baggeley on the medical aspects of the illness and by District Judge Elizabeth Batten on mental capacity. The authors would also particularly like to thank Caroline Bourke, solicitor at Anthony Gold, for her assistance.

The government have said they will not be taking forward in legislation any of the various recommendations of the Law Commission from their series of reports on personal injury, so it now seems certain that the Law Commission's recommendations on reform of the law of psychiatric injury from as long ago as 1998 will never be implemented. However, the Law Commission never sought to codify the common law, but to simply correct by legislation the 'wrong turn' it felt had been taken by the House of Lords. The common law will, however, continue to develop. To that extent it is necessary for practitioners to appreciate both the current limitations on claims and also the extent to which these might be open to change in appropriate cases in the future.

We thank our colleagues, at Anthony Gold Solicitors and at 2 Temple Garden respectively, but any errors remain the responsibility of the authors.

The law is stated as at 31 August 2011.

David Marshall and Jenny Kennedy

Anthony Gold Solicitors
The Counting House
53 Tooley Street
London SE1 9TY
020 7940 4000
www.anthonygold.co.uk

Rehana Azib

2 Temple Gardens
London EC4Y 9AY

020 7822 1200
www.2tg.co.uk

About the authors

David Marshall is a solicitor and partner with Anthony Gold Solicitors. He specialises in personal injury and employment law and has a particular expertise in claims for compensation for stress at work. He is recommended for personal injury work by both *Chambers* and *Legal 500*. He is a former president of the Association of Personal Injury Lawyers. He is the author of *Compensation for Stress at Work* (Jordans, 2009) and is Joint General Editor and a contributor to the *APIL Jordans Personal Injury Law, Practice and Precedents* looseleaf. He regularly lectures and blogs on personal injury law and practice.

Jenny Kennedy is a solicitor and partner in the Personal Injury and Clinical Negligence departments of Anthony Gold Solicitors. She is a former psychiatric nurse (RMN) and specialises in complex and serious injury claims. She is a member of the Association of Personal Injury Lawyers and both the Law Society's Personal Injury and Clinical Negligence Panels. She is on the joint editorial board of *Kemp & Kemp Personal Injury Law, Practice and Procedure* and is also a co-ordinator of *Personal Injury Practice*, published by Butterworths, and a regular lecturer on personal injury law and practice.

Rehana Azib is a barrister at 2 Temple Gardens, practising in personal injury and employment law with a particular emphasis on occupational stress, harassment and discrimination claims. She is recommended as a leading junior in the *Legal 500* for 2010 and 2011. She regularly writes articles for the New Law Journal and delivers seminars nationally on personal injury and employment issues. Rehana was awarded Young Achiever of the Year at the National Asian Women of Achievement Awards in 2009, has been a guest speaker on BBC World Radio on equality issues and is Patron of the International Law Firm Bird and Bird's Bursary Foundation. Prior to being called to the Bar, Rehana worked as a mental health advocate and trainer (focusing on ethnic minority issues) for a mental health charity.

Contents

Foreword	v
Preface	vii
About the Authors	ix
Table of Statutes	xvii
Table of Statutory Instruments	xix
Table of Cases	xxi

1 Liability and compensation for psychiatric injury: an overview — 1
  1 What is psychiatric injury? — 1
  2 A brief history — 8
  3 Why is psychiatric injury so controversial? — 12
  4 Causes of action — 15
      A Negligence — 15
      B Claims in contract — 17
      C Claims for psychiatric injury from other torts — 18
      D Criminal Injuries Compensation — 20
  5 Summary — 20

2 Primary victims of negligence: shock cases — 22
  1 Primary victims — 22
  2 Direct participants in events which also cause or risk physical injury to the victim — 22
      A Psychiatric injury associated with significant physical injury — 22
      B Soft-tissue injury and depression — 23
      C Brain injury and 'personality change' — 24
      D Serious psychiatric injury associated with minor physical injury — 25
      E Delayed onset of severe psychiatric injury accompanying physical injury — 26
  3 'Pure' psychiatric injury arising from an accident where physical injury to the claimant was foreseeable — 27
  4 'Pure' psychiatric injury with no physical injury and no shocking event — 35
  5 Rescuers — 36
  6 Other 'involuntary participants' — 40
  7 'Primary victims' in 'shock cases' — 45

3 Primary victims of negligence: non-shock cases — 46
  1 Introduction — 46
  2 Employer's liability: stress at work — 47
      A Breach of duty — 47
  3 Non-employer's liability — 58

4 Secondary victims of negligence — 60
  1 Secondary victims — 60
  2 The Hillsborough disaster — 60

xii *Contents*

		3	'Secondary victims'	62
		4	Reasonable foreseeability	65
			A 'Normal phlegm'	67
			B 'Eggshell personality'	67
			C 'Hindsight'	67
			D The requirement for 'shock'	68
			E Close ties of love and affection	70
			F Proximity in time and space	73
			G Means by which events are perceived	74
		5	Excluded categories of secondary victim	76
			A Self-harm by defendant	76
			B Recipients of news	77
		6	What did the Law Commission propose and was it necessary?	77
		7	Subsequent case law	79
			A Interpretation of proximity	79
			B Sudden, shocking event	80
			C Means of perception: broadcasters	80
			D Liability of primary victims to secondary victims	81
		8	Secondary victims—a summary	82
			A Distinction between primary and secondary victims	82
			B Reasonable foreseeability	82
			C Controls	82
			D The future	83
5	**Intentional acts and other liability**			**84**
	1	Assault and battery		84
		A Battery		84
		B Assault		84
		C Intentional infliction of harm		85
		D Criminal injures		86
		E Contract		88
	2	Statutory harassment		89
		A Potential defendants		90
		B Meaning of harassment		91
		C Harassment outside the workplace		95
		D Checklist for harassment claims under the PHA 1997		96
	3	Statutory discrimination		97
		A Protected characteristics		97
		B Disability and psychiatric injury		99
		C Direct discrimination		100
		D Indirect discrimination		100
		E Discrimination arising from a disability		101
		F Perceived and association discrimination		101
		G Practical considerations in a disability discrimination claim		101
		H Damages generally		103
		I Injury to feelings		103
		J Psychiatric injury		104
6	**The illness**			**105**
	1	Recognised psychiatric conditions, and diagnosis		105
	2	Types of injury		106
		A Post-traumatic stress disorder		106

		B	Anxieties and phobias	109
		C	Depression	110
		D	Adjustment disorders	112
		E	Somatisation and somatoform disorders	112
		F	Chronic pain	114
		G	Exacerbation of existing conditions (eg psychosis or bipolar disorder)	115
		H	Psychotic disorders	116
		I	Alcohol and substance misuse problems	117
	3		Head injuries—overlap with structural brain injury	118
	4		Whiplash etc—overlap with physical injury	118
	5		Pre-existing vulnerability	119
	6		Psychiatric treatments	120
	7		Children	121
	8		Psychiatric experts	122
		A	Psychiatrists and psychologists	122
		B	Psychometric tests	123
		C	Understanding medical notes and reports	124
		D	Miscellaneous difficulties with obtaining a psychiatric report	125
7	**Compensation**			**127**
	1		Background	127
	2		General damages: pain, suffering and loss of amenity (PSLA)	129
		A	General psychiatric damage	131
		B	Post-traumatic stress disorder	135
		C	Problematic medical/psychological conditions	136
	3		CICA and the tariff scheme	138
	4		Special damages	139
		A	Case managers/carers/buddies	140
		B	Short-term treatment interventions	142
	5		Practical effect on financial loss claims	143
			Mitigation	143
	6		Provisional damages	144
	7		Causation of damage: material contribution, apportionment and acceleration	145
		A	Material contribution	146
		B	Apportionment	146
		C	Acceleration	148
		D	Summary of causation of damage issues in psychiatric injury claims	149
8	**Practical steps**			**151**
	1		Instructions: identifying potential psychiatric injury	151
	2		Reviewing past medical history	153
			What records	154
	3		Building a team	156
		A	Counsel	157
		B	The client and their family as part of the team	158
		C	Legal expense insurers	159
	4		Choosing and instructing experts	159
		A	Which expert	160

	5	Handling the client	161
		A Difficult clients	161
		B Capacity	162
		C Mental Capacity Act	162
		D Coming off the record	163
	6	Rehabilitation	164
		A Case management outside of the Rehabilitation Code	166
		B Psychiatric rehabilitation facilities	166
		C Counselling and general psychiatric outpatient sessions	167
		D In-patient psychiatric care	167
	7	Attitudes of defendants: malingering, fraud and exaggeration	167
		A Malingering	169
		B How to detect malingering, fraud and exaggeration	170
	8	Costs and retainer issues	170
9	**The Mental Capacity Act 2005**		**174**
	1	Historical perspective	174
	2	The new legislation	175
	3	The Court of Protection	175
	4	The principles of the Mental Capacity Act 2005	176
		A Presumption of capacity	176
		B Practical steps to help P make the decision for himself	177
		C Unwise decisions	177
		D Best interests	177
		E Least restrictive option	178
	5	People who lack capacity	178
	6	Inability to make a decision	178
		A 'To understand the information relevant to the decision'	179
		B 'To retain that information'	179
		C 'To use or weigh that information as part of the process of making the decision'	179
		D 'To communicate his decision (whether by talking, using sign language or any other means'	180
	7	Passing the test for incapacity	180
	8	Best interests checklist	180
	9	Children who lack capacity	183
	10	Acts in connection with care or treatment	183
		A Powers of the court	184
		B Litigation capacity	185
	11	Managing property and affairs	186
	12	Making an application to the Court of Protection	188
		A Application for property and affairs deputyship	189
		B Application for personal welfare deputyship	191
		C Personal welfare decisions	191
		D Contested applications	192
	13	Costs	192
10	**The future**		**194**
	1	The Law Commission report	194
	2	The Australian experience	196
	3	The insurers	197
	4	Alternatives proposed for the United Kingdom	198

5		Possible future developments	199
	A	'Recognised psychiatric injury'	200
	B	The Page v Smith controversy	201
	C	Rescuers	201
	D	The requirement of foreseeability of psychiatric injury in stress at work cases	202
	E	Secondary victims' proximity: close ties of love and affection	203
	F	Secondary victims' proximity: 'shock' and space and time	203
	G	Secondary victims' proximity: means of perception	204
	H	Divisible/indivisible injury	204
6		Conclusion	205

Index   **207**

Table of Statutes

Administration of Justice Act 1982..	4.34
Civil Liability (Contribution) Act 1978	7.87
Disability Discrimination Act 1995	3.10; 5.44
s 4A(1)	3.11
18(2)	5.46
Sch 1	
para 4(1)	5.47
Employers' Liability (Compulsory Insurance) Act 1969	3.5
Enduring Powers of Attorney Act 1985	9.3, 9.7
Equality Act 2010	3.10, 3.14; 5.43, 5.44, 5.45, 5.47, 5.48, 5.55, 5.57, 5.61
s 10	5.44
13	5.49
14	5.43
15	5.54
(2)	5.54
29	5.45
119(2), (2)	5.64
123(1)	5.58
124	5.64
136	5.49, 5.53
Sch 1	5.44
Law Reform (Contributory Negligence) Act 1945	5.20
s 1	2.12
Law Reform (Personal Injuries) Act 1948	
s 2(4)	7.76
Limitation Act 1980	
s 11A	5.24
33	5.24, 5.59
(3)	5.59
38(1)	1.2

Mental Capacity Act 2005	8.51, 8.58, 8.62; 9.1, 9.2, 9.7, 9.8, 9.11, 9.12, 9.13, 9.14, 9.18, 9.37, 9.42, 9.47, 9.49, 9.58, 9.59, 9.60, 9.61, 9.62, 9.74
s 1	9.14, 9.61
(1)	9.2
(3)	9.32
2	9.25, 9.61
(1)	9.22
(2)	9.23
(3)	9.24, 9.39
(4)	9.34
(5)	9.47
(6)	9.48
3	9.61
(1)	9.25
(2)	9.27, 9.29, 9.39
(4)	9.26
4	9.38
(1), (3)	9.39
(6)	9.40
(7)	9.43
(8)	9.44
(9)	9.45
5	9.49
(1)–(3)	9.50
6	9.49, 9.51
(1)–(4), (6), (7)	9.51
15	9.52, 9.62
16	9.53, 9.62
(4)	9.54
18	9.68
(1)	9.48
(k)	9.62
(2)	9.48
(3)	9.48, 9.67
19	9.71
(1)(b)	9.71
(9)	9.72
42	9.9
47(1)	9.12
48	9.15
50(1)	9.89

xvii

Mental Capacity Act 2005 – *contd*
Sch 2.. 9.70
Sch 6
  para 43...................................... 9.12
Mental Health Act 1959
  Pt VIII (ss 100–121)..................... 9.3
Mental Health Act 1983............. 6.99; 7.69;
                                    8.77, 8.80
  s 12(2) 6.99
  Pt VII (ss 93–113)....................... 9.3, 9.58

Protection from Harassment Act
  1997............................ 1.17, 1.53; 3.12,
                         3.13; 5.4, 5.11, 5.24,
                         5.25, 5.26, 5.32, 5.33,
                         5.34, 5.38, 5.42; 1032
  s 1 .... 5.23
    (1) 5.23

Protection from Harassment Act
  1997 – *contd*
  s 2.. 5.31, 5.40
  3 .... 5.40
    (1) 5.23
    (2) 5.24
  6... 5.24
  7(2) 5.27
    (3) 5.28
    (4) 5.27

Race Relations Act 1976.................. 2.13
  s 56.. 1.52
Senior Courts Act 1981
  s 32A 7.78
Trustee Act 1925 .... 9.4

Table of Statutory Instruments

Civil Procedure (Amendment) Rules 2007, SI 2007/2204 .... 9.59
Civil Procedure Rules 1998, SI 1998/3132 .... 9.5, 9.8
   r 16.5 .... 8.92
   Pt 21 (rr 21.1–21.13) 9.58, 9.59
   r 21.4(1) 9.63
   21.5 .... 9.62
   21.6, 21.7 .... 9.63
   32.14 .... 8.90
   44.5 .... 8.104
Court of Protection Rules 2007, SI 2007/1744 .... 9.8, 9.95
   Pt 7 (rr 40–49) 9.79
   Pt 19 (rr 155–168) 9.98
   r 49 .... 9.79
   51, 52 .... 9.90

Court of Protection Rules 2007, SI 2007/1744 – *contd*
   89 .... 9.95
   156 .... 9.100, 9.102
   157 .... 9.100, 9.102
   158 .... 9.101, 9.102
   159 .... 9.102
Family Procedure Rules 2010, SI 2010/2955 .... 9.8
Lasting Powers of Attorney, Enduring Powers of Attorney and Public Guardian Regulations 2007, SI 2007/1253 .... 9.10
Management of Health and Safety at Work Regulations 1999, SI 1999/3242 .... 10.32
   reg 3 .... 3.10

Table of Cases

A

AB v Tameside and Glossop Health Authority [1997] 8 Med LR 91, CA 4.54
Alcock v Chief Constable of South Yorkshire [1992] 1 AC 310, [1991] 3 WLR 1057, [1991] 4 All ER 907... 1.25, 1.46, 1.56; 2.1, 2.20, 2.44, 2.45, 2.51, 2.54; 4.1, 4.2, 4.3, 4.4, 4.5, 4.6, 4.8, 4.9, 4.10, 4.11, 4.15, 4.17, 4.18, 4.19, 4.20, 4.28, 4.29, 4.30, 4.31, 4.33, 4.34, 4.35, 4.36, 4.37, 4.40, 4.41, 4.45 4.46, 4.47, 4.49, 4.50, 4.51, 4.53, 4.54, 4.55, 4.60, 4.63, 4.66, 4.68, 4.69; 7.4; 10.1, 10.6, 10.10, 10.20, 10.21, 10.22, 10.30, 10.34, 10.35, 10.38, 10.39, 10.40, 10.42
Al-Kandari v Brown [1988] QB 665, [1988] 2 WLR 671, [1988] 1 All ER 833 .... 3.22
Allen v London Borough of Southwark [2008] EWCA Civ 1478 .... 5.38
Armitage, Marsden & HM Prison Service v Johnson [1997] ICR 275, [1997] IRLR 162.. 5.65
Attia v British Gas plc [1988] QB 304, [1987] 3 WLR 1101, [1987] 3 All ER 455 ..... 1.24; 3.19

B

BJM v Eyre [2010] EWHC 2856 (QB).. 7.25
Bailey v Ministry of Defence [2008] EWCA Civ 883, [2009] 1 WLR 1052, [2008] LS Law Medical 481 .... 7.88
Barber v Somerset County Council [2004] UKHL 13, [2004] 1 WLR 1089, [2004] ICR 457 .... 2.24; 3.9; 7.90; 10.31
Barker v Corus UK Ltd [2006] UKHL 20, [2006] 2 AC 572, [2006] 2 WLR 1027...... 3.10
Bonnington Castings Ltd v Wardlaw [1956] AC 613, [1956] 2 WLR 707, [1956] 1 All ER 615 .... 2.11; 7.85
Bourhill v Young [1943] AC 92, [1942] 2 All ER 396, 1942 SC (HL) 78 .... 1.4, 1.21, 1.22, 1.25; 2.20; 3.22; 4.50
Brice v Brown [1984] 1 All ER 997, (1984) 134 NLJ 204.. 1.9
Bucanan v Broadleigh Developments Ltd (unreported, 8 July 2004).......................... 7.38
Butchart v Home Office [2006] EWCA Civ 239, [2006] 1 WLR 1155, [2007] Prison LR 99 .... 3.23

C

Caparo Industries plc v Dickman [1990] 2 AC 605, [1990] 2 WLR 358, [1990] 1 All ER 568 .... 1.39
Chadwick v British Transport Commission [1967] 1 WLR 912, [1967] 2 All ER 945, (1967) 111 SJ 562 .... 2.43, 2.47; 4.32
Chohan v Derby Law Centre [2004] IRLR 685... 5.59
Church v Ministry of Defence (1984) 134 NLJ 623... 3.16
Clark v Tull (t/a Ardington Electrical Services) [2003] UKHL 64, [2004] 1 AC 1067, [2003] 3 WLR 1571 .... 7.75
Collins v Wilcock [1984] 1 WLR 1172, [1984] 3 All ER 374, (1984) 79 Cr App R 229.... 5.2

xxii *Table of Cases*

Conn v Sunderland City Council [2007] EWCA Civ 1492, [2008] IRLR 324 .... 5.33
Cook v Sherwood [2006] CLY 3086 .... 7.34
Corr v IBC Vehicles Ltd [2008] UKHL 13, [2008] 1 AC 884, [2008] 2 WLR 499....... 2.12, 2.13, 2.34
Cox v Philips Industries Ltd [1976] 1 WLR 638, [1976] 3 All ER 161, [1976] ICR 138.. 1.48
Croft v Broadstairs & St Peter's Town Council [2003] EWCA Civ 676.................... 3.10
Cullin v London Fire & Civil Defence Authority [1999] PIQR P314........................ 2.53

D

Da'Bell v National Society for the Prevention of Cruelty to Children (NSPCC) [2010] IRLR 19 .... 5.66
Darg v Comr of Police for the Metropolis [2009] EWHC 684 (QB) 7.48
Daw v Intel Corpn (UK) Ltd [2007] EWCA Civ 70, [2007] 2 All ER 126, [2007] ICR 1318... 3.10
Dickens v O2 plc [2008] EWCA Civ 1144, [2009] IRLR 58, (2008) 105(41) LSG 91 .... 3.10; 7.89, 7.95, 7.97; 10.32, 10.44
Dodworth v Burford (1670) 1 Mod 29 .... 5.2
Donachie v Chief Constable of Greater Manchester [2004] EWCA Civ 405, [2004] Po LR 204, (2004) 148 SJLB 509.. 2.24, 2.25; 3.10
Donoghue v Stevenson [1932] AC 562, 1932 SC (HL) 31, 1932 SLT 31 .... 1.36, 1.37; 4.19
Dooley v Cammell Laird & Co Ltd [1951] 1 Lloyd's Rep 271.................................. 2.57; 4.32
Dowson v Chief Constable of Northumbria [2010] EWHC 2612 (QB)...................... 5.36
Dulieu v White & Sons [1901] 2 KB 669.. 1.3, 1.20
Dunnachie v Kingston-upon-Hull City Council [2004] UKHL 36, [2005] 1 AC 226, [2004] 3 WLR 310 .... 3.14

E

Eastwood v Magnox Electric plc [2004] UKHL 35, [2005] 1 AC 503, [2004] 3 WLR 322... 3.15
Edwards v Martin [2010] EWHC 570 (QB).. 2.8
Environment Agency v Ellis [2008] EWCA Civ 1117, [2009] PIQR P5, [2009] LS Law Medical 70 .... 7.92
Essa v Laing [2004] EWCA Civ 2, [2004] ICR 746, [2004] IRLR 313................ 1.52; 5.68
Evason v Essex Health Authority 8.106, 8.107

F

F v West Berkshire Health Authority [1990] 2 AC 1, [1989] 2 WLR 1025, [1989] 2 All ER 545 .... 5.3
F (a child) v Virgin Holidays (unreported, 20 August 2010) 7.30
Fairchild v Glenhaven Funeral Services Ltd (t/a GH Dovener & Son) [2002] UKHL 22, [2003] 1 AC 32, [2002] 3 WLR 89 .... 7.84
Farley v Skinner (No 2) [2001] UKHL 49, [2002] 2 AC 732, [2001] 3 WLR 899 ...... 1.48
Ferguson v British Gas Trading Ltd [2009] EWCA Civ 46, [2010] 1 WLR 785, [2009] 3 All ER 304... 5.39
Forsikringsaktieselskapet Vesta v Butcher [1989] AC 852, [1989] 2 WLR 290, [1989] 1 All ER 402 .... 5.20
Foumeny v University of Leeds [2003] EWCA Civ 557, [2003] ELR 443, (2003) 147 SJLB 508... 3.10
Frost v Chief Constable of South Yorkshire *sub nom* White v Chief Constable of South Yorkshire [1999] 2 AC 455, [1983] 3 WLR 1509, [1999] 1 All ER 1 ...... 1.9, 1.26, 1.31, 1.33, 1.46, 1.56; 2.27 2.28, 2.29, 2.30, 2.31, 2.32, 2.34, 2.37, 2.44, 2.49, 2.50, 2.52, 2.61; 3.17; 4.2, 4.4, 4.14, 4.15, 4.55, 4.60; 10.1, 10.6, 10.28, 10.49

G

Galli-Atkinson v Seghal [2003] EWCA Civ 697, [2003] Lloyd's Rep Med 285, (2004) 78 BMLR 22 .... 4.62
Galt v British Rlys Board [1983] 133 NLJ 870 .... 2.58
Garrod v North Devon NHS Primary Care Trust [2006] EWHC 850 (QB), [2007] PIQR Q1 .... 7.96
Gilbank v Miles [2006] EWCA Civ 543, [2006] ICR 1297, [2006] IRLR 538 .... 5.67
Grainger plc v Nicholson [2010] 2 All ER 253, [2010] ICR 360, [2010] IRLR 4 .... 5.44
Greatorex v Greatorex [2000] 1 WLR 1970, [2000] 4 All ER 769, [2000] All ER (D) 677 .... 4.68
Green v DB Group Services (UK) Ltd [2006] EWHC 1898 (QB), [2006] IRLR 764 .. 5.30; 10.32
Gregg v Scott [2005] UKHL 2, [2005] 2 AC 176, [2005] 2 WLR 268 .... 1.42
Grieves v FT Everard & Sons Ltd [2007] UKHL 39, [2008] 1 AC 281, [2007] 3 WLR 876 .... 1.47; 2.35, 2.41; 3.16, 3.17, 3.18

H

Hambrook v Stokes Bros [1925] 1 KB 141 .... 1.21; 4.2
Hamilton Jones v David & Snape (a firm) [2003] EWHC 3147 (Ch), [2004] 1 WLR 924, [2004] 1 All ER 657 .... 5.22
Hartman v South Essex Mental Health & Community Care NHS Trust *sub nom* Moore v Welwyn Components Ltd [2005] EWCA Civ 6, [2005] ICR 782, [2005] IRLR 293 .... 3.10; 7.96
Hatton v Sutherland *sub nom* Barber v Somerset County Council [2002] EWCA Civ 76, [2002] 2 All ER 1, [2002] ICR 613 .... 1.16; 3.8, 3.9; 7.89, 7.97; 10.44
Hevican v Ruane [1991] 3 All ER 65, (1991) 141 NLJ 235 .... 4.55
Heywood v Wellers (a firm) [1976] QB 446, [1976] 2 WLR 101, [1976] 1 All ER 300 .... 5.22
Hicks v Chief Constable of South Yorkshire Police [1992] 2 All ER 65, [1992] PIQR P433 .... 1.9
Hinz v Berry [1970] 2 QB 40, [1970] 2 WLR 684, [1970] 1 All ER 1074 .... 1.8
Holtby v Brigham & Cowan (Hull) Ltd [2000] 3 All ER 421, [2000] ICR 1086, [2000] PIQR Q293 .... 7.88
Home Office v Dorset Yacht Co Ltd [1970] AC 1004, [1970] 2 WLR 1140, [1970] 2 All ER 294 .... 1.37
Hone v Six Continents Retail Ltd [2005] EWCA Civ 922, [2006] IRLR 49 .... 3.10
Hotson v East Berkshire Area Health Authority [1987] AC 750, [1987] 3 WLR 232, [1987] 2 All ER 909 .... 7.84
Hunter v British Coal Corpn [1999] QB 140, [1998] 3 WLR 685, [1998] 2 All ER 97 .... 2.62, 2.63

I

ITW v Z [2009] EWHC 2525 (Fam), [2011] 1 WLR 344, [2010] 3 All ER 682 .... 9.42
Igen Ltd (formerly Leeds Careers Guidance) v Wong [2005] EWCA Civ 142, [2005] 3 All ER 812, [2005] ICR 931 .... 5.50
Intel Corpn (UK) Ltd v Daw [2007] EWCA Civ 70, [2007] 2 All ER 126, [2007] ICR 1318 .... 10.32

J

J v DLA Piper UK LLP [2010] ICR 1052, [2010] IRLR 936, (2010) 115 BMLR 107 .... 5.46,3.10
Jackson v Horizon Holidays Ltd [1975] 1 WLR 1468, [1975] 3 All ER 92, (1975) 119 SJ 759 .... 1.48
Jaensch v Coffey (1984) 54 ALR 417, 155 CLR 549 .... 4.51
James v Woodall Duckham Construction Co Ltd [1969] 1 WLR 903, [1969] 2 All ER 794, 6 KIR 464 .... 1.31
Jarvis v Swan Tours Ltd [1973] QB 233, [1972] 3 WLR 954, [1973] 1 All ER 71 .... 1.48

xxiv *Table of Cases*

Johnson v Gore Wood & Co (a firm) (No 1) [2002] 2 AC 1, [2001] 2 WLR 72, [2001] 1 All ER 481 .... 1.48; 5.22
Johnson v Unisys Ltd [2001] UKHL 13, [2003] 1 AC 518, [2003] 1 AC 518 .... 3.14
Johnston v NEI Internatiol Combustion Ltd [2007] UKHL 39 *see* Grieves v FT Everard & Sons Ltd
Johnstone v Bloomsbury Health Authority [1992]1 QB 333, [1991] 2 WLR 1362, [1991] 2 All ER 293... 3.6
Jones v Majid (unreported, 17 September 1999).. 2.6
Jones v Royal Devon & Exeter NHS Foundation Trust [2008] EWHC 558 (QB), [2008] 101 BMLR 154... 7.27
Jones v Ruth [2011] EWCA Civ 804, [2011] CILL 3085 .... 5.24
Jones v Wright *sub nom* Alcock v Chief Constable of South Yorkshire [1991] 3 All ER 88.. 4.47

K

KJM Superbikes Ltd v Anthony James Hinton [2008] EWCA Civ 1280, [2009] 1 WLR 2406, [2009] 3 All ER 76.. 8.90
Kenth v Heimdale Hotel Investments Ltd [2001] EWCA Civ 1283............................. 7.95
Kerby v Redbridge Health Authority [1994] PIQR Q1, [1993] 4 Med LR 178 .... 1.9
King v Bristow Helicopters [2002] UKHL 7, [2002] 2 AC 628, [2002] 2 WLR 578 ... 1.2
King v Phillips [1953] 1 QB 429, [1953] 2 WLR 526, [1953] 1 All ER 617 .... 1.22, 1.25; 2.20; 4.9
Kirk v Plotzer (unreported, 3 March 2008) 7.29
Krauth v Geller (1960) 157 A 2d 129 .... 2.46

L

Leach v Chief Constable of Gloucestershire [1999] 1 WLR 1421, [1999] 1 All ER 215, [1998] All ER (D) 399 .... 3.23
London Borough of Lewisham v Malcolm [2008] UKHL 43, [2008] 1 AC 1399, [2008] 3 WLR 194.. 5.54

M

McFarlane v EE Caledonia Ltd [1994] 2 All ER 1, [1994] 1 Lloyd's Rep 16, [1994] PIQR P154 .... 1.25; 2.20
McFarlane v Wilkinson *sub nom* Hegarty v EE Caledonia Ltd (2) [1997] 2 Lloyd's Rep 259, [1997] PNLR 578 .... 2.54; 4.14, 4.38
McKew v Hollad & Hannen & Cubbitts (Scotland) Ltd [1969] 3 All ER 1621, 1970 SC (HL) 20, 1970 SLT 68.. 4.19
McLoughlin v Jones [2001] EWCA Civ 1743, [2002] QB 1312, [2002] 2 WLR 1279.. 3.23
McLoughlin v O'Brian [1983] 1 AC 410, [1982] 2 WLR 982, [1982] 2 All ER 298 ... 1.5, 1.23, 1.30; 2.61; 4.2, 4.7, 4.26, 4.39, 4.41, 4.44, 4.47; 10.38
Majrowski v Guys & St Thomas's NHS Trust [2006] UKHL 34, [2007] 1 AC 224, [2006] 3 WLR 125 .... 5.26, 5.31, 5.32
Malcolm v Broadhurst [1970] 3 All ER 508... 2.19
Marcroft v Scrutton [1954] 1 Lloyd's Rep 395 .... 7.74
Masterman Lister v Brutton & Co [2002] EWCA Civ 1889, [2003] 1 WLR 1511, [2003] 3 All ER 162... 9.58, 9.60
Melville v Home Office [2005] EWCA Civ 6, [2005] ICR 782, [2005] IRLR 293 ...... 3.10
Mizon v Comcon International (unreported, 19 August 1999)....................................... 2.4
Monk v PC Harrington Ltd [2008] EWHC 1879 (QB), [2009] PIQR P3 .... 2.64
Moore v Ministry of Justice (unreported, 22 October 2009).. 7.39
Moore v Welwyn Components Ltd *see* Hartman v South Essex Mental Health & Community Care NHS Trust
Morgan v Staffordshire University [2002] ICR 475, [2002] IRLR 190 .... 5.46
Mullen v Accenture Services Ltd [2010] EWHC 2336 (QB)... 10.32

N

Nelson v Carillion Services Ltd [2003] EWCA Civ 544, [2003] ICR 1256, [2003] IRLR 428 .... 5.53
North Glamorgan NHS Trust v Walters [2002] EWCA Civ 1792, [2003] PIQR P16, [2003] Lloyd's Rep Med 49 .... 4.62

O

Ogwo v Taylor [1988] AC 431, [1987] 3 WLR 1145, [1987] 3 All ER 961 .... 2.46
O'Leary v Tunnelcraft Ltd [2009] EWHC 3438 (QB) 8.96
Osborn v Veitch (1830) 1 F & F 317, 175 ER 744 .... 5.5
O'Sullivan v Williams [1992] 3 All ER 385, [1992] RTR 402, (1992) 14 NLJ 717 ..... 3.21
Overseas Tankship (UK) Ltd v Morts Dock & Engineering Co (The Wagon Mound) [1961] AC 388, [1961] 2 WLR 126, [1961] 1 All ER 404................................. 1.22; 2.33
Owens v Liverpool Corpn [1939] 1 KB 394.. 3.22
Oxford University v Broughton [2008] EWHC 75 (QB) 5.40

P

P (Statutory Will), Re [2009] EWHC 163 (Ch), [2010] Ch 33, [2010] 2 WLR 253 ..... 9.42
Page v Smith [1996] AC 155, [1995] 2 WLR 644, [1995] 2 All ER 736 .... 1.6, 1.9, 1.25, 1.31, 1.56; 2.2, 2.10, 2.11, 2.14, 2.15, 2.16, 2.17, 2.21, 2.22, 2.26, 2.27, 2.29, 2.30, 2.32, 2.36, 2.37, 2.38, 2.41, 2.65; 3.10, 3.16, 3.17; 4.1, 4.2, 4.12, 4.15, 4.22, 4.23; 6.49; 7.8; 10.6, 10.20, 10.26, 10.31, 10.49
Page v Smith (No 2) [1996] 1 WLR 855, [1996] 3 All ER 272, [1996] PIQR P364..... 2.23
Paris v Stepney Borough Council [1951] AC 367, [1951] 1 All ER 42, [1950] UKHL 3 .... 2.18
Paterson v Surrey Police Authority [2008] EWHC 2693 (QB) 10.32
Patterson v MoD [1987] CLY 1194 .... 3.16
Petch v C & E Comrs [1993] ICR 789, (1993) 137 SJLB 120..................................... 3.6
Pratley v Surrey County Council [2003] EWCA Civ 1067, [2004] ICR 159, [2003] IRLR 794 .... 3.10

R

R v Cotesworth (1804) 6 Mod 172, 87 ER 928 .... 5.2
R v Criminal Injuries Compensation Board, ex p Johnson (Margaret) [1994] PIQR P469, [1995] COD 43 .... 1.9
R (a child) v Hibbert (unreported, 28 July 2010)... 7.33
Rahman v Arearose Ltd & University College London NHS Trust [2001] QB 351, [2000] 3 WLR 1184, (2001) 62 BMLR 84 .... 7.87
Ravenscroft v Rederiaktiebølaget Transatlantic [1991] 3 All ER 73, (1991) 141 NLJ 600.. 4.55
Rayment v Ministry of Defence [2010] EWHC 218 (QB), [2010] IRLR 768 .... 5.35
Reed v Sunderland Health Authority [1998] All ER (D) 447....................................... 7.23
Reeves v Comr of Police of the Metropolis [1999] QB 169, [1998] 2 WLR 401, [1998] 2 All ER 381.. 2.13
Reilly v Merseyside Regional Health Authority [1995] 6 Med LR 246....................... 1.9
Robertson & Rough v Forth Road Bridge Joint Board (No 2) 1995 SC 364, 1996 SLT 263, 1995 SCLR 466... 2.61
Rylands v Fletcher (1868) LR 3 HL 330 .... 1.54

S

St James & Seacroft University Hospital NHS Trust v Parkinson [2001] EWCA Civ 530, [2002] QB 266, [2001] 3 WLR 376.. 1.46
Saulle v Nouvet [2007] EWHC 2902 (QB), [2008] LS Law Medical 201, [2008] MHLR 59 .... 9.59
Simmons v British Steel [2004] UKHL 20, 2004 SC (HL) 94, 2004 SLT 595 .... 2.10, 2.24, 2.36, 2.41

xxvi Table of Cases

Sion v Hampstead Health Authority [1994] 5 Med LR 170, [1994] JPIL 241 .... 4.63
Smith v Leech Brain & Co Ltd [1962] 2 QB 405, [1962] 2 WLR 148, [1961] 3 All ER 1159.. 2.18
Smith v Jenkins (t/a Rod Jenkins Marine) [2003] EWHC 1356 (QB) 2.9
Spencer v First West Yorkshire Ltd (unreported, 9 December 2004) 7.40
Sougrin v Haringey Health Authority [1992] ICR 650, [1992] IRLR 416 .... 5.60
Stephens v Myers (1830) 4 C &P 349, 72 ER 735 .... 5.5
Stokes v Guest, Keen & Nettlefold (Bolts & Nuts) Ltd [1968] 1 WLR 1776, 5 KIR 401, (1968) 112 SJ 821 .... 3.11
Sunderland County Council v Conn [2007] EWCA CIv 1492, [2008] IRLR 324 .... 3.13
Sutherland v Hatton *see* Barber v Somerset County Council
Sykes v Ministry of Defence (The Times, 23 March 1984) 3.16

T

TP, Re (unreported, 2008) 7.37
Tame v NSW; Annetts Australian Stations Pty (2003) 211 CLR 317 (HCA) 10.7, 10.11, 10.12
Taylorson v Shieldness Produce Ltd [1994] PIQR P329 .... 4.62, 4.63
Thaine v London School of Economics [2010] ICR 1422 .... 7.91, 7.93, 7.97; 10.44
Thomas v National Union of Mineworkers (South Wales Area) [1986] Ch 20, [1985] 2 WLR 1081, [1985] 2 All ER 1 .... 5.4
Thomas v News Group Newspapers Ltd & Simon Hughes [2001] EWCA Civ 1233, [2002] EMLR 4, (2001) 98(34) LSG 43 .... 5.25; 5.37
Thompson v Smiths Ship Repairers (North Shields) Ltd [1984] QB 405, [1984] 2 WLR 522, [1984] 1 All ER 881 .... 7.88
Transfield Shipping v Mercator Shipping Inc (The Achilleas) [2008] UKHL 48, [2009] 1 AC 61, [2008] 3 WLR 345 .... 5.21
Turner, Turner & Jordan v IB [2010] EWHC 1508 (QB) 7.3, 7.46

U

Uttley v Uttley [2002] PIQR P12 .... 8.96

V

Vahidi v Fairstead House School Trust Ltd [2005] EWCA Civ 765, [2005] ELR 607 . 3.10
Veakins v Kier Islington Ltd [2009] EWCA Civ 1288, [2010] IRLR 132 .... 3.13; 5.34
Vento v Chief Constable of West Yorkshire [2002] EWCA Civ 1871, [2003] ICR 318, [2003] IRLR 102 .... 1.50; 5.66
Vernon v Bosley (No 1) [1997] 1 All ER 577, [1997] RTR 1, [1998] 1 FLR 297 .... 1.9
Vernon v Bosley (No 2) [1996] EWCA Civ 1217 .... 1.32
Victorian Rlys Comrs v Coultas (1888) LR 13 App Cas 222 .... 1.19, 1.20

W

W v Essex County Council [2001] 2 AC 592, [2000] 2 WLR 601, [2000] 2 All ER 237... 4.61
Wainwright v Home Office [2001] EWCA Civ 2081, [2002] QB 1334, [2002] 3 WLR 405 .... 5.9
Walker v Northumberland County Council [1995] 1 All ER 737, [1995] ICR 702, [1995] IRLR 35 .... 3.6, 3.7
Walters v Sloan (1977) 571 P 2d 609 .... 2.46
Ward v Leeds Teaching Hospital NHS Trust [2004] EWHC 2106 (QB), [2004] Lloyd's Rep Med 530 .... 4.64
Wardlaw v Bonnington Castings Ltd *see* Bonnington Castings Ltd v Wardlaw
White v Chief Constable of South Yorkshire see Frost v Chief Constable of South Yorkshire
Wikinson v Downton [1897] 2 QB 57 .... 1.20; 5.8, 5.11
Wilsher v Essex Area Health Authority [1988] AC 1074, [1988] 2 WLR 557, [1988] 1 All ER 871 .... 7.84

Wilson v Ministry of Defence [1991] 1 All ER 638, [1991] ICR 595............................ 7.82
Wong v Parkside Health NHS Trust [2001] EWCA Civ 1721, [2003] 3 All ER 932, (2002) 99(2) LSG 28.. 5.11

Y

YA (F) v A Local Authority [2010] EWHC 2770 (Fam), [2011] 1 WLR 1505, [2011] 1 FLR 2007 .... 9.12
Yearworth v North Bristol NHS Trust [2009] EWCA Civ 37, [2010] QB 1, [2009] 3 WLR 118... 3.20

1 Liability and compensation for psychiatric injury: an overview

1 What is psychiatric injury?

1.1 The concept that the law should compensate for psychiatric injury as well as for physical injury is controversial. The Law Commission, in their Consultation Paper on *Liability for Psychiatric Illness*[1], commented:

> 'We are aware from our preliminary consultations that there are strongly held views on this topic. On the one hand, there are those who are sceptical about the award of damages for psychiatric illness. They argue that such illness can easily be faked; that, in any event, those who are suffering should be able to "pull themselves together"; and that, even if they cannot do so, there is no good reason why defendants and, through them, those who pay insurance premiums should pay for their inability to do so … On the other hand, medical and legal experts working in the field, who are the people who most commonly encounter those complaining of psychiatric illness, have impressed upon us how life-shattering psychiatric illness can be and how, in many instances, it can be more debilitating than physical injuries'.

1   LCCP No 137, 1995.

1.2 In principle, English law allows for compensation for personal injuries where the claimant suffers only psychiatric injury as well as if the claimant had suffered a physical bodily injury. A good starting point is the definition of an action for 'personal injuries' in the Limitation Act 1980, s 38(1):

> 'personal injuries includes any disease and an impairment of a person's physical or mental condition…'

This definition of personal injuries which broadly equates psychiatric injury with physical injury is to be contrasted with claims for 'bodily injury' under the Warsaw Convention on carriage by air. The House of Lords in *King v Bristow Helicopters*[1] took a more restrictive view. They held that a claim for pure psychiatric injury could not be compensated under the terms of the Convention which required injury to 'the body'.

1   [2002] UKHL 7.

1.3 As early as 1901, in *Dulieu v White & Sons*[1], Kennedy J said:

> 'For my own part, I should not like to assume it to be scientifically true that a nervous shock which causes serious bodily illness is not actually accompanied by physical injury, although it may be impossible, or at least difficult, to detect the injury at the time

1

in the living subject. I should not be surprised if the surgeon or the physiologist told us that nervous shock is or may be in itself an injurious affection of the physical organism'.

1   [1901] 2 KB 669, [1900–1903] All ER Rep 353 at 358E.

1.4   In *Bourhill v Young*[1] Lord Macmillan took this further:

'The crude view that the law should take cognisance only of physical injury resulting from actual impact has been discarded, and it is now well recognised that an action will lie for injury by shock sustained through the medium of the eye or ear without direct contact. The distinction between mental shock and bodily injury was never a scientific one, for mental shock is presumably in all cases the result of, or at least accompanied by, some physical disturbance in the sufferer's system. And a mental shock may have consequences more serious than those resulting from physical impact'.

1   [1943] AC 92, [1942] 2 All ER 396 at 402E.

1.5   And in *McLoughlin v O'Brian*[1], Lord Bridge drew attention to the interrelation of physical and psychiatric injury:

'No judge who has spent any length of time trying personal injury claims in recent years would doubt that physical injuries can give rise not only to organic but also to psychiatric disorders. The sufferings of the patient from the latter are no less real and frequently no less painful and disabling than from the former. Likewise, I would suppose that the legal profession well understands that an acute emotional trauma, like a physical trauma, can well cause a psychiatric illness in a wide range of circumstances and in a wide range of individuals whom it would be wrong to regard as having any abnormal psychological make-up. It is in comparatively recent times that these insights have come to be generally accepted by the judiciary. It is only by giving effect to these insights in the developing law of negligence that we can do justice to an important, though no doubt small, class of plaintiffs whose genuine psychiatric illnesses are caused by negligent defendants'.

But he was also careful to note:

'The common law gives no damages for the emotional distress which any normal person experiences when someone he loves is killed or injured. Anxiety and depression are normal human emotions. Yet an anxiety neurosis or a reactive depression may be recognisable psychiatric illnesses, with or without psychosomatic symptoms. So, the first hurdle which a plaintiff claiming damages of the kind in question must surmount is to establish that he is suffering, not merely grief, distress or any other normal emotion, but a positive psychiatric illness'.

1   [1983] 1 AC 410, [1982] 2 All ER at 312h and 311j respectively.

1.6   Towards the end of the 20th century, in *Page v Smith*[1], Lord Lloyd said:

'As medical science advances, it is important that the law should not be seen to limp too far behind'

and:

'In an age when medical knowledge is expanding fast, and psychiatric knowledge with it, it would not be sensible to commit the law to a distinction between physical and psychiatric injury, which may already seem somewhat artificial, and may soon be altogether outmoded. Nothing will be gained by treating them as different "kinds" of personal injury, so as to require the application of different tests in law'.

Lord Browne-Wilkinson added:

'Finally I would endorse Lord Lloyd's remarks about the dangers of the court seeking to draw hard and fast lines between physical illness and its causes on the one hand and psychiatric illness and its causes on the other. Although medical science has not as yet progressed very far in elucidating the processes whereby psychiatric disorders come about, recent developments suggest a much closer relationship between physical and mental processes than had previously been thought. There is a substantial body of informed medical opinion which attributes some mental illness to physical causes such as chemical or hormonal imbalance. In the present case, for example, although all but one of the distinguished doctors who gave evidence were agreed that there was indeed an illness (however mysterious) called ME and that the plaintiff suffered from it, they had differing views as to its causes. One thought ME was linked to viral infection (physical) and stress (psychological): another to neuroendocrine disturbance (physical) and psychiatric disorder. In cases where distinguished doctors take differing views as to the aetiology of an illness it obviously presents great problems for the court to resolve what was the cause of the ecrudescence of such an illness'.

1   [1996] AC 155, [1995] 2 All ER 736 at 758f, 759e and 754b.

1.7   However, even today the general public (as opposed to most scientists) widely believe in a distinction between mind and body—that the mind or soul is a 'ghost in the machine'—so that a psychiatric injury is somehow qualitatively different to an injury to the body. The editors of the American *Diagnostic and Statistical Manual of Mental Disorder*[1] point out:

'The term mental disorder unfortunately implies a distinction between "mental" disorders and "physical" disorders that is a reductionist anachronism of mind body dualism. A compelling literature documents that there is much "physical" in "mental" disorders and much "mental" in "physical" disorders. The problems raised by the term "mental" disorders have been much clearer than its solution, and, unfortunately, the term persists in the title of DSM-IV because we have not found an appropriate substitute'.

1   DSM-IV (4th edn, 1994), published by the American Psychiatric Association.

1.8   Any physical injury to the body caused by negligence can in principle be compensated, even if minor scratches and bruises are unlikely to be litigated because the cost (or the effort for a litigant in person) is likely to be disproportionate to the damages. That is not the case for pure emotional or mental harm. One mechanism by which the courts restrict the ability to claim for psychiatric injury caused by the tort of negligence is to differentiate injury from 'normal reactions' of fear, grief and distress. Initially, the courts proceeded by way of a piecemeal extension of the kinds of damage which were compensatable as a psychiatric injury. In *Hinz v Berry*[1] Lord Denning held that:

'No damages are awarded for grief or sorrow…'

but that damages will be awarded:

'… for nervous shock, or, to put it in medical terms, for any recognisable psychiatric injury caused by breach of duty by the defendant'

4   *Liability and compensation for psychiatric injury: an overview*

and this enabled the claimant in this case to recover compensation for 'morbid depression'. No authority was cited by Lord Denning in his formulation 'recognised psychiatric injury', but it has been followed in subsequent decisions.

1   [1970] 2 QB 40.

1.9   So in *Brice v Brown*[1] the claimant recovered for 'hysterical personality disorder' and in *Vernon v Bosley (No 1)*[2] for 'pathological grief disorder', but the normal reactions of grief and 'shattered family plans' in *Kerby v Redbridge Health Authority*[3] were not compensated. The claimants in *White v Chief Constable of South Yorkshire Police*[4] (confusingly known up to the Court of Appeal stage as *Frost v Chief Constable of South Yorkshire Police*, so referred to here as *Frost/White*) could in principle receive compensation for 'post-traumatic stress disorder' and although the claim failed on other grounds (see Chapter 4) the nature of the injury as being one for which damages were recoverable was never in issue. But in *Reilly v Merseyside Health Authority*[5], where the claimant had been trapped in a lift, claustrophobia and fear where these did not fit the diagnostic criteria of post-traumatic stress disorder were not compensated. Nor was the fear of impending death[6] or distress occasioned by the discovery of the murdered body of a friend[7]. In *Page v Smith*[8] 'chronic fatigue syndrome' was held to be a recognised psychiatric condition (nowadays this may be controversial, with some viewing it as an illness with purely physical causes and effects).

1   [1984] 1 All ER 997.
2   [1997] 1 All ER 577.
3   [1993] 4 Med LR 178.
4   [1999] 2 AC 455.
5   [1995] 6 Med LR 246, CA.
6   *Hicks v Chief Constable of South Yorkshire Police* [1992] 2 All ER 65.
7   *R v Criminal Injuries Compensation Board, ex p Johnson* [1994] PIQR P469.
8   [1996] AC 155.

1.10   More recently the phrase 'recognised psychiatric injury' has been taken to mean in practice an illness which is categorised in either the American *Diagnostic and Statistical Manual of Mental Disorders*[1] or the *International Classification of Diseases and Related Health Problems*[2]. It should be noted that both publications are now significantly old. Revisions for medical purposes will no doubt be made in due course. If these extend the categories of recognised psychiatric injury, it will be interesting to see whether or not the courts follow suit. It should be noted that the various diagnostic criteria do not always exactly fit the legal requirements for recovery of compensation and nor do they always clearly distinguish between distress and illness. The editors of DSM-IV state:

'When the DSM-IV categories, criteria, and textual descriptions are employed for forensic purposes, there are significant risks that diagnostic information will be misused or misunderstood. These dangers arise because of the imperfect fit between the questions of ultimate concern to the law and the information contained in the clinical diagnosis. In most situations, the clinical diagnosis of a DSM-IV mental disorder is not sufficient to establish the existence for legal purposes of "mental disorder", "mental disability", "mental disease", or "mental defect". In determining whether an individual meets a specified legal standard additional information is usually required beyond that contained in the DSM-IV diagnosis. This might include information about the individual's functional impairments and how these impairments affect the particular abilities in question. It is precisely because impairments, abilities, and disabilities vary widely within each diagnostic category that assignment of the particular diagnosis does not imply a specific level of impairment or disability'.

1   DSM-IV (4th edn, 1994), published by the American Psychiatric Association.
2   ICD 10 (10th revision, 1993), published by the World Health Organisation.

1.11 The Law Commission consulted widely in respect of possible reforms to the law in relation to psychiatric injury in 1996. Their Consultation Paper concentrated largely on post-traumatic stress disorder (PTSD), which had been the most commonly recognised 'shock' claim. PTSD had first been described in the 1970s in relation to US army veterans returning form Vietnam and had been officially recognised in the DSM-III published in 1980. But in *Liability for Psychiatric Illness*[1], published in 1998, the Law Commission acknowledged that they had been too limited in their concentration on PTSD, particularly bearing in mind their view that the requirement for a shocking event before allowing recovery for a psychiatric injury should be abandoned.

1   Law Com no 249.

1.12 In their report the Law Commission also considered clinical depression:

'It is part of normal human experience to feel unhappy at times of adversity but, as we explained in our review of the present law, mere grief or distress is not compensatable at law. Depressive disorders are distinguished from more ordinary fluctuations in mood by the severity and duration of symptoms, and by the effect of these symptoms on nearly all activities. In broad terms, a depressive disorder is characterised by a cluster of symptoms including: depressed mood most of the day, nearly every day, for at least two weeks; loss of interest or pleasure in activities that are normally pleasurable; decreased energy; change in appetite; sleep disturbance; difficulties in concentrating; feelings of worthlessness; and recurrent thoughts of death'.

And adjustment disorders:

'The essential feature of an adjustment disorder is the development of clinically significant emotional or behavioural symptoms in response to an identifiable stressor. For a diagnosis under DSM-IV, the symptoms must occur within three months of the onset of the stressor, which may be of any severity (ranging from exposure to a natural disaster to the termination of a relationship). The diagnosis under ICD-10 can only be given if the symptoms occur within one month of exposure to the stressor, which must not be of an unusual or catastrophic type if this diagnosis is to be given.

63 Under both diagnoses the symptoms must not persist for more than six months after the cessation of the stressor. Individual predisposition or vulnerability is thought to play a greater role in the risk of occurrence and the shaping of the manifestations of an adjustment disorder than it does in PTSD, but it is still assumed that the condition would not have arisen without the stressor'.

And anxiety disorders:

'Anxiety disorders may be phobic disorders, where anxiety is evoked only (or predominantly) by certain well-defined situations which are not currently dangerous, or may be generalised disorders, where the essential feature is a generalised and persistent anxiety which is not restricted to any particular environmental circumstances. Coexistent adjustment and anxiety disorders are common, as are coexistent depressive and anxiety disorders ... Both phobic and generalised anxiety disorders have been found to be prevalent after trauma. For example, in the study mentioned above of patients presenting themselves at a hospital emergency department following road traffic accidents, 18 per cent were diagnosed as suffering phobic anxiety about travel at one year after the accident. Similarly, in the study mentioned above of patients attending a primary health care clinic one year after a major volcanic eruption in Columbia, although PTSD was the most prevalent diagnosis among the patients as a whole, when looking only at the group of indirect victims (those who had not experienced the disaster first hand, but who suffered as a result of the loss of a relative, friend, property, business or disruption to their community), the most prevalent diagnosis (22 per cent) was generalised anxiety disorder'.

1.13 However, the Law Commission did not recommend a statutory definition of 'psychiatric injury':

'We have concluded, however, that such a task would not be practicable. For example, it might at first sight appear that an obvious definition would be, "any diagnosis that is included in either of the two classificatory systems used by the psychiatric profession, the ICD-10 Classification of Mental and Behavioural Disorders and the Diagnostic and Statistical Manual of Mental Disorders". Such an approach, however, would not appear to be supported by many of the medical consultees, and the classificatory systems were not prepared for such legal purposes. As the Introduction to DSM-IV states, "(i)t is important that DSM-IV not be applied mechanically ... The specific diagnostic criteria included in DSM-IV are meant to serve as guidelines to be informed by clinical judgment and are not meant to be used in a cookbook fashion". In addition, we would risk excluding newly recognised disorders, which despite having gained the general acceptance of the psychiatric profession must wait for the publication of a revised edition before they can be included in the manuals... Conversely, such an approach might also be over-inclusive. That is, DSM-IV and ICD-10 would appear to include diagnoses that might not be recognised as psychiatric illnesses by the courts'.

The medical position is considered in more detail in Chapter 6, but it is clear that PTSD is no longer regarded as the only, or even the main, form of psychiatric injury to be compensated in tort.

1.14 In assessing whether a particular claimant is suffering from psychiatric injury, the court will always be reliant upon the expert evidence of relevant professionals, usually a consultant psychiatrist or consultant neuropsychiatrist or a clinical psychologist. Their assessment of the claimant's presentation and the diagnosis based upon the relevant published diagnostic criteria is usually essential as a prerequisite for liability.

1.15 It also should be noted that whilst most discussion of psychiatric injury relates to 'pure' psychiatric injury, or, in other words, a case where there has been no physical injury, in practice a psychological reaction to an accident often accompanies a physical injury of lesser or greater severity. Indeed such cases are far more common than pure psychiatric injury. In cases of psychiatric injury accompanying physical injury, recovery of compensation under a discrete head of loss will depend upon the claimant establishing a recognised psychiatric condition. However, because under English law compensation for pain and suffering and loss of amenity is not based on a tariff but is individually assessed by the judge hearing the case and is dependent upon, amongst other factors, the specific effect of the injury upon the claimant, in practice 'psychiatric' conditions which fall short of the medical definition may well contribute to the extent of the general damages awarded.

1.16 In *Hatton v Sutherland*[1] Hale LJ summarised the existing position for psychiatric injury caused by the tort of negligence:

> 'But although there have been great advances in understanding of the nature and causes of psychiatric ill-health, there are still important differences between physical and mental disorders.
>
> (1) The dividing line between a normal but unpleasant state of mind or emotion and a recognised psychiatric illness or disorder is not easy to draw. Psychiatric textbooks tell us that with a physical disease or disability, the doctor can presuppose a perfect or "normal" state of bodily health and then point to the ways in which his patient's condition falls short of this. There is probably no such thing as a state of perfect mental health. The doctor has instead to presuppose some average standard of functioning and then assess whether his patient's condition falls far enough short of that to be considered a disorder. However, there is now a considerable degree of international agreement on the classification of mental disorders and their diagnostic criteria, the two most commonly used tools being the most recent American Diagnostic and Statistical Manual of Mental Disorder, the DSM-IV (1994) and the World Health Organisation's ICD-10 Classification of Mental and Behavioural Disorders (1992).
>
> (2) While some of the major mental illnesses have a known or strongly suspected organic origin, this is not the case with many of the most common disorders. Their causes will often be complex and depend upon the interaction between the patient's personality and a number of factors in the patient's life. It is not easy to predict who will fall victim, how, why or when.
>
> (3) For the same reason, treatment is often not straightforward or its outcome predictable: while some conditions may respond comparatively quickly and easily to appropriate medication others may only respond, if at all, to prolonged and complicated "talking treatments" or behavioural therapy. There are strong divergences of views amongst psychiatrists on these issues.

In their report on *Liability for Psychiatric Illness* (Law Com no 249, 1998) at para 1.2, the Law Commission referred to the divergence of academic views on the approach the law should take:

> "At one end of the scale are those who argue that the same principles that apply to liability for physical injury should be applied to liability for psychiatric illness, and there is no legitimate reason to impose special restrictions in respect of claims for the latter [most forcefully by NJ Mullany and PR Handford in *Tort Liability for Psychiatric Damage*, 1993]. At the other extreme are those who argue that liability for psychiatric illness should be abandoned altogether. They say that the arbitrary rules which are required to control potential liability are so artificial that they bring the law into disrepute [cogently expressed by Dr J Stapleton, 'In Restraint of Tort', in P Birks (ed), *The Frontiers of Liability*, 1994]."

Both the law and the Law Commission have followed a middle course, in some cases treating a recognised psychiatric illness as no different in principle from a physical injury or illness, while in others imposing additional "control mechanisms" so that liability does not extend too far'.

1   [2002] EWCA Civ 76 at para 5.

1.17   Some specialised torts do allow recovery of damages for emotional and mental harm short of a 'recognised psychiatric injury'. So, for example, the statutory tort of discrimination under the equalities legislation allows for an award of compensation for 'injury to feelings' rather than requiring the discrimination to have caused recognised psychiatric injury as such, and compensation is payable under the Protection from Harassment Act 1997 for 'anxiety', but not intentionally inflicted mental injury (see Chapter 5). Even in contract, distress short of a 'recognised psychiatric injury' can be compensated (see para **1.47** below).

1.18   There seems to be no reason of principle which restricts compensation for emotional and mental harm caused by the tort of negligence to a 'recognised psychiatric injury'. It is rather the result of a combination of the piecemeal development of the law over the last century and the fear of the judiciary of opening the 'floodgates' to claims. This restriction is perhaps beginning to look rather anachronistic in the light of both scientific advances in the understanding of mental disorders and the recognition by Parliament that injury short of a 'recognised psychiatric injury' should be compensated in a number of statutory torts.

2   A brief history

1.19   Psychiatric injury claims were not a creature of the late 20th century. The English courts had to grapple with the issues as early as 1888, when the Privy Council heard an appeal from Australia in *Victorian Railways Comrs v Coultas*[1]. Mrs Coultas was permitted by an employee of the railway company to drive across a level crossing in her buggy when a train was approaching. There was no actual impact, but there was a very near miss. The plaintiff suffered severe nervous shock, which in turn produced illness and a miscarriage. She recovered damages for negligence at first instance, but the decision was reversed by the Privy Council on the ground that the damage was too remote. The Privy Council were clearly influenced by fear of opening floodgates:

> 'The difficulty which now often exists in cases of alleged physical injuries of determining whether they were caused by the negligent act would be greatly increased, and a wide field opened for imaginary claims'.

1   (1888) 13 App Cas 222.

1.20   This decision of the Privy Council was not followed (it had already been relaxed for deliberate harm cases in *Wikinson v Downton*[1]: see Chapter 5) in *Dulieu v White*[2], where:

> '... the plaintiff, then being in a state of pregnancy, was behind the bar of her husband's public-house, and that the defendants by their servant negligently drove a pair-horse van into the public-house. It goes on to allege in paragraph 4 that the plaintiff in consequence sustained a severe shock and was seriously ill, and on September 29 following gave premature birth to a child, and, in paragraph 5, that in consequence of the shock sustained by the plaintiff the said child was born an idiot'.

In allowing her to recover compensation for shock caused by physical fear to herself, and disapproving *Coultas*, the court held[3]:

> 'terror operates through parts of the physical organism to produce bodily illness ... The undoubted rule that merely mental pain unaccompanied by any injury to the person cannot sustain an action'

and

> 'It is not to be taken that in my view every nervous shock occasioned by negligence and producing physical injury to the sufferer gives a cause of action. There is I am inclined to think at least one limitation. The shock, where it operates through the mind, must be a shock which arises from a reasonable fear of immediate personal injury to oneself'.

1   [1897] 2 QB 57.
2   [1901] 2 KB 669, [1900–1903] All ER Rep 353 at 355A.
3   [1900–1903] All ER Rep 353 at 356B and 357D.

1.21 'Nervous shock' caused by fear of injury to others was compensated in *Hambrook v Stokes Bros*[1] when the claimant saw a runaway lorry careering down the hill towards where she had left her children. But in *Bourhill v Young*[2], where the claimant, a pregnant fishwife, heard the sound of an accident which she did not witness, and suffered severe nervous shock which stopped her working and which led to a still-born child, did not recover compensation. Ever since this decision the courts have sought to clarify when a claimant who is not directly involved in an accident can recover for psychiatric injury (see Chapter 4).

1   [1925] 1 KB 141.
2   [1943] AC 92.

1.22 In *King v Phillips*[1] a taxi driver reversed into a side road without checking that it was safe and hit a child's tricycle. The child was only slightly injured, but his mother saw and heard the incident from the window of her house 70 or so yards away suffered 'emotional injury'. The claim was rejected, the court finding that the slow reversing of the taxi was distinguishable from the runaway lorry in *Hambrook*. But Denning LJ did set out the following dictum:

> 'Howsoever that may be, whether the exemption for shock be based on want of duty or on remoteness, there can be no doubts that since *Bourhill v Young* [1943] AC 92 that the test for liability for shock is foreseeability of injury by shock'.

This was approved by the House of Lords in *The Wagon Mound No 1*[2].

1   [1953] 1 QB 429.
2   [1961] AC 388 at 426.

1.23 In *McLoughlin v O'Brian*[1] the House of Lords had the opportunity to revisit psychiatric injury claims. Mrs McLoughlin's husband and three children were seriously injured in a car accident. She was at home several miles away. Her youngest child died instantly, but she was told about the accident by a neighbour who was unclear as to the severity of the injuries each member of her family had sustained. Lord Wilberforce said[2]:

'English law, and common understanding, have moved some distance since recognition was given to this symptom as a basis for liability. Whatever is unknown about the mind-body relationship (and the area of ignorance seems to expand with that of knowledge), it is now accepted by medical science that recognisable and severe physical damage to the human body and system may be caused by the impact, through the senses, of external events on the mind. There may thus be produced what is as identifiable an illness as any that may be caused by direct physical impact'.

Lord Bridge held[3] that the claimant had to show a medically recognised psychiatric illness:

'Anxiety and depression are normal human emotions. Yet an anxiety neurosis or a reactive depression may be recognisable psychiatric illnesses, with or without psychosomatic symptoms. So, the first hurdle which a plaintiff claiming damages of the kind in question must surmount is to establish that he is suffering, not merely grief, distress or any other normal emotion, but a positive psychiatric illness'.

1 [1983] 1 AC 410, [1982] 2 All ER 298.
2 [1982] 2 All ER 298 at 301g.
3 [1982] 2 All ER 298 at 311j.

1.24 The phrase 'nervous shock' '*as lawyers quaintly persist in calling*' psychiatric injury was criticised by Bingham LJ in *Attia v British Gas plc*[1], as it is damage caused by the shock, not the 'shock' itself, that is compensatable.

1 [1988] QB 304.

1.25 In 1995 the issue of pure psychiatric injury returned to the House of Lords in *Page v Smith* when Lord Lloyd criticised Lord Denning's dictum in *King*[1]:

'The danger of any good phrase is that it gets repeated so often and applied so uncritically that in the end it tends to distort the law. Denning LJ's dictum is wrong in two respects. It is both too wide and too narrow. It is too wide where the plaintiff is the secondary victim, as she was in *King v Phillips*. For subsequent cases have shown that foreseeability of injury by shock is not the sole test (see *Alcock's case* [1992] 1 AC 310, 396 per Lord Keith of Kinkel and *McFarlane v EE Caledonia Ltd* [1994] 2 All ER 1). The test is also too narrow, where, as here, the plaintiff is the primary victim. There is nothing in *Bourhill v Young* to displace the ordinary rule that where the plaintiff is within the range of foreseeable physical injury the defendant must take his victim as he finds him. The whole point of *Bourhill v Young* was that the plaintiff was not within the range of foreseeable physical injury'.

Lord Browne-Wilkinson[2] concluded:

'In my view this case is bedeviled by the use of the description "nervous shock" to describe any injury suffered otherwise than by a chain of demonstrably physical causes. The law has long recognised tangible physical damage to the body of the plaintiff as a head of damage. Medical science has now advanced so far that the process whereby an impact causing direct physical injury to one limb or organ of the body can be demonstrated to have caused consequential physical damage to another limb or organ. Lawyers can readily accept that such consequential, physical damage is the consequence of the original impact. Hence there is a willingness to accept that all such tangible physical damage is foreseeable. Medical science has also demonstrated that there are other injuries the body can suffer as a consequence of an accident, such injuries not being demonstrably attributable directly to physical injury to the plaintiff. Injuries of this type may take two forms. First, physical illness or injury not brought about by a chain of demonstrable physical events but by mental or emotional stresses ie by a psychiatric route. Examples are a heart attack or a miscarriage produced by shock. In this case, the end product is a physical condition although it has been brought about by a process which is not demonstrably a physical one but lies in the mental or nervous system. The second form is psychiatric illness itself which is brought about by mental or emotional stresses, ie by a psychiatric route. Because medical science has so far been less successful in demonstrating the nature of psychiatric illness and the processes whereby it is brought about by the psychiatric route, the courts have been more reluctant to accept the risk of such illness as being foreseeable.

I am therefore of opinion that any driver of a car should reasonably foresee that, if he drives carelessly, he will be liable to cause injury, either physical or psychiatric or both, to other users of the highway who become involved in an accident. Therefore he owes to such persons a duty of care to avoid such injury. In the present case the defendant could not foresee the exact type of psychiatric damage in fact suffered by the plaintiff who, due to his ME, was "an eggshell personality". But that is of no significance since the defendant did owe a duty of care to prevent foreseeable damage, including psychiatric damage. Once such duty of care is established, the defendant must take the plaintiff as he finds him.

For the courts to impose different criteria for liability depending upon whether the injury is "physical" or "psychiatric" is likely to lead to a growing complication in straightforward personal injury cases. In my judgment, the law will be more effective if it accepts that the result of being involved in a collision may include both physical and psychiatric damage'.

However, this formulation of the law relating to psychiatric injury claims by direct participants in accidents has been much criticised (see Chapter 2).

1 [1996] AC 155, [1995] 2 All ER 736 at 764b.
2 [1995] 2 All ER 736 at 752c.

1.26 The law relating to secondary victims is even more confused (see Chapter 4). Psychiatric injury claims returned to the House of Lords in cases resulting from the Hillsborough disaster. In *White v Chief Constable of South Yorkshire Police*[1] (confusingly known up to the Court of Appeal stage as *Frost v Chief Constable of South Yorkshire Police*, so referred to here as *Frost/White*) Lord Hoffmann said:

'In order to give due weight to the earlier decisions, particularly at first instance, it is necessary to have regard to their historical context. They cannot be simply laid out flat and pieced together to form a timeless mosaic of legal rules. Some contained the embryonic forms of later developments; others are based upon theories of liability which had respectable support at the time but have since been left stranded by the shifting tides'.

These words are very important in the context of litigating psychiatric injury claims today. This brief historical survey is of use in tracing the origins of the current law and to an extent in assisting in ascertaining the extent of the current law and how it might apply to new factual circumstances, but there is a limit to the extent of the practical use today of the earlier decisions, however eminent the judges.

1 [1999] 2 AC 455, [1999] 1 All ER 1 at 41h.

12 *Liability and compensation for psychiatric injury: an overview*

3 Why is psychiatric injury so controversial?

1.27 It can therefore be seen that the courts have found the concept of compensation for psychiatric injury very controversial. Why is this?

1.28 First, the understanding of medical science and in particular the overlap between bodily and psychiatric injury has shifted considerably as medical science has developed. Second, the public perception of these developments has changed. Whereas in the past the reaction of the 'man on the Clapham omnibus' might have been to 'pull yourself together', there is a much greater understanding within society of 'nervous breakdowns' and depression. More treatments are available and well known to the public, even if many of these do not seem to them to be particularly good at treating long-term chronic psychiatric conditions. The judges are anxious to allow the common law to develop to enable recovery where this is just. However, they are also clearly anxious not to allow the law to proceed too fast so that it is completely out of step with the developing public opinion.

1.29 Third, with psychiatric injury there are no organic signs to substantiate the injury. Judges may be cautious about claims which are less susceptible of independent proof and often rely upon the unsupported assertion of a claimant. Diagnosis by a consultant psychiatrist is largely based on self-reporting of symptoms which the clinician must weigh against his personal experience and the relevant published diagnostic criteria. This creates a fear that exaggeration of symptoms will lead to over-compensation. In the same way, it is much more difficult for a judge to make an assessment of the current limitations a psychiatric condition is placing on a claimant, as opposed to a physical injury, and even more so as to the extent to which the prognosis for the injury is clear. Whereas with a physical injury a judge may well be able to take a view that there will be no significant recovery, even serious and chronic psychiatric conditions can sometimes spontaneously improve or be significantly mitigated by effective treatment in a way that is, in the current state of medical science, impossible with a spinal cord injury or an amputated limb. Judges are therefore much more cautious about long-term compensation on the assumption that there will be no recovery or improvement in psychiatric injury cases. However, as was pointed out by the House of Lords in *Frost/White*, psychiatric illness is not alone in this. The courts are, for example, well used to dealing with back injuries where there may be few organic signs and much is dependent upon the clinical presentation and the expert evidence.

1.30 In *McLoughlin v O'Brian*[1] the House of Lords noted that in consequence there was:

> '... a real need for the law to place some limitation upon the extent of admissible claims. It is necessary to consider three elements inherent in any claim: the class of persons whose claims should be recognised; the proximity of such persons to the accident; and the means by which the shock is caused'.

1   [1983] 1 AC 410, [1982] 2 All ER 298 at 304f.

1.31 In *Frost/White*[1], Lord Steyn noted four concerns which in combination may account for the differential treatment of psychiatric injury:

(i) establishing whether there is psychiatric injury, as opposed to some grief or other reaction which is real, but not compensatable:

> 'Firstly, there is the complexity of drawing the line between acute grief and psychiatric harm: see Hedley, Nervous Shock: Wider Still and Wider, 1997 CLJ 254. The symptoms may be the same. But there is greater diagnostic uncertainty in psychiatric injury cases than in physical injury cases. The classification of emotional injury is often controversial. In order to establish psychiatric harm expert evidence is required. That involves the calling of consultant psychiatrists on both sides. It is a costly and time-consuming exercise. If claims for psychiatric harm were to be treated as generally on a par with physical injury it would have implications for the administration of justice. On its own this factor may not be entitled to great weight and may not outweigh the considerations of justice supporting genuine claims in respect of pure psychiatric injury';

(ii) that the availability of compensation might encourage claims to an extent which the public would consider inappropriate and which, if this becomes the norm, might impede recovery:

> 'Secondly, there is the effect of the expansion of the availability of compensation on potential claimants who have witnessed gruesome events. I do not have in mind fraudulent or bogus claims. In general it ought to be possible for the administration of justice to expose such claims. But I do have in mind the unconscious effect of the prospect of compensation on potential claimants. Where there is generally no prospect of recovery, such as in the case of injuries sustained in sport, psychiatric harm appears not to obtrude often. On the other hand, in the case of industrial accidents, where there is often a prospect of recovery of compensation, psychiatric harm is repeatedly encountered and often endures until the process of claiming compensation comes to an end: see *James v Woodall Duckham Construction Co Ltd* [1969] 1 WLR 903 (CA). The litigation is sometimes an unconscious disincentive to rehabilitation. It is true that this factor is already present in cases of physical injuries with concomitant mental suffering. But it may play a larger role in cases of pure psychiatric harm, particularly if the categories of potential recovery are enlarged. For my part this factor cannot be dismissed';

(iii) 'floodgates':

> 'The third factor is important. The abolition or a relaxation of the special rules governing the recovery of damages for psychiatric harm would greatly increase the class of persons who can recover damages in tort. It is true that compensation is routinely awarded for psychiatric harm where the plaintiff has suffered some physical harm. It is also well established that psychiatric harm resulting from the apprehension of physical harm is enough: *Page v Smith* [1996] AC 155. These two principles are not surprising. In built in such situations are restrictions on the classes of plaintiff who can sue: the requirement of the infliction of some physical injury or apprehension of it introduces an element of immediacy which restricts the category of potential plaintiffs. But in cases of pure psychiatric harm there is potentially a wide class of plaintiffs involved';

(iv) the impact upon defendants and their insurers which might be thought disproportionate to their conduct:

> 'Fourthly, the imposition of liability for pure psychiatric harm in a wide range of situations may result in a burden of liability on defendants which may be disproportionate to tortious conduct involving perhaps momentary lapses of

concentration, eg in a motor car accident. The wide scope of potential liability for pure psychiatric harm is not only illustrated by the rather unique events of Hillsborough but also by of accidents involving trains, coaches and buses, and the everyday occurrence of serious collisions of vehicles all of which may result in gruesome scenes. In such cases there may be many claims for psychiatric harm by those who have witnessed and in some ways assisted at the scenes of the tragic events. Moreover, protagonists of very wide theories of liability for pure psychiatric loss have suggested that "workplace claims loom large as the next growth area of psychiatric injury law", the paradigm case being no doubt a workman who has witnessed a tragic accident to an employee: Mullany and Handford, Hillsborough Replayed (1997) 113 LQR 410, at 415'.

1   [1999] 2 AC 455, [1999] 1 All ER 1 at 32j–33h.

1.32 There is also a feeling that there might be a risk of misdiagnosis. In *Vernon v Bosley (No 2)*[1] Mr Bosley had claimed for psychiatric injury after watching rescuers make unsuccessful attempts to rescue his two daughters from a motor car which had been driven into a river in South Wales by the family's nanny. He said that he was suffering from post-traumatic stress disorder which had caused the failure of his business with losses claimed at more than £3 million. The defendant alleged that it was merely a grief reaction and that other factors contributed to his psychological problems and consequent financial losses. The judge awarded him £1.3 million on 30 January 1995. The defendant appealed and in a draft judgment handed down on 29 March 1996 the Court of Appeal indicated that they were dismissing the appeal on liability, but reducing the judge's award by about half, subject to agreement between the parties on certain figures. However, before the order was drawn up and sealed the defendant's QC received anonymously a copy of a judgment in the Family Division handed down on 6 January 1995 in respect of matrimonial proceedings involving Mr Bosley. This judgment indicated that evidence in the family proceedings indicated that Mr Bosley had largely recovered from his psychiatric injury by 1993. In these circumstances, the Court of Appeal allowed additional evidence to be adduced on this issue. Having heard further evidence from the psychiatrists, the Court of Appeal further reduced the award. The court was reluctant to find that there had been a deliberate attempt to mislead the trial judge, but they were clearly uncomfortable about the ease with which Mr Bosley was able to adduce evidence in respect of a different present condition and future prognosis at two trials within one month of each other.

1   [1996] EWCA Civ 1217.

1.33 That said, however, in *Frost/White*[1] the Court of Appeal commented that there was no greater risk in psychiatric injury than in 'cases involving back injuries where there is often a wide gap between observable symptoms and complaints'.

1   [1997] 1 All ER 540.

1.34 The Law Commission in *Liability for Psychiatric Illness*[1] pointed out:

'But while some medical commentators consider that fraud or exaggeration are commonplace and while undoubtedly cases of feigned psychosis or actual fabrication do arise, the medical literature suggests that such fraud or exaggeration is not common. The majority of studies indicate that if subjects with disabilities for which no organic cause can be found have not gone back to work before their court case they are unlikely to go back afterwards. This is the case whether they receive large amounts of compensation, small amounts or none at all…

Numerous tests have been developed which can help to ascertain whether an individual has faked or exaggerated psychological symptoms and whether he or she is a reliable informant. The tests are objective and are often scored by a computer. They should always be complemented by clinical evaluation, by an examination of the person's pre- and post-accident functioning, and by corroborative interviews with family members'.

1   Law Com no 249.

4   Causes of action

1.35 The law provides a number of potential causes of action for the victims of psychiatric injury.

A   Negligence

1.36 Claims are most frequently brought under the tort of negligence with regard to psychiatric injury resulting from 'accidents'. The tort of negligence is best encapsulated by the neighbour principle of Lord Atkin in *Donoghue v Stevenson*[1]:

> 'The rule that you are to love your neighbour becomes in law, you must not injure your neighbour: and the lawyer's question, Who is my neighbour? receives a restricted reply. You must take reasonable care to avoid acts or omissions which you can reasonably foresee would be likely to injure your neighbour. Who, then, in law is my neighbour? The answer seems to be – persons who are so closely and directly affected by my act that I ought reasonably to have them in contemplation as being so affected when I am directing my mind to the acts or omissions which are called into question'.

1   [1932] AC 562, HL.

1.37 In *Home Office v Dorset Yacht Co Ltd*[1] Lord Reid said:

> '*Donoghue v Stevenson* may be regarded as a milestone, and the well-known passage in Lord Atkin's speech should I think be regarded as a statement of principle. It is not to be treated as if it were a statutory definition. It will require qualification in new circumstances. But I think that the time has come when we can and should say that it ought to apply unless there is some justification or valid explanation for its exclusion'.

1   [1970] AC 1004, [1970] 2 All ER 294 at 297g, HL.

1.38 The necessary constituent elements for a claim in tort are:

(1) existence of a 'duty of care';
(2) 'breach' of that duty;
(3) reasonable 'foreseeability' that that breach will cause 'damage' (personal injury); and
(4) 'causation' of that 'damage' by that 'breach'.

16 *Liability and compensation for psychiatric injury: an overview*

1.39 The courts have always limited the impact of the duty of care arising under the neighbour principle by a number of different control mechanisms, nowadays usually stated as 'foreseeability', 'proximity' and 'justice and fairness'[1]. The most important of these controls in personal injury claims is 'foreseeability'. The duty of care only exists when it is reasonably foreseeable that the victim would suffer as a result the wrongdoing. It is essential that it is foreseeable that a victim within the same class of potential victims as the injured person might be injured, not any other class of person. It is not necessary that the defendant foresaw damage to the actual victim as an individual.

1   *Caparo Industries plc v Dickman* [1990] 2 AC 605, HL.

1.40 In the vast majority of personal injury cases the nature of the duty is clear. If it is foreseeable that physical injury will be caused to someone by way of negligent conduct, a duty of care will arise. For example, it is obvious that road users owe a duty of care to other road users as it is reasonably foreseeable that they will be injured by a failure to use reasonable care on the road. In other areas, such as employers' liability or maintenance of the highway, Parliament has intervened to deal with these issues rather than leaving it simply to the common law (although a common law claim, which will require foreseeability, might also be pleaded in the alternative). Another control mechanism in tort is 'proximity'. Physical injury caused physically sets its own boundaries and therefore the proximity of relationship between the wrongdoer and the victim is generally not of great relevance in establishing the duty of care in personal injury. A final control mechanism which can be imposed is for the court to ask whether it is fair and just to impose liability. This test once again comes close to conflating legal principles with policy justifications.

1.41 The control mechanisms are generally available as floodgates where the courts are concerned that there may be a flood of claims on the same or similar issue. It is at the boundaries of personal injury law that this becomes an issue; most cases are, of course, straightforward.

1.42 However, the principles behind this are difficult to ascertain. In *Gregg v Scott*[1], Lord Nicholls said:

> '"Floodgates" is not a convincing reason for letting injustice stand unremedied. This reason is invariably advanced whenever a development of the law is under consideration'.

1   [2005] UKHL 2.

1.43 As can be seen, English law has developed over the last 100 years to allow for compensation of psychiatric injury even where there is no accompanying physical injury. However, the progress of such remedies has not been straightforward. The courts have been anxious to impose control mechanisms to prevent the floodgates from opening and overwhelming numbers of pure psychiatric injury cases being brought. These control mechanisms are considered in Chapters 2, 3 and 4. However, the principal distinctions at present are between participants in shocking events and 'mere bystanders'.

1.44 The formulation of 'primary' and 'secondary' victims has been utilised but, as discussed below, has in many respects caused more problems than it solved. For example, when does a 'rescuer' become a participant? What the rescuer does and how proximate he is to the event and whether he is himself in any physical danger have all been mooted as possible restrictions to recovery of compensation. However, it is hard to escape the conclusion that in practice courts are allowing those they consider to be meritorious victims to recover and declining to allow recovery in more doubtful cases. This is not an approach which is easy of analysis or transparently fair.

1.45 There is also the question of victims of psychiatric injury in non-shock cases. In particular there are a number of claimants who suffer psychiatric injury as a result of prolonged stress at work. These have been described as 'primary' victims. However, the courts have developed a whole series of additional controls before the victims of psychiatric injury at work can recover compensation (see Chapter 3).

1.46 In *St James & Seacroft University Hospital NHS Trust v Parkinson*[1] Brooke LJ concluded:

> 'The researches of counsel have shown that recourse to the principles of distributive justice, familiar as they were to Aristotle, has only recently penetrated this field of English law. Lord Hoffmann drew on recent academic writings on the topic in his speech in *Frost v Chief Constable of South Yorkshire* [1999] 2 AC 455, where he was concerned to resolve the conundrum posed by the decision of the Court of Appeal in that case which had permitted police officers at the scene of the Hillsborough football tragedy to recover compensation for suffering post-traumatic stress disorder when such recovery was denied to relatives of the dead who had suffered in the same way.
>
> Lord Hoffmann took the view that the search for principle in this area of the law had been called off in the earlier Hillsborough case, *Alcock v Chief Constable of South Yorkshire Police* [1992] 1 AC 310. He considered that until there was legislative change the courts had got to live with the control mechanisms stated in the *Alcock* case and that any judicial developments had to take them into account. As a result, the House of Lords was engaged, not in the bold development of principle, but in a practical attempt, under adverse conditions, to preserve the general perception of the law as a system of rules which was fair between one citizen and another'.

1 [2001] EWCA Civ 530 at para 19.

B Claims in contract

1.47 In contract, it is necessary to show a breach of an express or implied contractual term and the courts will still require proof of foreseeability of damage and causation. In theory, however, claims in contract may not require the same proof of damage as in tort, namely a recognised psychiatric injury, as noted by the House of Lords in the pleural plaques case, *Johnston v NEI International Combustion Ltd*[1].

1 [2007] UKHL 39.

1.48 Until the 1970s it was thought that no compensation at all could be recovered in contract for distress or injured feeling arising from a breach of contract. However, in respect of the holiday cases[1] damages were awarded for loss of enjoyment of the holiday and in *Cox v Philips Industries Ltd*[2] the Court of Appeal extended this to employment contracts where the breach would be contemplated to give rise to 'vexation, distress and general disappointment'. This was not extended beyond consumer contracts[3] until the House of Lords upheld an award of £10,000 for distress and discomfort of the claimant who suffered from aircraft noise after a negligent survey even though there had been no diminution in value of the property[4].

1   *Jarvis v Swan Tours* [1973] QB 233, CA and *Jackson v Horizon Holidays Ltd* [1975] 1 WLR 1468, CA.
2   [1976] 1 WLR 638.
3   *Johnson v Gore Wood & Co (a firm)* [2002] 2 AC 1.
4   *Farley v Skinner* [2002] 2 AC 732.

1.49 It might perhaps be argued that the reason why in contract there is no need to establish a 'recognised psychiatric injury' is that there is no need for this control mechanism because, unlike claims under the tort of negligence where the numbers potentially contemplated under the duty of care are unlimited, the number of claimants is constrained by being limited to the parties to the contract. And, in practice, the difference between contractual and tortious remedies may not be that significant in most cases, as damages awarded in contract for anything less than a recognised psychiatric illness may be nominal (and effectively worthless).

C   Claims for psychiatric injury from other torts

1.50 The victims of statutory discrimination under the equalities legislation can recover both for 'injuries to feelings' (as is expressly allowed for by the legislation) but also for any associated 'psychiatric injury' if there is a recognised psychiatric injury supported by medical evidence. In the leading case on compensation for injury to feelings, *Vento v Chief Constable of West Yorkshire*[1], the Court of Appeal explored the different awards to be made for 'injury to feelings' and 'psychiatric injury' to a claimant:

> 'Common sense requires that regard should also be had to the overall magnitude of the sum total of the awards of compensation for non-pecuniary loss made under the various headings of injury to feelings, psychiatric damage and aggravated damage. In particular, double recovery should be avoided by taking appropriate account of the overlap between the individual heads of damage. The extent of overlap will depend on the facts of each particular case'.

and, by way of example of how this operates in practice, in the particular appeal in *Vento* the Court of Appeal said:

> 'In our judgment, taking account of the level of awards undisturbed on recent appeals to the Appeal Tribunal and of the JSB Guidelines, the fair, reasonable and just award in this case for non-pecuniary loss is a total of £32,000, made up as to £18,000 for injury to feelings, £5,000 aggravated damages and £9,000 for psychiatric damage, which took the form of clinical depression and adjustment disorder lasting for three years (and against which there was no appeal). We also bear in mind that there was no finding by the employment tribunal that the injury to Ms Vento's feelings would continue after the psychiatric disorder had passed. During the period of psychiatric disorder there must have been a significant degree of overlap with the injury to her feelings'.

1   [2002] EWCA Civ 1871 at paras 68 and 63.

1.51 It is unnecessary for the claimant to establish that psychiatric injury was foreseeable. It is enough to establish breach of the statutory provision and causation of damage as a result. However, it is not always straightforward for the tribunal to distinguish between the upset caused by unlawful discrimination and consequent psychiatric illness, particularly where the latter is an exacerbation of an existing condition or the acceleration of a vulnerability to that condition.

1.52 *Essa v Laing*[1] was a discrimination claim brought by a black Welshman who had been singled out from the other workers on the Millennium Stadium by the foreman, who racially insulted him. A key issue in this case was whether foreseeability was a necessary component of the statutory tort of discrimination. If the claim had been brought at common law Mr Essa, having no previous psychiatric history known to his employers, would almost certainly have lost his case by failing to establish foreseeability. However, the Court of Appeal in *Essa* held (per Pill LJ):

> 'I see no need to superimpose the requirement or pre-requisite of reasonable foreseeability upon the statutory tort in order to achieve the balance of interests which the law of tort requires. It is sufficient if the damage flows directly and naturally from the wrong. While there is force in the submission that, to prevent multiplicity of claims and frivolous claims, a control mechanism beyond that of causation is needed, reliance upon the good sense of employment tribunals in finding the facts and reaching conclusions on them is a sufficient control mechanism, in my view. As a mechanism for protecting a defendant against damages which, on policy grounds, may appear too remote, a further control by way of a reasonable foreseeability test is neither appropriate nor necessary in present circumstances'.

Clarke LJ agreed with Pill LJ, adding:

> 'In all the circumstances I agree with Pill LJ that there is no need to add a further requirement of reasonable foreseeability and that the robust good sense of employment tribunals can be relied upon to ensure that compensation is awarded only where there really is a causal link between the act of discrimination and the injury alleged. No such compensation will of course be payable where there has been a break in the chain of causation or where the claimant has failed to take reasonable steps to mitigate his loss'.

Rix LJ dissented. Although Clark LJ had sympathy with Rix LJ's view, he (Clark LJ) ultimately agreed with Pill LJ and said:

> '… it seems to me that that balance is best achieved by affording compensation for injury caused by the act of discrimination. Such an approach affords justice to the claimant who has been unlawfully discriminated against and is not unjust to the perpetrator because he deliberately made the racist remark. Like Rix LJ, I am intrigued by the just and equitable phraseology found in section 56 of the 1976 Act. Although no-one placed reliance upon it in the course of the argument, it seems to me that for the reasons already given, in the particular circumstances of this statutory tort, justice and equity are best served by holding that a simple test of causation is sufficient. The position might be different if there were a real risk that, without a further requirement of reasonable foreseeability, the floodgates of unmeritorious claims might be opened. I adhere to my view that there is no such real risk'.

1   [2004] ICR 746 at paras 37, 53 and 63.

20 *Liability and compensation for psychiatric injury: an overview*

1.53 The same principle applies to claims for damages for the statutory tort of harassment created by the Protection from Harassment Act 1997.

1.54 Claims for psychiatric injury brought under non-statutory torts other than negligence also have fewer controls. The Law Commission says[1]:

> 'We recognise that one could argue that any special rules that apply in relation to recovery for psychiatric illness for negligence should extend to recovery for psychiatric illness for other torts, such as public or private nuisance, breach of statutory duty or liability under *Rylands v Fletcher*. If not, a plaintiff who is unable to recover damages in negligence because of the application of special restrictions, might be able to avoid their application and make a successful claim by framing the action for damages under another tort. However, not all the reasons advanced for restricting liability for psychiatric illness in negligence apply with equal force to other torts. One of the most frequently cited arguments for limiting liability for psychiatric illness in negligence claims is the fear of a proliferation of claims arising from a single event. The weight of this objection is considerably weaker in relation to claims for the tort of private nuisance, breach of statutory duty and possibly *Rylands v Fletcher* liability. Further reasons may be put forward for not extending any special restrictions on liability in negligence to other torts. For example, damages are recoverable without special restrictions in private nuisance for mental distress caused by the interference with the enjoyment of one's own land, so that to impose limitations on recovery for psychiatric illness would seem odd'.

The other tortious remedies for psychiatric injury are dealt with in Chapter 5.

1   Law Com no 249.

D   Criminal Injuries Compensation

1.55 The statutory scheme established by the government for compensation of the victims of crime compensates those who have suffered psychiatric injury (see Chapter 5).

5   Summary

1.56 The law relating to compensation for psychiatric injury is controversial, confused and subject to change as the common law develops:

- the current law on recoverability for 'primary victims' in 'shock' cases is set out in Chapter 2, including an analysis of *Page v Smith*[1] and the distinction between rescuers, involuntary participants and mere bystanders after *Frost/White*[2];
- the current law on recoverability for 'primary victims' in 'non-shock' cases is set out in Chapter 3, particularly claims for 'stress' at work claims for psychiatric injury arising from overwork or bullying;
- the current law on recoverability for 'secondary victims' is set out in Chapter 4 including an analysis of *Alcock*[3] and a survey of subsequent case law;
- the other potential causes of action for the victims of psychiatric injury are set out in Chapter 5, including the statutory torts of discrimination and harassment, statutory schemes such as the Criminal Injuries Compensation scheme, through other torts, such as assault, and in contract;

- in Chapter 6, Dr Martin Baggeley examines the medical definitions of psychiatric injury in more detail;
- the awards for general damages for pain, suffering and loss of amenity for various kinds of psychiatric injury are considered in Chapter 7, along with the vexed questions of apportionment and acceleration;
- best practice in the handling of psychiatric injury cases is discussed in Chapter 8;
- the legal issues of capacity and psychiatric injury are set out in Chapter 9;
- finally, Chapter 10 is devoted to looking at the many unresolved issues in litigating psychiatric injury claims, and offers some pointers as to the likely ways ahead.

1 [1996] AC 155.
2 *White v Chief Constable of South Yorkshire Police* [1999] 2 AC 455, HL; *Frost v Chief Constable of South Yorkshire Police*, CA.
3 *Alcock v Chief Constable of South Yorkshire Police* [1992] 1 AC 310

2 Primary victims of negligence: shock cases

1 Primary victims

2.1 The concept of the 'primary victim' was introduced by Lord Oliver in *Alcock v Chief Constable of South Yorkshire Police*[1]:

> 'Broadly [victims] divide into two categories, that is to say, those cases in which the injured plaintiff was involved, either mediately or immediately, as a participant, and those in which the plaintiff was no more than the passive and unwilling witness of injury caused to others'.

1 [1992] 1 AC 310, [1991] 4 All ER 907 at 923a.

2.2 This was considered further by Lord Lloyd in *Page v Smith*[1]:

> 'he [Lord Oliver in *Alcock*] referred to those who are involved in an accident as the primary victims, and to those who are not directly involved, but who suffer from what they see or hear, as the secondary victims'.

It is therefore crucial, but in practice is often difficult, to determine whether a claimant is a primary or a secondary victim.

The House of Lords in *Page* thought that their approach was a simple one, but unfortunately it has since caused confusion.

1 [1996] 1 AC 155, [1995] 2 All ER 736 at 755g.

2 Direct participants in events which also cause or risk physical injury to the victim

2.3 It is at least relatively uncontroversial that a claimant who suffers a physical injury as a direct participant in an accident should also be able to recover compensation for associated psychiatric injury. There are several distinct situations which serve as good examples of this principle, but the factual possibilities are unlimited.

A Psychiatric injury associated with significant physical injury

2.4 The combination of serious physical injury and post-traumatic stress disorder following a major accident is very common. For example, in *Mizon v Comcon International*[1], the claimant was an engineer at sea when an engine exploded, trapping him in the engine room, which was on fire. He received severe burns to face, hands and forearms. He had to undergo several operations involving skin grafts, and still had significant residual scarring at the date of trial. As well as his physical injuries he developed post-traumatic stress disorder, depression and a phobia of fires. He suffered a personality change as a result, he was prescribed medication, counselling had been ineffective and the prognosis was poor. The judge awarded him £55,000 for pain, suffering and loss of amenity (of which £28,000, just over half, was expressly for the psychological injury). The total award was £245,403 and it would seem from the case report that the principal reason for his being unable to return to work was the psychiatric injury rather than the physical injuries.

This is a good example of a situation where the shocking nature of the accident which led to post-traumatic stress disorder and other psychiatric illnesses and where the claim for compensation for psychiatric injury as a primary victim is unlikely to be challenged. Although the claimant had suffered serious physical injuries it was the psychiatric consequences which led to the bulk of the compensation. As well as post-traumatic stress disorder, other psychiatric injury related to serious physical injury can include phobias which arise specifically from the circumstances of the accident (such as the fear of fire in *Mizon*).

1   19 August 1999, HHJ Bowers at Kingston-upon-Thames County Court, reported in Kemp & Kemp *The Quantum of Damages* at C2–001.

B   Soft-tissue injury and depression

2.5   Another common situation is where the claimant has suffered a disabling physical condition, often a back injury, and as a result has also developed clinical depression. Sometimes this involves the trigger of an inherent disposition to depression, or the recurrence of a past depression which had previously been asymptomatic. It is often difficult to disentangle the effect of the physical injury from the effect of the psychiatric injury. This is particularly so in the case of soft tissue whiplash-type injury to the back and neck where there are few or no objective signs of the physical injury. However, the claimant presents with continuing pain and/or loss of function which is often associated with clinical depression.

2.6   For example, in *Jones v Majid*[1], the claimant had suffered soft tissue injuries in a road traffic accident. The discomfort from the physical injuries ceased after 6–9 months. The claimant, however, continued to suffer from driving phobia, panic attacks and became suicidal. She claimed that she was suffering from post-traumatic stress disorder resulting from the accident, but she did not meet the diagnostic criteria for this. She had some previous history of depression, although that was in remission at the time of the accident. The judge found that she was genuinely suffering from a disabling depressed state of mind which amounted to moderately severe depression. However, he limited her claim to seven years from the accident and awarded damages for pain, suffering and loss of amenity of £18,000 (to include the whiplash injury which, on the facts, might have merited perhaps £1,500 on its own).

1   (17 September 1999, unreported), HHJ Swanson at Barnsley County Court, reported in Kemp & Kemp *The Quantum of Damages* at C1–010.

C Brain injury and 'personality change'

2.7 It is not always easy to distinguish between organic brain damage which has caused a physical change in the brain and which has consequently led to a personality change (eg damage to the frontal lobe of the brain) and psychiatric injury which has led to the same effect. Sometimes the organic damage may be suspected by neurological experts, but be impossible to show on brain imaging. The experts will often have to concede that similar effects might be caused by psychiatric injury. The clinical presentation of the claimant is crucial and ultimately the court, if it accepts the claimant as genuine, is not likely to be overly concerned as to whether this was caused by physical or psychiatric injury. Neuropsychiatric evidence is likely to be crucial.

2.8 If structural brain damage is accepted, the injury, which is often similar in symptoms to a psychiatric injury, might be described by the court as 'organic personality change'.

In *Edwards v Martin*[1] the claimant suffered a serious brain injury:

> 'The claimant was admitted to hospital unconscious and suffered prolonged post-traumatic amnesia. He was initially detained in hospital for 12 days, but required readmission on 4 August and suffered a generalised tonic fit two or three days later. (This was an isolated incident suggestive of post-traumatic epilepsy; there has been no repeat.) Importantly, MRI scanning revealed significant organic brain damage, in the form of multiple foci of signal loss throughout the cerebral hemispheres. This organic brain damage is permanent and is agreed to be responsible for the cognitive and behavioural impairments and personality disorder which the claimant has since displayed'.

However, the neurologists were agreed:

> 'that the head injury was severe even though it has not resulted in any continuing neurological impairment'.

It was agreed that there were multiple neuropsychiatric effects including:

> 'memory loss; fatigue, inertia and lack of motivation; irritability and temper; rigid and at times obsessive thinking; total loss of libido; depression and phobic anxiety'

although there were significant issues as to their severity. The defendants conducted surveillance. The judge concluded:

> 'I am satisfied that there has been no conscious exaggeration on the claimant's part. He has shown little or no interest in this litigation at any time. There is specific evidence of his lack of interest in, and carelessness with, his financial affairs; such matters cause him stress, from which it is his instinct to escape. In the early stages he was keen to return to work, and did so much too soon ... For a long time he lacked insight into the extent of the effects of his injury upon his life and relationships. From the early medical reports it appears that he tended to minimise his problems, or to be unaware of them'.

1 [2010] EWHC 570 (QB).

2.9 However, by contrast, in *Smith v Rod Jenkins Marine*[1] the claimant had suffered a fracture to the right temporal bone and fractures to the right jaw and cheekbone. The claimant contended that the head injury had caused him to be permanently unfit for work and to be in permanent need of a significant level of care to enable him to lead a reasonably normal life. He alleged that he was depressed, verging on suicidal, subject to mood swings and suffered poor concentration and a lack of enjoyment of life. The defendants adduced surveillance evidence. A neuropsychologist called by the claimant had found that he had suffered only a moderate head injury, although he accepted the claimant was suffering from post-concussion syndrome. The judge concluded that the claimant's symptoms were not caused by organic brain injury and nor had he suffered post-traumatic stress disorder. There was a degree of continuing mental disorder attributable to the effects of post-concussion syndrome. However, the judge found that the claimant had consciously exaggerated his disability.

1   [2003] EWHC 1356 (QB).

D   Serious psychiatric injury associated with minor physical injury

2.10 Provided that a psychiatric injury is a medical consequence of a physical injury the wrongdoer is liable for the full extent of the psychiatric injury. In *Simmons v British Steel*[1], the claimant suffered a relatively minor physical injury (unlike in *Page v Smith*[2] where there was no associated physical injury at all):

> 'The pursuer sustained injuries on 13 May 1996 in the course of his employment as a burner at Clyde Bridge Steel Works, Cambuslang. He tripped and fell from the burning table and struck his head on a metal stanchion. There was a severe impact, but fortunately the pursuer was wearing protective head gear. So his head injury was not as serious as it might have been. Nevertheless he sustained a severe blow to the head. He was dazed and shaking, and developed a swelling on the right side of his head. This was accompanied by headaches, disturbance to his eyesight and suppuration from his right ear'.

But he also suffered a far more significant psychiatric injury:

> 'After the accident the pursuer experienced an exacerbation of a pre-existing skin condition, and he developed a change in his personality which has resulted in a severe depressive illness. He has not returned to work since the accident. While there has been some improvement in his condition, it is likely to be several years before he is fit to do so. These further consequences have turned out to be much more serious than the immediate effects of the head injury. The Lord Ordinary found that the pursuer's pre-existing skin condition was exacerbated and that he was suffering from a depressive illness and a complete change in his personality'.

The psychiatric injury may have been caused directly by the accident or as a result of frustration and anger which followed the accident. The claimant had warned his employer of the possibility of such an accident beforehand, which contributed to the severity of his anger afterwards when it happened in those same circumstances to him. At first instance the claim for damages for psychiatric injury failed as the judge was not satisfied that the psychiatric injury had been caused by the accident, but rather as a result of his subsequent absence from work and his resentment towards his employer. For all practical purposes, the judge had felt that the loss was too 'remote' to be compensated.

1   [2004] UKHL 20.
2   [1996] 1 AC 155. See para **2.14** below.

2.11 On the appeal in the House of Lords, drawing an analogy with *Wardlaw v Bonnington Castings Ltd*[1] (a case on causation of physical injury where there were two potential causative sources, one negligent and one non-negligent), the court held (per Lord Hope):

> 'In this case there were several causes of the pursuer's anger. It was enough that one of them arose from the fault of the defenders... The conclusion which I would draw from the evidence is that it made a material contribution to the development of the skin condition and to the depressive mental illness which resulted from it'.

Lord Rodger pointed out that the claimant was undoubtedly a primary victim under Lord Lloyd's classification in *Page v Smith*. He doubted that in cases of psychiatric injury it was often possible in practice to divide the causes and that:

> 'regret, fear for the future, frustration at the slow pace of recovery and anger are all emotions that are likely to arise, unbidden, in the minds of those who suffer injuries in an accident.'

1   1956 SC (HL) 26.

E Delayed onset of severe psychiatric injury accompanying physical injury

2.12 Sometimes the onset of the severe psychiatric injury might be remote in time from the accident which caused physical injury.

In *Corr v IBC Vehicles Ltd*[1], the claimant was the widow and executrix of Mr Corr who had been seriously injured in an accident at work. He was hit on the side of his head by an automated robot arm on the car part production line on which he worked. He was nearly decapitated and his right ear was severed. He suffered from post-traumatic stress disorder and depression. Proceedings were commenced three years later, just within the limitation period, but still had not been concluded six years after the accident when he committed suicide.

It had been agreed by the experts that that the depression caused by the accident had driven him to suicide. Evidence before the court suggested that about 10% of severely depressed people seek to take their own lives. The court therefore held, whether or not this was a strictly necessary ingredient for a claim, that suicide here was foreseeable. Nor was it treated as a *novus actus interveniens* on the ground that the suicide was not a voluntary act, but inextricably linked with the breach of duty.

The Lords were more exercised about whether there should be an apportionment between the parties by way of a finding of contributory fault. Finding suicide to be 'contributory fault' might be thought harsh, but under the Law Reform (Contributory Negligence) Act 1945, s 1:

Psychiatric injury arising from accident where physical injury was foreseeable

'... the damages ... shall be reduced to such extent as the court thinks just and equitable having regard to the claimant's share in the responsibility for the damage'.

1   [2008] UKHL 13.

2.13 In *Corr v IBC Vehicles Ltd*[1], the Lords (Lord Scott dissenting) made no reduction, but that was largely on the basis that evidence on the issue had not been fully adduced.

Lord Bingham[2] (with whom Lord Walker agreed) would not have allowed any reduction for contributory fault:

'For reasons already given, I do not think that any blame should be attributed to the deceased for the consequences of a situation which was of the employer's making, not his. Consistently with my rejection of arguments based on novus actus and unreasonable conduct, I would similarly absolve the deceased from any causal responsibility for his own tragic death. I would accordingly assess his contributory negligence at 0%. That, in my opinion, reflects the responsibility of the deceased for his own loss (see *Reeves v Commissioner of Police of the Metropolis* [1999] QB 169, 198)'.

But Lord Neuberger[3] (with whom Lords Scott and Mance agreed) said:

'In my judgment, in a case such as this, it would represent a failure to take into account the importance of personal autonomy, and would be inconsistent with the reasoning in *Reeves*, if we were to hold that, save where the deceased was of entirely sound mind at the relevant time, it would be inappropriate in principle to reduce the damages awarded under the 1976 Act on the grounds of contributory negligence, where the deceased had taken his own life. The mere facts that his mental state was impaired to some extent by a condition for which the defendant was responsible, and that he would not have killed himself but for that impairment, cannot, in my opinion, without more justify rejecting the contention that there could have been a degree of "fault" on his part'.

Lord Scott would have reduced the damages by 20%; Lord Neuberger felt that any reduction would be between 0% and 50%, depending on the extent to which the claimant's capacity for independent thought had been impaired by the defendant's negligence. Future claims in these circumstances will, in all likelihood, face a reduction for contributory fault.

1   [2008] UKHL 13.
2   At para 22.
3   At para 64.

3 'Pure' psychiatric injury arising from an accident where physical injury to the claimant was foreseeable

2.14 In *Page v Smith*[1], the House of Lords held that in case where there is a foreseeable risk of physical injury, then any psychiatric injury which also occurs as a result of the accident is compensatable, even if the psychiatric injury or its extent would not be reasonably foreseeable to the defendant. That physical injury did not in fact occur is irrelevant. The facts of *Page* were as follows (per Lord Lloyd[2]):

> '... the plaintiff, a schoolteacher by profession, was driving at approximately 30 miles per hour when suddenly, without warning, the defendant, coming in the opposite direction, turned right across the white line. The plaintiff braked hard, but the two vehicles were so close that he could not avoid a collision. The impact was severe enough to cause considerable damage to both vehicles. Nevertheless, the plaintiff was able to drive his car home. The judge said: "I find on the balance of probabilities that there was a collision of moderate severity. It must have been a frightening experience for Mr Page and I have no doubt that he did suffer nervous shock in the broad sense of the word." Three hours later the plaintiff felt exhausted. He took to his bed. The exhaustion continued...'

1 [1996] 1 AC 155, [1995] 2 All ER 736.
2 [1995] 2 All ER 736 at 756c.

2.15 It should be noted that, as is sometimes assumed, the collision was not a low velocity collision. In his dissenting judgment Lord Jauncey had argued that in finding for the claimant, the Lords would be extending the potential liability to, for example, psychiatric injury to a hysterical person following a minor bump whilst parking, but Lord Lloyd[1] dismissed this argument, stressing the need for physical injury to be foreseeable (even if not in fact suffered):

> 'There is another limiting factor. Before a defendant can be held liable for psychiatric injury suffered by a primary victim, he must at least have foreseen the risk of physical injury. So that if, to take the example given by my noble and learned friend Lord Jauncey of Tullichettle...there could be no question of his being held liable for the onset of hysteria. Since he could not reasonably foresee any injury, physical or psychiatric, he would owe the plaintiff no duty of care. That example is however, very far removed from the present case'.

1 [1996] 1 AC 155, [1995] 2 All ER 736 at 760f.

2.16 In *Page* the speeds involved were about 30mph and there was considerable damage to both vehicles. However, the claimant did not sustain any physical injury. That such physical injury might have occurred was, however, reasonably foreseeable to the defendant (per Lord Lloyd[1]):

> 'It was enough to ask whether the defendant should reasonably have foreseen that the plaintiff might have suffered a physical injury as a result of the defendant's negligence, so as to bring him within the range of the defendant's duty of care. It was unnecessary to ask as a separate question, whether the defendant should reasonably have foreseen injury by shock; and it is irrelevant that the plaintiff did not, in fact, suffer any external physical injury'.

And hindsight should not be used

> 'Liability for physical injury depends on what was reasonably foreseeable by the defendant before the event. It could not be right that a negligent defendant should escape liability for psychiatric injury just because, though serious physical injury was foreseeable, it did not in fact transpire. Such a result in the case of a primary victim is neither necessary, logical nor just. To introduce hindsight into the trial of an ordinary running-down action would do the law no service'.

1 [1996] 1 AC 155, [1995] 2 All ER 736 at 761c and 759h.

2.17 The claimant was obviously a primary victim (per Lord Lloyd[1]):

> 'He was himself directly involved in the accident, and well within the range of foreseeable physical injury'.

It was accepted that the claimant had an 'eggshell personality' (per Lord Browne-Wilkinson[2]):

> 'In the present case the defendant could not foresee the exact type of psychiatric damage in fact suffered by the plaintiff who, due to his ME, was "an eggshell personality"'.

1   [1996] 1 AC 155, [1995] 2 All ER 736 at 755c.
2   At 753j.

2.18 In the tort of negligence generally, whilst the type of damage must be foreseeable, the extent need not be. The wrongdoer is, of course, not liable if the injury pre-exists and developed subsequently entirely independently of the accident. The 'eggshell skull principle' arose from the decision in *Smith v Leech Brain & Co Ltd*[1]. In that case the type of injury suffered by the claimant (a burn to the lip) was a 'personal injury' as was the subsequent injury (the development of a cancer). They were not different kinds of damage. The claimant could recover compensation for the cancer even though he only developed this following the burn to the lip because of his own particular genetic predisposition which could not have been known to the wrongdoer. *Paris v Stepney Borough Council*[2] further illustrates the point. The claimant was blind in his left eye and this was known to his employers. He was therefore particularly vulnerable in respect of any injury to his right eye. The employer therefore owed him as an individual a particular duty to supply him with safety goggles to protect his right eye from injury, even though it was accepted that there was no general duty in this respect with regard to fully-sighted employees. They did not do so and were held negligent when he was left totally blind following an accident at work. It is, of course, easier to establish knowledge of a particular physical disability than a pre-existing vulnerability to a psychiatric condition (although, even in *Paris*, the evidence was that the employer had not been aware of the disability at the commencement of employment).

1   [1962] 2 QB 405.
2   [1950] UKHL 3.

2.19 In *Page* Lord Lloyd relied on the 'eggshell skull rule' in respect of 'eggshell personalities', citing *Malcolm v Broadhurst*[1], although the editors of *Clerk and Lindsell on Torts*[2] state:

> 'However, there are likely to be many more "eggshell personalities" than "eggshell skulls" and it is questionable whether a rule developed with physical injury in mind should be applied to psychiatric injury'.

1   [1970] 3 All ER 508.
2   (20th edn, 2010) p 458.

2.20 Lord Lloyd proceeded to distinguish the earlier dictum of Lord Denning in *King v Phillips*[1], namely:

Primary victims of negligence: shock cases

'Howsoever that may be, whether the exemption for shock be based on want of duty or on remoteness, there can be no doubts that since *Bourhill v Young* [1943] AC 92 that the test for liability for shock is foreseeability of injury by shock'

by stating[2] that Lord Denning's dictum was:

'... both too wide and too narrow. It is too wide where the plaintiff is the secondary victim, as she was in *King v Phillips*. For subsequent cases have shown that foreseeability of injury by shock is not the sole test (see *Alcock's case* [1992] 1 AC 310, 396 per Lord Keith of Kinkel and *McFarlane v EE Caledonia Ltd* [1994] 2 All ER 1). The test is also too narrow, where, as here, the plaintiff is the primary victim. There is nothing in *Bourhill v Young* to displace the ordinary rule that where the plaintiff is within the range of foreseeable physical injury the defendant must take his victim as he finds him. The whole point of *Bourhill v Young* was that the plaintiff was not within the range of foreseeable physical injury'.

And Lord Lloyd[3] rejected any limitation to persons of normal fortitude or phlegm:

'Since the number of potential claimants is limited by the nature of the case, there is no need to impose any further limit by reference to a person of ordinary phlegm. Nor can I see any justification for doing so'.

1   [1953] 1 QB 429 at 441.
2   [1996] 1 AC 155, [1995] 2 All ER 736 at 764b.
3   [1995] 2 All ER 736 at 760d.

2.21 Lord Browne-Wilkinson[1], in agreeing with the majority of the court, summarised their view:

'I am therefore of opinion that any driver of a car should reasonably foresee that, if he drives carelessly, he will be liable to cause injury, either physical or psychiatric or both, to other users of the highway who become involved in an accident. Therefore he owes to such persons a duty of care to avoid such injury. In the present case the defendant could not foresee the exact type of psychiatric damage in fact suffered by the plaintiff who, due to his ME, was "an eggshell personality". But that is of no significance since the defendant did owe a duty of care to prevent foreseeable damage, including psychiatric damage. Once such duty of care is established, the defendant must take the plaintiff as he finds him'.

1   [1996] 1 AC 155, [1995] 2 All ER 736 at 753j.

2.22 However, two members of the House of Lords gave dissenting judgements, Lord Jauncey[1] saying:

'The rule that a tortfeasor is entitled to assume that his victim is of normal fortitude is designed to limit the class of bystanders to whom a duty is owed and is neither relevant nor necessary in the case of participants. Taking your victim as you find him however is relevant, not to the existence of a duty owed to him but rather to the question of damages payable in respect of breach of a duty otherwise established'.

1   [1996] 1 AC 155, [1995] 2 All ER 736 at 748e.

2.23 The *Page* case was remitted to the Court of Appeal to determine whether in fact the claimant's condition had been caused by the accident and the court upheld the trial judge's conclusions that it had[1].

1   *Page v Smith (No 2)* [1996] 1 WLR 855.

Psychiatric injury arising from accident where physical injury was foreseeable 31

2.24 It does not matter, following *Simmons v British Steel*[1], whether the psychiatric injury was caused directly by the incident giving rise to the anticipation of physical injury or as a result of feelings about the incident. In *Donachie v Chief Constable of the Greater Manchester Police*[2] the claimant was a policeman who suffered psychiatric injury after being assigned to attach a tagging device to the underside of a car in circumstances where he risked serious injury or death if he were caught. In allowing his appeal, the Court of Appeal held:

> '… the judge, in the passages from his judgment that I have set out in paragraph 19 above, wrongly relied on *Sutherland v Hatton*, a claim for occupational stress induced psychiatric injury that failed because there was no reasonably foreseeable risk of injury of any sort. This case was one in which, as I have said, there was a reasonable foreseeability that the Chief Constable's breach of duty would cause physical injury to Mr Donachie, though not of the kind he actually suffered, and via the unforeseeable psychiatric injury actually caused by his negligence. He was thus a primary victim in respect of whom there was a reasonable foreseeability of physical injury and, in consequence, in respect of whom it was not necessary to prove involvement in an "event" in the form of an assault or otherwise'.

1 [2004] UKHL 20.
2 [2004] EWCA Civ 405 at para 23.

2.25 The court went further to emphasise that a single shocking event was not necessarily required[1]:

> 'I should add that, even if it had been necessary to look for an "event" in this case sufficient to enable Mr Donachie to rely as a primary victim on reasonable foreseeability of psychiatric, as distinct from physical injury, I would have had sympathy with Mr Turner's submission that the circumstances in which he had been placed as a police officer, coupled with his fear engendered by those circumstances of physical injury, are indistinguishable in principle from occurrence of such injury. If A puts B in a position which A can reasonably foresee that B would fear physical injury, and B, as a result, suffers psychiatric injury and/or physical injury, B is, in my view, a primary victim. If it were necessary to characterise the onset of the fear causative of such injury as "an event", I would do so. There is all the difference in the world between a person like Mr Donachie, put in such a position by the tortfeasor, and someone who happens to learn from afar and/or a significant time afterwards of an event in which he had no involvement, the discovery of which he claims to have caused him psychiatric injury'.

1 [2004] EWCA Civ 405 at para 24.

2.26 The Law Commission in their report no 249 commented on *Page*:

> 'Many have welcomed this decision. Although the decision was given after the publication of the consultation paper, so that we did not have an opportunity to ask consultees for their views, several did comment in any event. On the whole, the responses, especially from practitioners, were very favourable to the decision. They suggested that it rendered the law simpler and more certain… Also welcomed was the fact that liability for psychiatric injury would also turn on the fortuitous absence of a physical injury'.

2.27 However, the decision in *Page* has also caused much controversy. When, three years later, a differently-composed House of Lords heard the appeals in *Frost/White*,

32 *Primary victims of negligence: shock cases*

Lord Goff (who would have in fact allowed the appeals by the professional rescuers in *Frost/White*) was particularly scathing:

> '... the decision of your Lordships' House in *Page v Smith* constituted a remarkable departure from these generally accepted principles. The case was concerned with a traffic accident, in which the defendant's car collided with the plaintiff's car—a collision described as one of "moderate severity". Indeed nobody in either car suffered any physical injury, and the plaintiff (who was not even bruised by his seat belt) was able to drive his damaged car away after the accident ... Lord Lloyd of Berwick ... departed from the previous understanding of the law in a number of respects'[1].

1   [1999] 2 AC 455, [1999] 1 All ER 1 at 14f.

2.28 Lord Goff argued that, as the driver of one of the cars involved in the accident, Mr Page was clearly a 'primary victim' so the special control mechanisms to deal with bystanders or 'secondary victims' were irrelevant, so that:

> 'On the then-accepted principles, the only question for consideration was whether the defendant could reasonably foresee that, in the circumstances which in fact occurred, a person of ordinary fortitude in the position of the plaintiff would suffer psychiatric injury'[1].

1   [1999] 2 AC 455, [1999] 1 All ER 1 at 15b.

2.29 Lord Goff went on to point out that the majority of the House of Lords in *Page* had found as a subsidiary ground for their decision that on the facts of *Page* this had indeed been established. But in their primary grounds for the decision, in Lord Goff's opinion, the majority in *Page* had:

> '... dethroned foreseeability of psychiatric injury from its central position as the unifying feature of this branch of the law ... by invoking the distinction between primary and secondary victims'[1].

1   [1999] 2 AC 455, [1999] 1 All ER 1 at 15d.

2.30 Lord Goff accepted that the Lords in *Page* had recognised that in the case of secondary victims (see Chapter 4):

> '... the law insists on certain "control mechanisms", to limit the number of potential claimants...'

but he concluded that with regard to primary victims that the majority in *Page* had changed the law as:

> 'Before the decision of your Lordships' House in *Page v Smith*, the requirement of reasonable fortitude was regarded as being of general application, in cases concerned with primary victims as well as those concerned with secondary victims'[1].

1   [1999] 2 AC 455, [1999] 1 All ER 1 at 17f.

2.31 However, giving a contrary view, Lord Griffiths in *Frost/White* welcomed the decision in *Page* as 'a sensible development of the law', pointing out, as discussed elsewhere[1]:

> 'If some very minor physical injury is suffered and this triggers a far more serious psychiatric disorder no one questions that damages are recoverable for the psychiatric disorder'[2].

Lord Griffiths therefore felt that the law should make no distinction between a situation where a minor physical injury leads to a subsequent serious psychological injury and a situation where a physical injury was contemplated, but not in fact suffered, and the claimant subsequently develops a psychiatric injury by reason of the shock:

> 'If the victim of the negligence escapes minor physical injury but the shock or fear of the peril in which he is placed by the defendant's negligent conduct causes psychiatric injury I can see no sensible reason why he should not recover for that psychiatric damage'[3].

1   See para **2.10**.
2   [1999] 2 AC 455, [1999] 1 All ER 1 at 5f.
3   [1999] 1 All ER 1 at 5g.

2.32 A key reason for this is, Lord Griffiths considered, the continuing development of our understanding of psychiatric injury and the fact that:

> 'As medical science advances we realise how difficult it is to separate out the physical and psychiatric consequences of trauma, and I believe the law would do better to regard both as personal injury as *Page v Smith* requires in the case of primary victims, that is victims who are imperilled or reasonably believe themselves to be imperilled by the defendant's negligence'[1].

1   [1999] 2 AC 455, [1999] 1 All ER 1 at 5h.

2.33 Subsequent academic debate had concentrated particularly on whether the Lords decision in *Page* contradicted the Privy Council's unambiguous endorsement in *The Wagon Mound No 1*[1] of Denning LJ's statement of principle which was 'clearly seen as an all-purpose test for personal injury actions'[2].

1   [1961] AC 388.
2   Nicholas Mullany in (1995) 3 Journal of Law and Medicine 112.

2.34 This debate has also continued in more recent decisions. Lord Neuberger in *Corr v IBC Vehicles Ltd*[1] suggested that he would welcome an opportunity to revisit *Page* in an appropriate case:

> 'The first point concerns the somewhat controversial decision of this House in *Page v Smith* [1996] AC 155. As Lord Bingham has explained, neither party has criticised that decision, let alone invited the House to review it. At least for my part, I understood that was the position of the employer because, even if we had been persuaded that *Page* was wrongly decided, that would not have ensured the success of this appeal. I agree. Accordingly, not least in the light of the trenchant observations of Lord Goff of Chieveley in *Frost v Chief Constable of South Yorkshire Police* [1999] 2 AC 9 455 at 473D to 480F, I would not want to appear to prejudge any decision as to the correctness of the majority view in *Page*, if it comes to be challenged before your Lordship's House on another occasion'.

1   [2008] UKHL 13 at para 54.

34 Primary victims of negligence: shock cases

2.35 In the pleural plaques cases, *Johnston v NEI International Combustion Ltd*[1], the House of Lords decided that *Page* did not apply to a claim for psychiatric injury by a worker who developed a depressive illness as a result of his fear of having been exposed to asbestos when in fact there had been no asbestos-related physical injury.

Lord Mance pointed out that the circumstances in *Page* were very different, as:

'… it concerned psychiatric injury arising as an immediate consequence of an obvious accident, in which the claimant could foreseeably have been physically injured at the time'[2].

1   [2007] UKHL 39.
2   At para 104.

2.36 Some members of the House of Lords queried whether *Page* should be limited to its facts (per Lord Hope):

'The labels that were identified in *Page v Smith* should not be extended beyond what was in contemplation in that case. The category of primary victim should be confined to persons who suffer psychiatric injury caused by fear or distress resulting from involvement in an accident caused by the defendant's negligence or its immediate aftermath. A person like Mr Grieves who suffers psychiatric injury because of something that he may experience in the future as a result of the defendant's past negligence is in an entirely different category. The immediacy that is characteristic of the situation that applies to primary victims as contemplated in *Page v Smith* [1996] AC 155 is lacking in his case'[1],

or even revisited entirely (per Lord Mance):

'I would leave open the correctness of *Page v Smith* for another day. I see some force in the criticisms that have been levied against it, and I am not confident that it does not cause uncertainty and argument (the latter indeed in this case). On the one hand psychiatric illness resulting over time from the exacerbation of a physical condition contributed to by anger about the occurrence of a past accident (in which the claimant did, it is true, suffer a physical injury) was held recoverable irrespective of foreseeability in *Simmons v British Steel plc* [2004] ICR 585, in reliance on *Page v Smith*. On the other hand, the present case establishes that psychiatric illness arising from the stress of belated discovery of a continuing risk of future physical illness arising from past exposure to asbestos dust is not actionable, in the absence of specific foreseeability. Some artificiality may be a necessary result of the controls on which the law insists in this area. But this distinction, although one that I endorse if necessary, is not, I think, particularly happy. However, it is unnecessary to say more about it in this case'[2].

1   [2007] UKHL 39 at para 54.
2   At para 104.

2.37 Lord Hoffmann, however, said:

'Counsel for the defendant invited the House to depart from the decision in *Page v Smith* on the ground that it was wrongly decided. It has certainly had no shortage of critics, chief of whom was Lord Goff of Chieveley in *Frost v Chief Constable of South Yorkshire Police* [1999] 2 AC 455, supported by a host of academic writers. But I do not think that it would be right to depart from *Page v Smith*. It does not appear to have caused any practical difficulties and is not, I think, likely to do so if confined to the kind of situation which the majority in that case had in mind. That was a foreseeable event (a collision) which, viewed in prospect, was such as might cause physical injury or psychiatric injury or both. Where such an event has in fact happened and caused psychiatric injury, the House decided that it is unnecessary to ask whether it was foreseeable that what actually happened would have that consequence. Either form of injury is recoverable'[1].

1   [2007] UKHL 39 at para 32.

2.38 Lord Hoffmann took the view that the claimants in *Johnson* were in fact seeking to extend the principle in *Page* and that this should not be permitted:

'In the present case, the foreseeable event was that the claimant would contract an asbestos-related disease. If that event occurred, it could no doubt cause psychiatric as well as physical injury. But the event has not occurred. The psychiatric illness has been caused by apprehension that the event may occur. The creation of such a risk is, as I have said, not in itself actionable. I think it would be an unwarranted extension of the principle in *Page v Smith* to apply it to psychiatric illness caused by apprehension of the possibility of an unfavourable event which had not actually happened'[1].

Page was, therefore, in the event distinguished rather than overruled by *Johnston*.

1   [2007] UKHL 39 at para 33.

2.39 There remains, however, an obvious tension at the highest level of the judiciary which has clearly still not been resolved. On the one hand, the 'modernisers' see the scientific advances in medicine and the understanding of psychiatric illness as demanding that psychiatric injury be treated in the same way as any other personal injury for 'primary victims' (at least in so far as direct participants in an accident, rescuers in physical danger and 'involuntary participants' are concerned). By contrast, the 'conservatives' remain concerned about psychiatric illness and would wish to limit recovery to those cases where it is reasonably foreseeable that even those persons of 'ordinary phlegm' might suffer psychiatric injury (ie 'truly' shocking events rather than a simple collision of two vehicles at 30mph causing no physical injury).

2.40 Notwithstanding the criticisms, however, the decision in *Page* has now stood for 15 years and it seems unlikely to be displaced entirely. The view 'thus far but no further' is perhaps the best summary of the present position.

4 'Pure' psychiatric injury with no physical injury and no shocking event

2.41 As we have seen, in *Johnston v NEI International Combustion Ltd*[1] (the pleural plaques decision) the Lords held that the presence of symptomless pleural plaques did not give rise to a cause of action as there is in law no 'injury'. This is so even if the claimant develops a recognised psychiatric injury as a result, because to found such a claim it is necessary for the claimant to also suffer a shock with a foreseeable physical injury, however slight[2], even if the physical injury does not in fact transpire. If there is no alarming accident, a psychiatric injury alone was not a reasonably foreseeable consequence of the breach of duty. Lord Scott said:

'But in *Simmons*, as in *Page v Smith*, the illness was prompted by the pursuer's reaction to a very unpleasant event that had actually occurred, not by his contemplation of the risk that something unpleasant might occur in the future. Moreover, his claim was for a psychiatric illness brought on by an accident in which he had suffered a far from trivial physical injury. In my view *Simmons* is not authority for the application of *Page v Smith* in this case'[3].

The claimants' 'aggregation' argument, that symptomless changes to the body combined with anxiety should constitute injury, was dismissed. The decision was highly controversial: the negligent exposure to asbestos was admitted, the claimants did suffer 'scarring', albeit internal rather than external, and all developed at least the anxiety that the knowledge of their exposure to asbestos and potential development of an asbestos related condition inevitably induced.

1 [2007] UKHL 39.
2 *Page v Smith* [1996] 1 AC 155.
3 [2007] UKHL 39 at para 97.

5 Rescuers

2.42 The category of 'rescuers' has also caused some controversy in respect of claims for psychiatric injury. Rescuers might be said to be those people who come upon the scene of a shocking event and pitch in to help the victims. It might therefore have been thought unremarkable that some such rescuers might develop psychiatric injury as a result of the horrors they witnessed.

2.43 The first major reported 'rescuer case' was *Chadwick v British Transport Commission*[1]. Ninety people were killed in a railway accident at Lewisham, a couple of hundred yards from Mr Chadwick's house, when a moving train ran into the back of a stationary train in fog. The accident happened at 6pm and Mr Chadwick immediately went to help and did not return home until 3am. The carnage was significant; as well as the dead there were numerous severely injured people, many of whom were fearful that movement of carriages would cause further serious injury.

Mr Chadwick was a hard-working and successful owner of a window-cleaning business. He had had pre-existing 'psycho-neurotic' symptoms arising in 1941, but he had suffered no other such symptoms until after the accident in 1958. As a result of the accident, the medical evidence was that he had suffered a 'major stress reaction' which led to his admission as a psychiatric in-patient. The judge accepted the medical evidence that 'this is something which is known to result from major catastrophes such as such as earthquakes, fires, floods and major accidents and disasters'.

Waller J did feel that 'there was clearly an element of personal danger', but held that he had 'to deal with the case on the basis that it was the horror of the whole experience which caused his reaction'.

The judge held:

'In the present case, the defendants were negligent towards their passengers. As a result, passengers were injured and put in peril. All that could reasonably have been foreseen. It could also be foreseen that somebody might try and rescue passengers and suffer injury in the process, and in my opinion the defendants owed a duty to Mr Chadwick who was within the area of contemplation'[2].

And he also considered that 'Once the possibility of rescue occurs, the precise manner of rescue is immaterial'.

Mr Chadwick's estate therefore succeeded in recovering compensation.

1   [1967] 2 All ER 945.
2   [1967] 2 All ER 945 at 952A.

2.44 In *Alcock v Chief Constable of South Yorkshire Police*[1], the court included within the ambit of 'primary victims':

> 'not only to those threatened... by [the defendant's] careless acts but also to those who, as a result, are induced to go to their rescue and suffer injury in so doing'.

However, in *Frost v Chief Constable of South Yorkshire Police/White v Chief Constable of South Yorkshire Police*[2], police officers who attended the scene of the Hillsborough disaster and had suffered psychiatric injury brought claims for compensation. The House of Lords in *Alcock* had earlier rejected the claims of relatives who suffered psychiatric injury on the grounds that they were secondary victims who did not pass the 'control' tests (see Chapter 4). In terms of liability, it had been established that the failure of the police force (although not, of course, the individual police officer rescuers) had been responsible for the failings which led to the deaths of the Hillsborough victims.

1   [1992] 1 AC 310, [1991] 4 All ER 907 at 923g.
2   [1999] 2 AC 455.

2.45 Underlying the rejection of the rescuers' claims was undoubtedly the feeling that to allow the claims of the police officer rescuers would sit:

> 'uneasily with the denial of the claims of the relatives ... in *Alcock* ... [which might] perplex the man on the underground'[1].

And Lord Hoffmann said a result which gave the police officers compensation but not the relatives 'would be quite unacceptable'.

1   [1999] 2 AC 455, [1999] 1 All ER 1 at 34c.

2.46 All of the Lords rejected the so-called 'fireman's rule', which applies in some US states and which prevents claims where an occupation requires the claimant to run the risk of injury, following *Ogwo v Taylor*[1], although that case had also involved physical injury (per Lord Goff):

> 'I must mention the position of people such as policemen or firemen, who might be thought to be less prone to suffer psychiatric injury at the sight of the sufferings of others than members of the general public. In two States of the United States there has developed a principle of policy known as the fireman's rule, under which it has been held that there is no "duty owed to the fireman to exercise care so as not to require the special services for which he is trained and paid": see *Krauth v Geller* (1960) 157 A

2d 129 NJ p 131, per Weintraub CJ. The fireman's rule was subsequently affirmed by the Supreme Court of California in *Walters v Sloan* (1977) 571 P 2d 609. In *Ogwo v Taylor* [1988] AC 448, however, it was held by your Lordships' House that the American fireman's rule had no place in English law. That case was concerned with a claim in respect of physical injury, but I can see no reason why the same conclusion should not be reached in the case of a claim for psychiatric injury'[2].

However, he went on to say that although not precluded from bringing a claim under English law, so far as professional rescuers are concerned:

'... it is generally accepted that, in considering whether psychiatric injury suffered by a plaintiff is reasonably foreseeable, it is legitimate to take into account the fact that the plaintiff is a person, such as for example a policeman, who may by reason of his training and experience be expected to have more resilience in the face of tragic events in which he is involved, or which he witnesses, than an ordinary member of the public possesses who does not have the same background. This is as far as it goes; and, as I shall explain in due course, it does not, in my opinion, affect the result in the wholly exceptional circumstances of the present case. It follows that, unlike Waller J, I would not, except in the limited manner I have indicated, think it necessary to identify a class of 'professional' rescuers to which special rules apply'[3].

1   [1988] AC 431.
2   [1999] 2 AC 455, [1999] 1 All ER 1 at 12e.
3   [1999] 1 All ER at 12g.

2.47 The Lords in *Frost/White* distinguished *Chadwick v British Transport Commission* on the basis that there the rescuer was in physical danger as the carriage might collapse during the rescue, although, as we have seen, it is questionable whether the judge in *Chadwick* in fact based his decision on this footing. This distinction was doubted by Lord Goff as the rescuers, as employees (or quasi-employees like police officers), had no choice but to get involved. Lord Goff, dissenting, felt:

'it is in any event misleading to think in terms of one class of plaintiffs being "better off" than another. Tort liability is concerned not only with compensating plaintiffs, but with awarding such compensation against a defendant who is responsible in law for the plaintiff's injury. It may well be that one plaintiff will succeed on the basis that he can establish such responsibility, whereas another plaintiff who has suffered the same injury will not succeed because he is unable to do so'[1].

1   [1999] 2 AC 455, [1999] 1 All ER 1 at 28a.

2.48 The Law Commission also rejected this approach in their report *Liability for Psychiatric Injury*[1]:

'It should not be a condition of a rescuer's entitlement to recover damages for psychiatric injury that he or she is in physical danger',

but its recommendations for a change in the law have never been implemented.

1   Law Com no 249.

2.49 The editors of *Clerk and Lindsell* suggest[1]:

'A possible compromise between the majority and the minority view in *White*, might be to accept the narrow "endangerment" requirement as a justification for allowing recovery where illness was foreseeable but to recognise "participation" as a justification for allowing recovery where illness was foreseeable but the remaining requirements for secondary victim recovery were not met'.

1   (20th edn, 2010) p 460.

2.50 The police officers had also formulated their claims as primary victims relying on their quasi-employment relationship with the Chief Constable (who had admitted negligence which had led the deaths and injuries to spectators) on the basis that he had a duty to protect their healthy and safety at work (see Chapter 3). In his dissenting judgment Lord Goff expressed this as follows:

'… it is not difficult for us to grasp that the atmosphere of this wholly exceptional tragedy, in the aftermath of which the officers became involved, and the length of time during which the officers were exposed to the consequences of the tragedy, were potent forces which are highly relevant to the question whether, in each of their cases, psychiatric injury was a consequence of their involvement which was reasonably foreseeable by their "employer" who was responsible for their safety at work'[1].

1   [1999] 2 AC 455, [1999] 1 All ER 1 at 30d.

2.51 But in rejecting their claims as 'employees' (primary victims in a 'stress at work claim'), the majority agreed with Lord Hoffmann's purely pragmatic conclusion:

'In principle, therefore, I do not think it would be fair to give police officers the right to a larger claim merely because the disaster was caused by the negligence of other policemen. In the circumstances in which the injuries were caused, I do not think that this is a relevant distinction and if it were to be given effect, the law would not be treating like cases alike'[1].

And Lord Steyn resorted to the 'floodgates' argument:

'One is considering the claims of police officers who sustained serious psychiatric harm in the course of performing and assisting their duties in harrowing circumstances. That is a weighty moral argument: the police perform their duties for the benefit of us all. The difficulty is, however, twofold. First, the pragmatic rules governing the recovery of damages for pure psychiatric harm do not at present include police officers who sustain such injuries while on duty. If such a category were to be created by judicial decision, the new principle would be available in many different situations, eg doctors and hospital workers who are exposed to the sight of grievous injuries and suffering. Secondly, it is common ground that police officers who are traumatized by something they encounter in their work have the benefit of statutory schemes which permit them to retire on pension. In this sense they are already better off than bereaved relatives who were not allowed to recover in *Alcock*. The claim of the police officers on our sympathy, and the justice of the case, is great but not as great as that of others to whom the law denies redress'[2].

1   [1999] 2 AC 455, [1999] 1 All ER 1 at 45b.
2   [1999] 1 All ER 1 at 37c.

2.52 It is difficult to reconcile this decision with the general law on liability of employers to protect their employees from psychiatric injury caused by their employer's breaches discussed in Chapter 3, but as a result of *Frost/White* an employee bystander who suffers psychiatric injury at an horrific event caused by the negligence of his employee cannot recover compensation on the basis of his employment relationship with the wrongdoer unless he can bring himself into the category of 'rescuer' or 'involuntary participant'.

2.53 However, in *Cullin v London Fire and Civil Defence Authority*[1] the Court of Appeal refused to strike out claims for firefighter rescuers. The defendants had argued that the collapse of a wall which had killed the firefighters' colleagues had not endangered the claimants themselves and that they had therefore not been in fear of their own safety. In rejecting the appeal, the court said that first it was necessary look at the totality of the evidence and that, second, there was under *Frost/White* no need to establish that the psychiatric injury was caused by the perception of physical danger.

1 [1999] PIQR P314.

2.54 *Frost/White* left open the question of whether the rescuer must actually be within the range of physical risk or whether it is sufficient for him to reasonably believe this to be so. Several cases arising from the Piper Alpha disaster explored this further. In 1988, the Piper Alpha oil platform in the North Sea exploded killing 164 men. The Court of Appeal in *McFarlane v EE Caledonia Ltd (1) Hegarty v EE Caledonia Ltd (2)*[1] considered whether two employees could recover compensation for the post-traumatic stress disorder they had developed following the disaster. Both men worked on the rig during the day and were housed on a boat 550 metres away at night, which is where they were at the time of the explosion. The Court of Appeal held that a rescuer who believed he was in danger should be able to recover. But Brooke LJ rejected this claim on the basis that once it was established that the rescue vessel had never been in danger the claimant's fear for his life must have been irrational, in other words he was neither in danger nor reasonably believed himself to be so. The claimant must (per Lord Steyn in *Frost/White*):

> 'satisfy the threshold requirement that he objectively exposed himself to danger or reasonably believed he was doing so'.

1 [1997] 2 Lloyd's Rep 259.

6 Other 'involuntary participants'

2.55 Lord Oliver in *Alcock v Chief Constable of South Yorkshire Police* included as 'primary victims':

> 'cases where the negligent act of the defendant has put the [claimant] in the position of being, or thinking that he is about to be or has been, the involuntary cause of another's death or injury and the illness stems from the shock to the [claimant] of the consciousness of this supposed fact'[1].

1 [1992] 1 AC 310, [1991] 4 All ER 907 at 924a.

2.56 The Law Commission stated that:

'[as] the floodgates objection does not apply in relation to involuntary participants, there would appear to be no reason to restrict their right of recovery'[1].

1   Law Com no 249.

2.57   In *Dooley v Cammell Laird & Co Ltd*[1] the claimant was a crane driver. A defective rope on the crane snapped, causing the load to fall to the deck of the ship, where the claimant's fellow employees were working. No one was in fact hurt, but the claimant suffered psychiatric injury. The court held that he was entitled to compensation. He could be described as a primary victim as he was a direct participant, as the person driving the crane when the rope snapped, even though he was physically removed from the consequences to the others on the deck.

1   [1951] 1 Lloyd's Rep 271.

2.58   In *Galt v British Railways Board*[1] a train driver succeeded in a claim for nervous shock. He thought he had struck and killed men on the track. This led to chest pains at the time and subsequently a heart attack. He had a predisposition to this, but had been symptomless prior to the accident.

1   [1983] 133 NLJ 870.

2.59   In *Wigg v British Railways Board*[1], the plaintiff train driver recovered damages for the shock and trauma he suffered soon after his train was brought to an abrupt halt by the emergency brakes as it was leaving a station. A passenger trying to board a train had been dragged along the platform until he fell between it and the train. The driver found him and stayed with him for ten minutes until help arrived, when he began to tremble from shock.

1   (1986) Times, 4 February.

2.60   In *Young v Charles Church (Southern) Ltd*[1] the Court of Appeal allowed an appeal in respect of a claimant who was working alongside a man who was electrocuted and killed when a pole he was holding came into contact with an overhead power line. The claimant was about 6–10 feet away with his back turned when the accident happened. He heard a loud bang and a hissing noise, and turned round to see that the pole held by his colleague had struck the electric wiring and that the ground round his colleague had burst into flames. The majority of the Court of Appeal held that he was a primary victim and the whole Court of Appeal held that they were bound by the decision in *Frost* to hold that the plaintiff's psychiatric injury was a foreseeable consequence of his employers' breach of duty of care.

1   [1997] EWCA Civ 1523.

2.61   However, in *Frost/White*, Lord Goff considered the Scottish case of *Robertson and Rough v Forth Road Bridge Joint Board*[1] where:

'The accident occurred while the men were in the course of removing a large thin piece of metal sheeting which had been found lying on the south-bound carriageway. It was being taken off the bridge on the open platform of a Ford Transit pick-up van. Smith was sitting on the top of the metal sheet on the back of the van, Robertson was driving the van and Rough was following a few feet behind in a small patrol van which he was driving. In the course of their journey to the south end of the bridge a sudden and violent gust of wind caused the sheet and Smith to be thrown violently off the back of the van and over the side of the bridge'[2].

The Scottish court rejected the claim as (per Lord Goff in *Frost/White*) the case was:

'not as one of active participation in the event, but as one where the pursuers were merely bystanders or witnesses, in which event the ordinary rule stated by Lord Oliver in *McLoughlin v O'Brian* must apply and, as the pursuers did not comply with the control mechanisms applicable in the case of claimants who were only witnesses, their claim must fail. The case therefore provides authority that, in a claim by an employee against his employer for damages for psychiatric injury arising from the death of or injury to another, his claim will fail if he is simply a bystander who witnesses the event, and is not an active participant in it (or, I would add, its aftermath)'[3].

Lord Goff points out:

'It was perhaps open to the Lord President to take the view that the two pursuers were at the time actively involved with Mr Smith in the operation of removing the sheet from the bridge, in which event the reclaiming motion would no doubt have been granted; but he took a different view of the facts of the case'[4].

1   1995 SC 364.
2   Ibid at 264 (per Lord Hope of Craighead).
3   [1999] 2 AC 455, [1999] 1 All ER 1 at 23b.
4   [1999] 1 All ER 1 at 23c.

2.62 Similarly, in *Hunter v British Coal Corpn*[1], the majority of the Court of Appeal disallowed the claim. The claimant had been working deep underground with a colleague in North Selby coal mine. They were trying to make safe a dangerous hydrant, which had been damaged by a vehicle which the claimant had been driving in treacherous conditions. The claimant left to get some additional equipment:

'When he was 20–30 yards outbye he heard an almighty bang, like a bomb going off, and the sound of water screaming through the pipes. He looked back and saw a large cloud of dust. He shouted "I'll get the water" and hurried off outbye to find a stop valve and shut off the water. As he hurried outbye he was saying to himself: "I hope that Tommy is out of that". J12 is about 307 metres from the accident scene, and when he got there he managed to turn the stop valve, with help from others, and shut the water off. It took him a good ten minutes to turn the water off. As he was doing this, he heard a message over the tannoy to the effect that a man had been injured'[2].

The claimant then heard that his colleague was dead. The accident was a freak incident but the plaintiff felt responsible and guilty for being the survivor. The claimant believed he was the cause of a fatal accident (in fact, he was not, although he was the involuntary agent of the events which occurred), but only got to the scene 15 minutes later:

'Although he knew it was a freak accident, he has felt particularly responsible and guilty about it, and he has been profoundly affected by the experience. He has not been able to sleep properly at night, and he has been preoccupied by his concerns in the daytime. He has not recovered emotionally from the experience'[3].

Other 'involuntary participants' 43

The medical evidence was that he was suffering from 'survivor guilt':

> 'His reaction was partly connected with the severity of the injury to his fellow worker and partly with his feelings of personal responsibility. His feeling of guilt was an abnormal or atypical bereavement reaction. It was a form of "survivor guilt", which is a common feature of the psychopathology of survivors in armed conflict. His ability to socialise was sufficiently impaired to regard him as having a mental illness of mild severity'[4].

1   [1999] QB 140, [1998] 2 All ER 97.
2   [1998] 2 All ER 97 at 100h.
3   [1998] 2 All ER 97 at 101c.
4   [1998] 2 All ER 97 at 101j.

2.63 Brooke LJ (with whom Vinelott LJ agreed) was not prepared to find that Mr Hunter was a participant and thus a primary victim:

> 'I am wholly unpersuaded that Mr Hunter is to be treated as a participant in the accident, as the law now stands, and the concept that he still believed himself to be still psychologically involved as a participant in an accident which had occurred at least a quarter of an hour before he was told that his workmate had died is not one which is currently recognised by English law. It must of course be remembered that a direct victim can recover even if he/she is not a person of ordinary fortitude, so that this control mechanism would be wholly absent in "survivor's guilt" cases if Mr Berrisford's submissions are correct. Employers will then be liable for damages suffered by the most nervous of their employees in such circumstances, since they must take their direct, or primary, victims as they find them'[1].

He dismissed the appeal holding that:

> 'The law requires a greater degree of physical and temporal proximity ... before [the claimant] could properly be treated as a direct or primary victim'.

Hobhouse LJ dissented, as he believed that the employee's participation in the event justified his being classified as a primary victim:

> 'In my judgment, the effect of these statements of the law is to identify as the relevant factor the physical participation of the plaintiff in the event which resulted from the employer's breach of duty, which participation caused the plaintiff to believe that he was responsible for his fellow employee's death or injury. If so, the employer is liable for the nervous shock and psychiatric injury caused to the plaintiff as a result of his having participated in the event. It puts the plaintiff into the same class as a "primary" victim; it puts him and his injury within the scope of the duty of care which the employer owes to him'[2].

Hunter has been described as a 'harsh decision'[3], but Mr Hunter did not seek leave to appeal to the House of Lords.

1   [1999] QB 140, [1998] 2 All ER 97at 109b.
2   [1998] 2 All ER 97at 121g.
3   See, for example, Kemp & Kemp *The Quantum of Damages* at Vol 1, 32–025.

2.64 In *Monk v PC Harrington*[1] a temporary working platform, during the construction of the new Wembley Stadium, was dislodged by a crane, falling sixty feet and killing one man and injuring another. Mr Monk was a foreman on the construction site:

> 'Mr Monk heard that there had been an accident on his portable radio immediately after it had occurred (probably at about 8.25 am). He made his way to the scene and crawled underneath the fallen platform to see if, as a first aider, he could help Patsy O'Sullivan. Mr O'Sullivan was gravely injured and there was little or nothing that Mr Monk could do to help him. He therefore turned his attention to the other injured man, Ray Carroll, and did his best to comfort him. At one point Mr Monk went back under the platform and knelt next to Patsy O'Sullivan and shouted his name to see if could get a reaction, but he got none. Mr Monk then went back to Ray Carroll and stayed with him trying to calm him until the ambulance arrived'.

The decision was perhaps coloured by the view of the judge that:

> 'Having heard Mr Monk's evidence tested in cross-examination by Mr Watt-Pringle QC who appeared for PCH, it is clear to me that I need to approach Mr Monk's evidence with considerable caution and cannot regard it as a reliable record of what he actually witnessed on 15 January 2004. That is scarcely surprising given that the accident occurred some 4½ years ago and given the strong emotions which it aroused in Mr Monk both at the time and afterwards, continuing to this day'[2].

Although the judge accepted that he was rescuer, he was not able to recover compensation on that ground as the judge rejected his evidence that he was ever in personal danger:

> 'I therefore reject as improbable Mr Monk's evidence that he believed he was putting his own physical safety at risk when he went to the aid of Mr O'Sullivan and Mr Carroll; alternatively, if he did have such a belief, it was not a reasonable one. It follows that Mr Monk cannot establish that he was a primary victim on the basis of his involvement as a rescuer'[3].

The claimant also believed that he was the cause of the accident where a platform fell onto fellow workers as he had supervised its construction:

> 'It was Mr Monk's evidence that, on hearing this, his first thought was that the peri-platform had been put in wrong and that this was the cause of the accident and that he was somehow to blame. Mr Monk also said that after the accident he felt guilty, and that initially this was because he was blaming himself for what had happened, thinking that it was because the platform had been wrongly installed. Only later did he discover that the accident was not his fault'[4].

But, as his belief was not reasonable, he did not recover:

> '... while I find that the traumatic effect of the accident on Mr Monk was increased by a belief that he might have caused the accident, I do not consider that there was any reasonable basis for such a belief ... His response was, as I find, a more basic and nonspecific feeling of guilt – that simply because he was ultimately in charge of the platforms, he might somehow be implicated in the accident. This was a genuine anxiety, but no more reasonable than his subsequent persistent fears that another accident would happen for which he might be blamed'[5].

However, it is clear that the judge's view of the claimant's evidence in *Monk* was a significant factor.

1   [2008] EWHC 1879 (QB) at para 4.
2   At para 21.
3   At para 28.
4   At para 36.
5   At para 45.

7 'Primary victims' in 'shock cases'

2.65 As can be seen, the 'simple' classification in *Page v Smith* of direct participants and the rules which govern recoverability for them as primary victims has turned out to be far from simple.

The following types of primary victim, who can be said in some way to be 'participants' and who can recover compensation for their psychiatric injury, have been examined in this chapter:

- direct participants in events which also cause physical injury to the victim, however minor, see paras **2.3–2.13**;
- direct participants who suffer 'pure' psychiatric injury from an accident where physical injury was foreseeable, but not where there was no 'shocking event' (paras **2.14–2.40**);
- 'rescuers' but not 'bystanders' (paras **2.44–2.54**);
- 'involuntary participants' of various kinds (paras **2.55–2.64**).

2.66 There is another category of 'primary victims', however, for whom the need to establish foreseeability on the part of the wrongdoer of the risk of psychiatric injury still applies. These are the employment cases where there is no single 'accident' or 'shocking' event. These are considered in Chapter 3. In Chapter 4 the position of so-called 'secondary' victims is considered.

3 Primary victims of negligence: non-shock cases

1 Introduction

3.1 Psychiatric injury in the context of non-shock claims is a tricky area of law for practitioners and courts to navigate their way around. The most significant area in which there has been a rapid expansion of non-shock claims is in the context of occupational stress, which is unsurprising given the current economic climate, the consequent redundancies and business closures, and the additional pressures upon those remaining in employment.

3.2 The common feature of occupational stress cases is that there is rarely, if ever, a single event which causes the relevant injury, and litigating such claims will often involve a detailed examination of events occurring over several months or even years prior to the illness developing. It is also important to remember that stress of itself is not a medical condition, nor is it one that the courts will be prepared to compensate as a stand-alone condition. Practitioners must be careful to distinguish between the two and recognise that liability will only attach once the stress has developed into an actual psychiatric condition.

3.3 It is only once the crucial distinction between 'stress' and an actual injury has been identified, that practitioners can then go on to examine the presence of the factors necessary to establish liability, such as whether and what breaches have occurred, whether those breaches have caused or materially contributed to the condition and whether it was or ought to have been reasonably foreseeable to the potential tortfeasor that such a condition would or was likely to develop as a result of those breaches.

3.4 An expert diagnosis will inevitably be required in every case, whether by a suitably qualified treating physician, or a medico-legal expert. It is also advisable that a chronology of events occurring in the personal life of a claimant is created, to deal with the issue of contributory or material causes other than occupational stress. One of the strongest weapons in a defendant employer's armoury is causation, and the potential existence of stressful personal events outside the workplace which may independently have caused or materially contributed to the development of a psychiatric condition. A claimant practitioner would be wise to pre-empt this potential defence and ensure that they are fully appraised of any significant events which may have occurred in the claimant's personal life and which may or did have an impact on the claimant's mental health.

2 Employer's liability: stress at work

A Breach of duty

(1) Development of case law

3.5 Historically, the concept of work-related stress was an unfamiliar one to the courts, particularly in the context of cases where there had been no precipitating accident or event which had triggered an adverse psychiatric response. It is perhaps unsurprising that in our modern climate, with increased economic pressures, businesses finding it more difficult to sustain and thrive, fewer available jobs, the threat of redundancy and an overall cut-throat job market, individuals are placed under greater strain at work with increased workloads and ever-present pressure to perform. The concept of allowing employees to be compensated for stress-related conditions arising out of their work may have been a slow one to develop, but in the last twenty years, the courts have shown an increased willingness to recognise such claims. Further, given that employers are required to have compulsory insurance in place in respect of their employees by virtue of the Employers' Liability (Compulsory Insurance) Act 1969, the financial structures are in place for the employer rather than the State, to bear the economic burden of treating the condition and consequences of such claims.

3.6 The progress of psychiatric injury claims in the context of the workplace can easily be traced chronologically through case law. *Johnstone v Bloomsbury Health Authority*[1] and *Petch v Customs and Excise Commissioners*[2] laid down the groundwork for the first award of psychiatric injury for work stress in *Walker v Northumberland County Council*[3]. *Johnstone* and *Petch* dealt predominantly with the question of the nature of the duty of care owed to the employee. In *Johnstone,* a case about physical injury arising out of long working hours where the terms of the claimant's contract of employment required him to work and 'be available' for up to 88 hours per week, the Court of Appeal held that the employer was under a duty to take reasonable care not to injure the claimant's health. In *Petch* the employer admitted that, upon the claimant employee's return to work following a mental breakdown in 1974 and prior to his ultimate retirement on ill-health grounds, they owed him a duty to take reasonable care to ensure that the duties allotted to him upon his return to work did not damage his health further. However, evidentially, the claimant failed on two counts. First, on the grounds of foresight of his first breakdown as he failed to show that his employers were or ought to have been aware that he was showing signs of an impending breakdown in 1974. Second, he failed to establish breach of duty upon his return to work, as the court found that the steps taken by the employer to manage the claimant's condition and concerns were sensible.

1 [1992] 1 QB 333.
2 [1993] ICR 789.
3 [1995] ICR 702.

3.7 *Walker v Northumberland County Council*[1] was the first English case in which the courts awarded compensation for occupational stress-related psychiatric harm. This was a claim by a social services officer against his local authority employer, who had suffered a nervous breakdown as a result of his duties as the leader of a

48 *Primary victims of negligence: non-shock cases*

team tasked with investigating cases of child abuse. He suffered a second breakdown, which led to his retirement on health grounds, which he alleged was as a result of the employer's failure to take reasonable steps to avoid exposing him to a workload that endangered his health, such as providing him with an assistant. Coleman J held that it was:

> 'clear law that an employer has a duty to provide his employee with a reasonably safe system of work and to take reasonable steps to protect him from risks which are reasonably foreseeable ... there is no reason why risk of psychiatric damage should be excluded from the scope of an employer's duty of care or from the co-extensive implied term in the contract of employment'.

Therefore, the claimant was entitled to damages for his second nervous breakdown, based on the breach of the employer's duty to provide a safe system of work. Whilst it was not reasonably foreseeable prior to the first breakdown that the claimant's workload would give rise to a material risk of mental illness, following the claimant's return to work, the defendant ought to have foreseen the risk of a further breakdown if the claimant was exposed to the same level of work. He only received assistance with his workload for a limited period and then was forced to catch up with the backlog of work as well as deal with new cases. Coleman J held that the employer was in breach for failing to provide additional assistance. However, it was recognised that issues of causation and foreseeability would often arise in the context of such claims.

1   [1995] 1 All ER 737, [1995] ICR 702.

3.8 However, it became clear that guidance was required by the courts and by employers that continued to value the protection from psychiatric harm in the workplace but also recognised the realities of that workplace and in particular, the need for employees to be aware of the precise nature and extent of their duties and the expectations of their role in the context of guarding against psychiatric injury. Such guidance was comprehensively provided by the Court of Appeal in *Hatton v Sutherland*[1], the leading case on occupational stress claims.

1   [2002] ICR 613.

(2) The Hatton guidelines and their practical application

3.9 *Hatton v Sutherland*[1] concerned appeals by employers in four separate cases, all of whom had had damages awarded against them for stress-induced psychiatric illness. Two of the claimants were comprehensive school teachers, the other two being an administrative assistant and a factory operative. Three of the four appeals were allowed. Hale LJ recognised the need to return to basic principles of duty of care, foreseeability, breach of duty and causation and set out a series of principles designed to give clear guidance to the lower courts (and no doubt to employers) as to how to approach occupational stress claims. These guidelines were unanimously endorsed by the House of Lords in *Barber v Somerset County Council*[2], an appeal by one of the unsuccessful teachers whose damages were overturned by the Court of Appeal in *Hatton*. Whilst the guidelines set clear principles, and limits to occupational stress claims, it is essential to remember that occupational stress cases are fact-specific and unique to the personal characteristics and circumstances of each individual, therefore there is a degree of subjectivity as to the correct outcome in any one case, and opinions may very well differ despite the uniform application of the guidelines. This was amply demonstrated in *Barber*.

1   [2002] ICR 613.
2   [2004] ICR 457.

3.10 The guidance and its implication in practise can be summarised as follows:

(1) There are no special control mechanisms applying to claims for psychiatric injury illness or injury arising from the stress of doing the work the employee is required to do. The ordinary principles of employers' liability apply.

Health and safety legislation is a useful reference in this respect. Claimants will often plead a breach of statutory duty to add further weight to a stress claim and in particular, the Management of Health and Safety at Work Regulations 1999, reg 3, which requires employers to make a suitable and sufficient assessment of the risk to health and safety of his employees to which they are exposed at work. A risk assessment argument is particularly useful in the context of employees who have experienced a breakdown or other stress-related sickness absence following which they return to work. It is incumbent upon employers to perform some form of assessment identifying the risks (and in particular the factors which caused or contributed to the condition) and removing or minimising the risk factors, balancing the other elements of the *Hatton* guidelines. From an employer's perspective, it can be argued that a risk assessment would have no causal relevance to the claim if, for example, it would not have identified the factors which caused or contributed to the condition or if, when balancing the competing interests of the employee and the organisation as a whole, it would not have been reasonable or viable to implement the measures required to reduce the risk. It is still strongly advised that employers perform a risk assessment of an employee upon their return to work following a stress-related absence.

However, compliance with health and safety regulations does not automatically lead to a finding that there has been no overall breach of the duty of care owed to the claimant. In contrast, a breach of statutory regulations may be more indicative of a breach of the employer's general duty of care.

(2) The threshold question is whether this kind of harm to this particular employee was reasonably foreseeable, which requires: (a) an injury to health as opposed to occupational stress which is (b) attributable to stress at work as opposed to other factors.

It is important to remember that there is no medical condition of 'stress'. As Hale LJ point out in *Hatton*, there is a very clear distinction to be made between a stress reaction and an actual injury to health. All of us have doubtless experienced stress during our working lives, but stress of itself is not sufficient to attract tortious liability and a compensatory award. It is crucial for practitioners to identify the point at which 'work stress' deteriorates into a diagnosable clinical disorder, and the factors causative of that deterioration.

For claimant and defendant practitioners alike, defining that point can often be determinative of whether liability attaches. It is crucial in every stress case to establish a detailed factual chronology of events from the first time the claimant began to experience feelings of stress to the point at which the condition deteriorates, such as the employee being signed off sick, being prescribed medication or, better still from a litigation point of view, being formally diagnosed. Caution should be exercised in relying too heavily on the diagnosis of a GP of 'depression', as often that term can be used in its generic sense to simply denote a stress reaction as opposed to a medical condition. There is a recent example of the courts demonstrating a willingness to attach greater weight to the evidence and diagnosis of a GP, in the context of the employment tribunal. In *J v DLA Piper UK LLP*[1], the employment tribunal was required to determine the preliminary issue of whether the claimant's psychiatric condition qualified as a disability under the Disability Discrimination Act 1995. Although the claimant was required to satisfy the narrow definition of disability under the Act, the tribunal was troubled by the lack of a formal diagnosis of the claimant's condition, something which neither the occupational health psychiatrists, nor even the employer's own medico-legal expert could conclusively decide. The only firm diagnosis available to the tribunal was that of the claimant's treating GP who had had the benefit of contemporaneous examination of the claimant and who was clear that the claimant satisfied the diagnostic criteria of depression. This case is unique in the sense that out of four experts, including the employer's own psychiatric consultant, no one was able to either definitively diagnose or rule out a psychiatric condition, save for the GP. Whilst it is questionable how much weight the civil courts will be prepared to attach to a GP's diagnosis where it is more usual to obtain the opinion of a more senior clinician, this case provides a valuable lesson as to the importance of ensuring that an actual injury has occurred in the medical sense, and identifying the point in time at which that occurs.

(3) Foreseeability depends on what the employer knows (or ought reasonably to know) about the individual employee. Because of the nature of mental disorder, it is harder to foresee than physical injury, but may be easier to foresee in a known individual than in the population at large. An employer is usually entitled to assume that the employee can withstand the normal pressures of the job unless he knows of some particular problem or vulnerability.

In *Pratley v Surrey County Council*[2] the claimant suffered an immediate breakdown upon her return from holiday. It was held reasonable for the defendant to have postponed a reduction in the claimant's workload until her return from holiday as, even though it was foreseeable that the claimant would suffer a breakdown in the future if her workload was not decreased, it was not foreseeable that she would have had the breakdown that she did.

Croft v Broadstairs & St Peter's Town Council[3] is authority for the proposition that the fact an employee is undergoing counselling is not necessarily sufficient warning of psychiatric vulnerability if the defendant does not know that the claimant is at risk of psychological harm. It was found as a fact that the disciplinary warning given to the claimant which caused her to have a nervous breakdown would not have been sent if the relevant council members had been aware of her psychiatric vulnerability.

Whilst employers are inevitably required to be vigilant, it must be remembered that foresight of stress is not of itself sufficient—the employer must foresee the risk of harm to the health of the employee, not just that the employee will become 'stressed' by work-related factors.

(4) The test is the same whatever the employment: there are no occupations which should be regarded as intrinsically dangerous to mental health.

This emphasises the point that the nature of breach and foreseeability is determined by the characteristics of the individual employee and his personal circumstances, strengths and weaknesses. If a claimant wishes to argue that a unique or higher duty of care is owed by his employer, this must be in the context of a particular vulnerability or characteristic unique to the claimant and known to the employer either prior to or at the material time, rather than in the context of the employee's role or job description.

(5) Factors likely to be relevant in answering the threshold question include:
   (a) the nature and extent of the work done by the employee:
       • Is the workload much more than is normal for that particular job?
       • Is the work particularly intellectually or emotionally demanding for this employee?
       • Are demands being made of this employee unreasonable when compared with the demands made of others in the same or comparable jobs?
       • Or are there signs that others doing this job are suffering harmful levels of stress?
       • Is there an abnormal level of sickness or absenteeism in the same job or the same department?
   (b) Signs from the employee of impending harm to health:
       • Has he a particular problem or vulnerability?
       • Has he already suffered from illness attributable to stress at work?
       • Have there recently been frequent or prolonged absences which are uncharacteristic of him?
       • Is there reason to think that these are attributable to stress at work, for example because of complaints or warnings from him or others?

This list is not exhaustive but is certainly valuable in highlighting some of the key indicators of an actual or impending risk to the health of the employee. If an employee has had a previous episode of stress, employers should be on red alert for any or all of the above indicators in order to prevent a recurrence. Again, this is where the performance of a risk assessment would greatly assist.

(6) The employer is generally entitled to take what he is told by his employee at face value, unless he has good reason to think to the contrary. He does not generally have to make searching inquiries of the employee or seek permission to make further inquiries of his medical advisers.

In *Hartman v South Essex Mental Health and Community Care NHS Trust*[4], it was held on the facts of that case that it was not appropriate to attribute to the employer the knowledge of the defendant's occupational health department that the claimant had a history of depression. The Court of Appeal held that where an employee is referred to the employer's occupational health department, such information is to be treated as confidential and cannot be attributed to an employer's knowledge of either disability or psychiatric problems unless the employee waives their right to confidentiality. Further, in *Melville v The Home Office*[5] it was noted that the presence of an occupational health service for employees, or even a particular group of employees, should not lead to the conclusion that it could foresee the risk of psychiatric injury to any individual or class of employee.

Since the introduction of the Equality Act 2010, it is now unlawful for employers to make pre-employment health enquiries of prospective employees. The purpose of this is to avoid the discrimination of an employee on the grounds of their disability. Employers will therefore be reliant upon the employee's voluntary disclosure of any relevant medical history which may include previous episodes of a psychiatric disorder or a particular medical vulnerability to psychiatric injury. Inadvertently, the Equality Act 2010 may also have provided employers with an additional defence to foreseeability: foresight of harm may be even more difficult for a claimant to establish if they had a known psychiatric history or vulnerability which they chose not to disclose to their employer, and where there was no other reasonable basis upon which the employer ought reasonably to have known of it. From a practical perspective and in order to protect both the employee from a relapse and the employer from a potential claim, the employer may ask questions of an employer as to the relevant medical history once the employee commences employment, which would assist in highlighting any particular vulnerabilities or risk factors at the earliest stage.

Another avenue of recovery for psychiatric loss is under the rule in *Page v Smith*[6] where psychiatric injury (which is in itself unforeseeable) arises out of a foreseeable risk of physical injury. This was the case in *Donachie v Chief Constable of Greater Manchester Police*[7] where the extreme stress due to the risk of physical endangerment arising out of a negligently-run police surveillance operation caused a psychiatric injury.

(7) To trigger a duty to take steps, the indications of impending harm to health arising from stress at work must be plain enough for any reasonable employer to realise that he should do something about it.

In *Hone v Six Continents Retail Ltd*[8] Dyson LJ considered that the key to determining reasonable foreseeability was Hale LJ's seventh proposition.

(8) The employer is only in breach of duty if he has failed to take the steps which are reasonable in the circumstances, bearing in mind the magnitude of the risk of harm occurring, the gravity of the harm which may occur, the costs and practicability of preventing it and the justifications for running the risk.

Even hard-stretched employers and smaller companies should have some scope to redistribute tasks and reduce the workload of vulnerable employees. Increased monitoring or supervision of a vulnerable employee may also be less costly options.

(9) The size and scope of the employer's operation, its resources and the demands it faces are relevant in deciding what is reasonable; these include the interests of the other employees and the need to treat them fairly, for example in any redistribution of duties.

Where the only effective way of reducing the risk of harm to an individual employee would involve a large-scale change in management decisions, the courts are slow to say that an employer should have taken such a step, for example in *Foumeny v University of Leeds*[9], where it was held that it was not necessary for the employer to have reversed the merger of departments and restored the claimant to his previous position as head of department. Further, in *Vahidi v Fairstead House School Trust Ltd*[10], no liability was found against the employer of a teacher who was required to make fundamental changes to her methods of teaching.

(10) An employer can only reasonably be expected to take steps which are likely to do some good: the court is likely to need expert evidence on this.

In *Dickens v O2 plc*[11], Smith LJ noted that the offer of counselling was not so much of benefit in this case, as the claimant did not hide her work-related stress and had no need for confidentiality. The relevant steps are unique to the particular employee and therefore the employer may wish to consider departing from a general company policy, such as automatic referral of employees experiencing stress to counselling, and consider alternatives in the context of the individual.

(11) An employer who offers a confidential advice service, with referral to appropriate counselling or treatment services, is unlikely to be found in breach of duty.

Melville v The Home Office established that the foreseeability test may be met in the absence of knowledge of a claimant's vulnerability if the employee is exposed to a traumatic event and the employer does not provide appropriate counselling. However, caution should be exercised in taking this too literally, as in practice the courts have discouraged employers from relying too heavily on the literal wording of the *Hatton* guidelines. For example, in *Daw v Intel Corp (UK) Ltd*[12], Pill LJ was keen to stress that employers cannot escape liability by clinging to the strict wording of the *Hatton* judgment. In particular, it was held that the provision of a counselling service could not be seen as a panacea to liability. In doing so, the court supported the House of Lords' judgment in *Barber* to the effect that there is an overriding duty on management to identify and address work situations that create a risk of psychiatric injury due to stress. This approach was also followed in the judgment of Smith LJ in *Dickens v O2 plc*[13], where it was held that where there is an absence of steps other than a referral to a counselling service, this did not satisfy the employer's duty of care.

(12) If the only reasonable and effective step would have been to dismiss or demote the employee, the employer will not be in breach of duty in allowing a willing employee to continue in the job.

This was endorsed in *Barber*. The difficulty arises where the psychiatric vulnerability is known but the employer is faced with very limited options. In *Hatton,* Hale LJ considered that if there were no reasonable and effective steps open to the employer but to fire or demote the employee, then the employer would not be in breach for allowing a willing employee to continue in their job.

Employers should also note that dismissing or demoting an employee could expose the employer to potential claims of unfair and constructive dismissal in the employment tribunal. If an employee has had previous episodes of psychiatric injury and qualifies for protection under the Equality Act 2010 (under the protected characteristic of disability), dismissal or demotion may also constitute disability discrimination. An employee is under a duty to take such steps as are reasonable to prevent any provision, criterion or practice applied by him or on his behalf, from placing the disabled person concerned at a substantial disadvantage in comparison to those persons who are not disabled[14]. The duty is only triggered where the employee is placed at a substantial disadvantage and the extent to which that adjustment would prevent the disadvantage will also need to be examined.

(13) In all cases, therefore, it is necessary to identify the steps which the employer both could and should have taken before finding him in breach of his duty of care.

This requires a key balancing exercise between the protection of the individual employee, and the constraints of the organisation. Employers must not neglect their general duty of care towards the remainder of their workforce, and where steps which could have been taken to protect an individual claimant would have caused the employer to discriminate against or otherwise breach its duties in respect of other employees this constitutes a potential defence to breach of duty.

(14) The claimant must show that that breach of duty has caused or materially contributed to the harm suffered. It is not enough to show that occupational stress has caused the harm.

The claimant must demonstrate that the psychiatric illness is not due simply to stress at work but due to the employer's specific breach of duty. It is insufficient for a claimant to simply state that stress was suffered as a result of the breach of duty. However, the employee does not have to prove that the breach of the duty was the sole cause of the psychiatric illness, but rather that it made a material contribution to the same.

(15) Where the harm suffered has more than one cause, the employer should only pay for that proportion of the harm suffered which is attributable to his wrongdoing, unless the harm is truly indivisible. It is for the defendant to raise the question of apportionment.

Although *Hatton* allowed for apportionment on the basis that psychiatric harm could be a divisible injury, this was doubted by Smith LJ in *Dickins v O2 plc*, who stated that where it is not scientifically possible to say how much the contribution of one factor was to an injury, it would be inappropriate to apportion damages across the board. The more appropriate approach may be to reduce certain heads of damage to reflect the fact that psychiatric injury may have occurred at some point in the future. The risk is that this approach may confuse the cases of apportionment and those of acceleration, which are two distinct arguments. Apportionment is appropriate where there are competing contributory factors at or around the material time that the injury is sustained and would apply to all damages awarded as a result of that injury. In contrast, if a defendant is arguing that the claimant, by reason of a pre-existing medical history or vulnerability, would have most likely suffered an episode of psychiatric illness in any event at some point in the future, this will require an assessment of the losses specifically relating to the period of acceleration and damages may be capped by reference to that period of time.

Smith LJ's views that psychiatric illness is an indivisible harm were given without her Ladyship having heard arguments by counsel on the subject, as the trial judge's decision to award 50% of damages to reflect the contribution of non-tortious causes to the injury was not appealed by either party. However, following *Barker v Corus*[15], there could be apportionment based on the defendant's contribution to the risk of the claimant developing psychological injury.

The real difficulty is an evidential one. It may be a very difficult task to separate the relative contributions of tortious and non-tortious factors, particularly where these are multiple. Expert evidence will be crucial in this respect and it is important that a medico-legal expert on behalf of a party provides as much detail as possible, not only in assessing the impact and contribution of competing causes, but in attempting to provide the likely prognosis in the absence of such non-tortious factors and in assessing the impact of the employer's breach of duty as against what might have occurred in its absence[16].

(16) The assessment of damages will take account of any pre-existing disorder or vulnerability and of the chance that the claimant would have succumbed to a stress related disorder in any event.

This follows on from (15) of the *Hatton* guidelines but deals more with acceleration of an inevitable psychiatric condition rather than causation.

1 [2010] UKEAT 0263/09/1506.
2 [2003] IRLR 794.
3 [2003] EWCA Civ 676.
4 [2005] IRLR 293, CA.
5 [2005] EWCA Civ 6, [2005] ICR 782.
6 [1996] 2 AC 155.
7 [2004] EWCA Civ 405.
8 [2005] EWCA Civ 922, [2006] IRLR 49 at [15].
9 [2003] EWCA Civ 557, [2003] ELR 443.
10 [2005] EWCA Civ 765, [2005] ELR 607.
11 [2008] EWCA Civ 1144.
12 [2007] EWCA Civ 70, [2007] 2 All ER 126.
13 [2008] EWCA Civ 1144.
14 Disability Discrimination Act 1995, s 4A(1), now replaced by the EqA 2010, s 19.
15 [2006] UKHL 20.
16 Considered further in Chapter 7 at **para 7.83**.

3.11 Whilst the guidelines are extremely useful in setting out the various elements of breach, causation and foreseeability in a logical and coherent way, the overall benchmark is still the conduct of the reasonable and prudent employer taking positive thought for the safety of its workers in the light of what it knows or ought to know, as Swanwick J reminded us in *Stokes v Guest, Keen and Nettlefold (Bolts and Nuts) Ltd*[1], subsequently endorsed in *Barber*.

1   [1968] 1 WLR 1776.

(3) Other avenues: harassment and employment law

Harassment

3.12 Claimants should also consider a potential claim under the Protection from Harassment Act 1997 (PHA 1997) (discussed in Chapter 5). The advantages of pursuing a statutory harassment claim are multiple. The limitation period of six years is more generous than the three-year period for personal injury claims. Further, there is no requirement either of foreseeability of harm or for an actual psychiatric injury; damages may be awarded for anxiety or emotional distress in the absence of a formal clinical disorder. No defence is open to the employer that all reasonable steps were taken to prevent the harassment.

3.13 However, the threshold of conduct required to amount to harassment is a high one. It appears from the case law[1] that the major limitation to harassment claims is the need for the harassing act itself to amount to the standard required under the PHA 1997. In *Veakins v Kier Islington Ltd* the Court of Appeal held that, while it must be kept in mind that harassment is an offence for which criminal liability is possible, the test does not have to be that a criminal prosecution must be the likely result of the conduct complained of. The conduct complained of does have to go beyond the normal annoyances of life and constitute 'oppressive and unacceptable conduct'. For this reason a PHA 1997 claim is only going to be available in certain factual contexts and where there has been more than one such act.

1   *Sunderland County Council v Conn* [2008] IRLR 324, CA and *Veakins v Kier Islington Ltd* [2009] EWCA Civ 1288.

Employment law

3.14 Following *Johnson v Unisys Ltd*[1], if the employment relationship is terminated, whether by dismissal or resignation, the employee's only remedy in the absence of a discrimination claim is an unfair dismissal claim, where the compensation is limited to financial losses up to the statutory cap[2]. This is irrespective of whether the relationship of mutual trust and confidence has been breached. The cap was £68,400 from 1 February 2011. The cap only applies to unfair dismissal claims. There is currently no statutory cap on awards for discrimination claims and there may be situations where claimants can establish that by reason of their psychiatric illness, they are disabled within the meaning of the Equality Act 2010, and can therefore bring a discrimination claim.

1   [2003] 1 AC 518, HL.
2   *Dunnachie v Kingston-upon-Hull City Council* [2004] UKHL 36, [2005] 1 AC 226.

3.15 However, if the obligation of mutual trust and confidence is broken prior to the immediate steps leading to the dismissal or resignation (ie outside the *Johnson* 'area of exclusion') then the employee is not precluded from bringing a claim for personal injury (including psychological injuries) arising out of that breach of duty[1]. In theory, the claimant will also be able to bring a claim in respect of the dismissal itself where it is alleged that the dismissal is unfair, although any compensation awarded must be carefully scrutinised to ensure there is no double recovery between the concurrent claims.

1   *Eastwood v Magnox Electric plc* [2004] UKHL 35, [2005] 1 AC 503.

(4) Pleural plaques (discontinuity on time)

3.16 The question of whether damages for psychological injury as a result of pleural plaques were recoverable was explored in *Grieves v FT Everard & Sons*[1]. Pleural plaques had previously been seen as actionable damage due to a trio of cases against the Ministry of Defence in 1980s[2]. In *Grieves* the claimant had developed a recognised psychiatric illness as a result of his anxiety over the risk of contracting a future illness caused by the inhalation of asbestos fibres. It was argued on his behalf that he was a primary victim of the defendant's negligence in exposing him to asbestos dust. Therefore, on the basis of *Page v Smith*[3], it was not necessary for psychiatric illness to be foreseeable due to the inhalation of asbestos fibres, but all that was required was the foreseeability of a physical injury, namely an asbestos-related disease.

1   [2007] UKHL 39.
2   *Church v MoD* (1984) 134 NLJ 623; *Sykes v MoD* (1984) Times, 23 March; *Patterson v MoD* [1987] CLY 1194.
3   [1999] 2 AC 455.

3.17 The House of Lords dismissed the claimant's appeal as they considered that *Page* could be distinguished. The most pertinent judgment on this point is that of Lord Hope who provided two reasons:

(i)   The claimant was not a primary victim as envisaged in *Page v Smith*, as there was no immediacy between the negligent act complained of and the injury suffered. Lord Hope at [54] stated that:

> '[t]he category of primary victim should be confined to persons who suffer psychiatric injury caused by fear or distress resulting from involvement in an accident caused by the defendant's negligence or its immediate aftermath. A person like Mr Grieves who suffers psychiatric injury because of something that he may experience in the future as a result of the defendant's past negligence is in an entirely different category.'

Lord Hope considered that, in light of Lord Steyn's comment in *Frost v Chief Constable of South Yorkshire Police*[1], the limits of recovery for psychiatric injuries should not be extended any further by the common law (except, seemingly, in the case of employer's liability). It would be inappropriate to extend the conception of a primary victim from the focal meaning enunciated in *Page*.

(ii) The causal chain between the result of the negligence (the inhalation of asbestos) and the psychological illness was much greater than in *Page*. In *Page* the illness was the immediate result of an alarming incident. In *Grieves* the injury was not the result of any stress arising immediately out of the negligence itself but as a result of being informed about the risk of physical injury the claimant faced some years later.

1   [1999] 2 AC 455 at 500.

3.18   In *Grieves v FT Everard & Sons* Lord Scott mentioned in particular[1] that all of the claimants (including those who did not suffer a psychiatric illness as Mr Grieves did) could potentially have a claim in contract, as damage does not have to be shown in order to establish a cause of action for breach of contract; all that is necessary is to prove the breach. His Lordship considered that in negligently exposing the employees to asbestos dust the employers would have breached the implied contractual duty to provide a safe working environment. However in reality, compensation in contract may be limited (or precluded) by the stricter rules on remoteness in relation to psychological injuries arising from asbestos inhalation.

1   [2007] UKHL 39 at [74].

3   Non-employer's liability

3.19   In *Attia v British Gas plc*[1] it was held as a preliminary issue that damages could be recovered in respect of psychiatric illness arising out of the claimant witnessing the destruction of her property. The claimant alleged that the defendant had negligently allowed a fire to destroy her home and she suffered a psychiatric illness as a result of witnessing the fire. The Court of Appeal held that if the illness was a foreseeable consequence of the claimant witnessing this fire (which was a question of fact on the medical evidence) then the illness would be regarded as foreseeable as a matter of law.

1   [1988] QB 304, CA.

3.20   It is arguable that the majority of these cases award damages in situations where the physical damage is directly witnessed by the claimant. By contrast, in *Yearworth v North Bristol NHS Trust*[1] the Court of Appeal considered whether to award damages where a claimant developed a recognised psychiatric condition as a result of being informed that the sperm he had stored for possible future use was negligently destroyed by the defendant. Although the court decided the case on a matter of bailment, it considered that this case could be differentiated from *Attia* on the basis that in the latter case the claimant had seen the damage to property, whereas here the claimant had only been informed of the sperm's destruction. However, the court went on to query whether it was actually a valid distinction even though it matched the provisions for secondary victims of personal injury following *Alcock*.

1   [2009] EWCA Civ 37, [2010] QB 1.

3.21   The above cases involve situations where the property damage in question occurred to property owned by the claimant. Questions are raised as to whether recovery for psychiatric injury would be permitted where such injury was consequent upon damage to property belonging to another. In *O'Sullivan v Williams*[1] a county court judge would not have denied recovery for psychiatric injury caused by damage to the claimant's boyfriend's motor car on the basis that it was not her property. Despite the judge's views, claimants claiming damages in respect of psychiatric injury occurring as a result of property damage to the property of another will most likely face an uphill struggle.

1   [1992] 3 All ER 385.

3.22 Further examples of recovery in the non-employer's liability context include *Owens v Liverpool Corpn*[1], where relatives recovered damages when a tramcar negligently drove into the side of a hearse containing a deceased man and caused them mental shock. However, it is important to note this case was expressly disapproved of by three members of the House of Lords in *Bourhill v Young*[2]. In *Al-Kandari v Brown*[3] the defendant solicitors were found liable for causing psychiatric illness to the claimant though their failure to prevent her children being abducted.

1   [1939] 1 KB 394.
2   [1942] AC 100.
3   [1988] QB 665.

3.23 Recovery has also been permitted in the context of law enforcement. In *Leach v Chief Constable of Gloucestershire Constabulary*[1] a volunteer who attended interviews with a multiple mass murderer obtained compensation for psychiatric injury, alleging that the police had negligently failed to arrange counselling. In *Butchart v Home Office*[2] a prisoner recovered compensation having been placed in a cell with another prisoner who committed suicide, having been known to have suicidal tendencies. In *McLoughlin v Jones*[3] a solicitor was liable to compensate a claimant who suffered psychiatric injury following imprisonment as a result of negligence on the conduct of a criminal defence.

1   [1998] All ER (D) 399.
2   [2006] 1 WLR 1155, CA.
3   [2001] EWCA Civ 1743.

4 Secondary victims of negligence

1 Secondary victims

4.1 This chapter examines the vexed question of the extent to which the victims of negligence should be compensated by the wrongdoer for psychiatric injury suffered when they are not directly involved in the accident or event. Describing them as 'secondary victims' adopts the terminology used by Lord Oliver in *Alcock v Chief Constable of South Yorkshire Police*[1] and by Lord Lloyd in *Page v Smith*[2], although the use of the phrase itself not uncontroversial and, as is noted below, there are arguably differences in the exact meaning of the phrases as used in the two cases.

1 [1992] 1 AC 310, [1991] 4 All ER 907.
2 [1996] 1 AC 155.

4.2 As discussed in Chapter 1, a 'secondary' victim was compensated for psychiatric injury in *Hambrook v Stokes Bros*[1] and the principle was affirmed by the House of Lords in *McLoughlin v O'Brian*[2]. However, the modern law in relation to secondary victims arises principally from the series of claims arising from the Hillsborough disaster which reached the House of Lords in *Alcock*, the various criticisms of the decision and most notably the report of the Law Commission *Liability for Psychiatric Illness*[3], and the subsequent comments on *Alcock* in *Page v Smith* and *Frost v Chief Constable of South Yorkshire Police/White v Chief Constable of South Yorkshire Police*[4].

1 [1925] 1 KB 141.
2 [1983] 1 AC 410.
3 [1998] EWLC 249.
4 [1999] 2 AC 455.

2 The Hillsborough disaster

4.3 Lord Keith sets out the background to the cases in *Alcock v Chief Constable of South Yorkshire Police*:

'The litigation with which these appeals are concerned arose out of the disaster at Hillsborough Stadium, Sheffield, which occurred on 15 April 1989. On that day a football match was arranged to be played at the stadium between the Liverpool and the Nottingham Forest football clubs. It was a semi-final of the FA Cup. The South Yorkshire police force, which was responsible for crowd control at the match, allowed an excessively large number of intending spectators to enter the ground at the Lemmings Lane end, an area reserved for Liverpool supporters. They crammed into pens 3 and 4 below the West Stand, and in the resulting crush 95 people were killed and over 400 physically injured. Scenes from the ground were broadcast live on television from time to time during the course of the disaster, and recordings were broadcast later'[1].

The handling of the crowds prior to the game and as the disaster unfolded, as well as the media and public reaction to the disaster, remains controversial to this day. A public online petition demanding the release of cabinet papers relating to the disaster attracted more than 100,000 signatures by July 2011.

1   [1992] 1 AC 310, [1991] 4 All ER 907 at 910f.

4.4   Litigation was brought against the Chief Constable of South Yorkshire Police as being the authority responsible for safety at the ground. He admitted liability in negligence in respect of the deaths and physical injuries. However, claims by two groups of claimants proved to be difficult to resolve, namely those by relatives of the deceased which were brought in *Alcock* and those by police officers present at the ground brought in a group of cases known as *Frost/White* (confusingly the cases are reported as *Frost v Chief Constable of South Yorkshire* up to the Court of Appeal and as *White v Chief Constable of South Yorkshire* in the House of Lords. For consistency we have used the short case reference *Frost/White*).

4.5   So far as the *Alcock v Chief Constable of South Yorkshire Police* appeals are concerned, Lord Keith described them as follows:

> 'Sixteen separate actions were brought against him by persons none of whom was present in the area where the disaster occurred, although four of them were elsewhere in the ground. All of them were connected in various ways with persons who were in that area, being related to such persons or, in one case, being a fiancée. In most cases the person with whom the plaintiff was concerned was killed, in other cases that person was injured, and in one case turned out to be uninjured. All the plaintiffs claim damages for nervous shock resulting in psychiatric illness which they allege was caused by the experiences inflicted on them by the disaster… For purposes of his judgment Hidden J assumed in the case of each plaintiff that causation was established, leaving that matter to be dealt with, if necessary, in further proceedings. In the result, he found in favour of ten out of the sixteen plaintiffs before him and against six of them. The defendant appealed to the Court of Appeal in the cases of nine out of the ten successful plaintiffs, and the six unsuccessful plaintiffs also appealed to that court. On 3 May 1991 the Court of Appeal (Parker, Stocker and Nolan LJJ) gave judgment allowing the defendant's appeals in the cases of the nine formerly successful plaintiffs and rejecting the appeals of the six unsuccessful ones. Ten only of these fifteen plaintiffs now appeal to your Lordships' House, with leave granted in the Court of Appeal'[1].

1   [1992] 1 AC 310, [1991] 4 All ER 907 at 910g.

4.6   So, although a minority of the claimants had succeeded before the trial judge, all the claims were rejected in the Court of Appeal. The cases involved a variety of factual issues, summarised by Lord Jauncey:

> 'Of the six appellants who were successful before Hidden J only one, who lost two brothers, was present at the ground. The others saw the disaster on television, two of them losing a son and the remaining three losing brothers. Of the four appellants who were unsuccessful before the judge, one who lost his brother-in-law was at the ground, one who lost her fiancé saw the disaster on television, another who lost her brother heard

initial news while shopping and more details on the wireless during the evening and a third who lost a grandson heard of the disaster on the wireless and later saw a recorded television programme. Thus all but two of the appellants were claiming in respect of shock resulting from the deaths of persons outside the categories of relations so far recognised by the law for the purposes of this type of action'[1].

1   [1992] 1 AC 310, [1991] 4 All ER 907 at 934h.

4.7   Lord Ackner set out the issues to be determined:

'Since the decision of your Lordships' House in *McLoughlin v O'Brian*[1] if not earlier, it is established law that:

1   A claim for damages for psychiatric illness resulting from shock caused by negligence can be made without the necessity of the plaintiff establishing that he was himself injured or was in fear of personal injury.
2   A claim for damages for such illness can be made when the shock results:
   a)   From death or injury to the plaintiff's spouse or child or the fear of such death or injury and
   b)   The shock has come about through the sight or hearing of the event, or its immediate aftermath.

To succeed in the present appeals the plaintiffs seek to extend the boundaries of this cause of action by:

1   Removing any restrictions on the categories of persons who may sue;
2   Extending the means by which the shock is caused, so that it includes viewing the simultaneous broadcast on television of the incident which caused the shock;
3   Modifying the present requirement that the aftermath must be "immediate"'[2].

1   [1983] AC 410.
2   [1992] 1 AC 310, [1991] 4 All ER 907 at 916d.

3   'Secondary victims'

4.8   In *Alcock v Chief Constable of South Yorkshire Police* Lord Oliver set out his definition of a secondary victim. The first point to note is that although the phrase might be (mis)understood to mean that the claimant does not have to establish a duty of care towards him by the wrongdoer, this is not so:

'Although it is convenient to describe the plaintiff in such a case as a "secondary" victim, that description must not be permitted to obscure the absolute essentiality of establishing a duty owed by the defendant directly to him—a duty which depends not only upon the reasonable foreseeability of damage of the type which has in fact occurred to the particular plaintiff but also upon the proximity or directness of the relationship between the plaintiff and the defendant'[1].

1   [1992] 1 AC 310, [1991] 4 All ER 907 at 926a.

4.9   Although there does not in fact have to actually be a primary victim for the 'secondary victim' to establish liability:

'There may, indeed, be no primary "victim" in fact. It is, for instance, readily conceivable that a parent may suffer injury, whether physical or psychiatric, as a result of witnessing a negligent act which places his or her child in extreme jeopardy but from which, in the event, the child escapes unharmed. I doubt very much, for instance, whether *King v Phillips* [1953] 1 QB 429, where a mother's claim for damages for shock caused by witnessing a near accident to her child was rejected, would be decided in the same way today in the light of later authorities'[1].

1 [1992] 1 AC 310, [1991] 4 All ER 907 at 926h.

4.10 The 'secondary victim' has to establish that the wrongdoer owes him a duty of care. The phrase 'secondary' in Lord Oliver's definition relates to the way in which the claimant experienced the breach of duty:

'Broadly they divide into two categories, that is to say, those cases in which the injured plaintiff was involved, either mediately or immediately, as a participant, and those in which the plaintiff was no more than the passive and unwilling witness of injury caused to others. In the context of the instant appeals the cases of the former type are not particularly helpful, except to the extent that they yield a number of illuminating dicta, for they illustrate only a directness of relationship (and thus a duty) which is almost self-evident from a mere recital of the facts'[1].

1 [1992] 1 AC 310, [1991] 4 All ER 907 at 923a.

4.11 In Lord Oliver's view, rescuers were not 'secondary victims':

'Into the same category, as it seems to me, fall the so called "rescue cases" ... These are all cases where the plaintiff has, to a greater or lesser degree, been personally involved in the incident out of which the action arises, either through the direct threat of bodily injury to himself or in coming to the aid of others injured or threatened'[1].

He therefore considered that primary victims could include claimants who feared for their own safety, rescuers and involuntary participants in events (see Chapter 2).

1 [1992] 1 AC 310, [1991] 4 All ER 907 at 923g.

4.12 However, in the subsequent decision of a differently constituted House of Lords in *Page v Smith*[1], whilst emphasising the crucial importance of determining whether a claimant is a primary or secondary victim, Lord Lloyd described primary victims as those *'directly involved in the accident'* and *'well within the range of foreseeable physical injury'*. This might be considered to be a narrower group than those envisaged by Lord Oliver, and would exclude most 'involuntary participants'. However, *Page* involved a driver who was indisputably 'directly involved' as the driver of one of the cars, so any distinction in meaning was not relevant to the decision in *Page*. The Law Commission pointed out that:

'In *Page v Smith*, Lord Lloyd used the primary/secondary victim classification for different purposes. He thought that the law should not commit itself to a distinction between physical injury and psychiatric illness which, he said, may already be somewhat artificial, and may soon be altogether outmoded. Nothing would be gained by treating them as different "kinds" of personal injury, so as to require the application of different tests in law. Whether the plaintiff suffered a physical injury or psychiatric illness the test of liability is therefore the same: whether the defendant could reasonably foresee that his conduct would expose the plaintiff to risk of personal injury. In the case of a primary victim the question will almost always turn on whether the foreseeable injury is physical, whereas in the case of a secondary victim the question will usually turn on whether the foreseeable injury is psychiatric. But it is the same test in both cases, with different applications. However, in the case of secondary victims the law requires not only foreseeability but also imposes certain control mechanisms in order as a matter of policy to limit the number of potential claimants. Lord Lloyd gave two examples of the control factors to which he was referring. First, that the psychiatric illness should have been reasonably foreseeable in a person of "normal fortitude" and, secondly, that hindsight may be used in applying the foreseeability test'[2].

1   [1996] 1 AC 155.
2   Law Com no 249.

4.13 The Law Commission agreed that Lord Oliver's categorisation was helpful:

'We consider that this approach is justifiable, even where it results in the plaintiff being able to recover damages for psychiatric illness suffered pursuant to the injury of a loved one caused by the defendant in circumstances where the defendant would not be liable in negligence to the physically injured person. For example, the plaintiff may suffer psychiatric illness as a result of injuries inflicted by the defendant on a person who has agreed an exclusion clause exempting the defendant from liability for the injuries. This does not necessarily mean, however, that the defendant should be able to ignore the claims of any others who might foreseeably be injured by his or her acts, including those with a close tie of love and affection to the injured person. Likewise, the defendant may be able to rely on the defence of ex turpi causa to defeat an injured person's claim for damages, whereas there may be no similar public policy justification to deny the claim of a loved one who suffers psychiatric illness as a result'[1].

1   Law Com no 249.

4.14 However, the Law Commission also pointed out that in practice courts had often found it difficult to work out whether claimants were in fact primary or secondary victims. Quite apart from the police officer Hillsborough cases in *Frost/ White* (some of which at that time been decided in favour of the claimants by the Court of Appeal) and the issue as to whether someone was a bystander or a rescuer[1], the test proposed by Lord Lloyd in *Page* seemed to require proximate physical danger, something which was not necessary in employment cases, for example for stress at work (as discussed in Chapter 3).

The Law Commission did consider whether the confusion was such that they should recommend a statutory definition of primary and secondary victims, but concluded:

'It seems to us, however, that this would not be appropriate. Indeed, since we have no objections to the results of cases, we are not convinced that legislation would solve the problem. A provision saying something like, "Courts shall not use the distinction between primary and secondary victims" would be both odd and probably unworkable. Nevertheless we hope and expect that through this Report the courts will be encouraged to consider abandoning attaching practical consequences to whether the plaintiff may be described as a primary or secondary victim .... We therefore recommend that although a legislative provision on this would not be appropriate, we tend to the view that the courts should abandon attaching practical significance, in psychiatric illness cases, to whether the plaintiff may be described as a primary or a secondary victim'[2].

However, the distinction still remains in practice.

1 See, for example, *Hegarty v EE Caledonia Ltd* [1997] 2 Lloyd's Rep 259, discussed in Chapter 2.
2 Law Com no 249.

4.15 In *Frost/White*, in his dissenting judgment, Lord Goff doubted whether Lord Lloyd had in fact departed from the categorisation of Lord Oliver in *Alcock* and, even if he had done so, this was not binding as it was obiter in the context of the facts in *Page*:

> 'I am however satisfied that in neither of these passages did Lord Lloyd intend to reach any such conclusion (which would, in any event, have been no more than an obiter dictum)'[1].

1 [1999] 2 AC 455, 1999] 1 All ER 1 at 19d.

4 Reasonable foreseeability

4.16 One important issue is whether it is simply necessary for psychiatric injury to the secondary victim to be 'reasonably foreseeable' to the wrongdoer, and that the various proximity tests are merely aids to establishing this, or whether the proximity restrictions stand alone as additional requirements over and above the requirement to prove reasonable foreseeability.

4.17 The starting point of a requirement to establish reasonable foreseability of psychiatric injury for secondary victims was set out by the court in *Alcock v Chief Constable of South Yorkshire Police* and this was accepted by the Law Commission:

> 'We consider that, at least where the plaintiff is outside the area of reasonably foreseeable physical injury, the plaintiff should, as at common law, be under an obligation to show that his or her psychiatric illness was a reasonably foreseeable consequence of the defendant's conduct. We consider that reasonable foreseeability of harm to the plaintiff is fundamental to all negligence claims and should only be rejected if there are compelling policy reasons for doing so. There would not appear to be any here'[1].

1 Law Com no 249.

4.18 The next question is whether the proximity tests were indeed additional controls for public policy reasons. Lord Jauncey said:

> 'I start with the proposition that the existence of a duty of care on the part of the defendant does not depend on foreseeability alone. Reasonable foreseeability is subject to controls'[1].

1 *Alcock v Chief Constable of South Yorkshire Police* [1992] 1 AC 310, [1991] 4 All ER 907 at 933e.

4.19 Lord Ackner put this in the context of the neighbour principle:

> 'Although it is a vital step towards the establishment of liability, the satisfaction of the test of reasonable foreseeability does not, in my judgment, ipso facto satisfy Lord Atkin's well-known neighbourhood principle enunciated in *Donoghue v Stevenson* [1932] AC 562, 580. For him to have been reasonably in contemplation by a defendant he must be:

"... so closely and directly affected by my act that I ought reasonably to have them in contemplation as being so affected when I am directing my mind to the acts or omissions which are called in question".

The requirement contained in the words "so closely and directly affected... that" constitutes a control upon the test of reasonable foreseeability of injury. Lord Atkin was at pains to stress at pp 580–582 that the formulation of a duty of care, merely in the general terms of reasonable foreseeability, would be too wide unless it were "limited by the notion of proximity" which was embodied in the restriction of the duty of care to one's "neighbour"'[1].

Lord Ackner concluded:

I do not find it surprising that in this particular area of the tort of negligence, the reasonable foreseeability test is not given a free rein. As Lord Reid said in *McKew v Holland and Hannen and Cubitts (Scotland) Ltd* [1969] 3 All ER 1621 at 1623:

"A defender is not liable for the consequence of the kind which is not foreseeable. But it does not follow that he is liable for every consequence which a reasonable man could foresee"'[2].

[1] *Alcock v Chief Constable of South Yorkshire Police* [1992] 1 AC 310, [1991] 4 All ER 907 at 918f.
[2] [1991] 4 All ER 907 at 918c.

4.20 Lord Oliver was more reflective as to the reasons why the court imposes additional proximity controls for psychiatric injury of secondary victims over and above the basic requirement of reasonable foreseability:

'... there is, on the face of it, no readily discernible logical reason why he who carelessly inflicts an injury upon another should not be held responsible for its inevitable consequences not only to him who may conveniently be termed "the primary victim" but to others who suffer as a result. It cannot, I think, be accounted for by saying that such consequences cannot reasonably be foreseen. It is readily foreseeable that very real and easily ascertainable injury is likely to result to those dependent upon the primary victim or those upon whom, as a result of negligently inflicted injury, the primary victim himself becomes dependent...

What is more difficult to account for is why, when the law in general declines to extend the area of compensation to those whose injury arises only from the circumstances of their relationship to the primary victim, an exception has arisen in those cases in which the event of injury to the primary victim has been actually witnessed by the plaintiff and the injury claimed is established as stemming from that fact. That such an exception exists is now too well established to be called in question. What is less clear, however, is the ambit of the duty in such cases or, to put it another way, what is the essential characteristic of such cases that marks them off from those cases of injury to uninvolved persons in which the law denies any remedy for injury of precisely the same sort...

The answer has, as it seems to me, to be found in the existence of a combination of circumstances from which the necessary degree of "proximity" between the plaintiff and the defendant can be deduced. And, in the end, it has to be accepted that the concept of "proximity" is an artificial one which depends more upon the court's perception of what is the reasonable area for the imposition of liability than upon any logical process of analogical deduction'[1].

[1] [1992] 1 AC 310, [1991] 4 All ER 907 at 925c–g.

4.21 The practitioner needs to consider the various controls placed on secondary victims who suffer psychiatric injury, whether this is seen as an interpretation of what constitutes 'reasonable foreseeability', or as additional proximity controls for reasons of 'public policy'.

A 'Normal phlegm'

4.22 Where the claimant (a 'secondary victim') has suffered psychiatric illness as a result of an injury or fear of injury to another person, in assessing whether psychiatric illness is reasonably foreseeable, the wrongdoer, unless he or she has special knowledge to the contrary, may assume that the plaintiff is a person of 'customary phlegm' and has 'a normal standard of susceptibility'. This is different to the test for the 'primary victim' in *Page v Smith*, where only foreseeability of physical injury is required (see Chapter 2).

4.23 In *Page v Smith* Lord Lloyd considered that the requirement that the claimant must prove that the psychiatric illness was foreseeable in a person of normal fortitude was a special control mechanism adopted as a matter of policy for secondary victims, implying that he regarded the requirement as a special limiting factor over and above an application of the usual foreseeability test. Also in *Page* Lord Ackner commented that 'normal fortitude' is an 'imprecise phrase'. The Law Commission concluded:

> 'Any attempt to fix upon criteria of what constituted such fortitude would be very difficult. We therefore think that allowing the defendant to assume that the plaintiff is a person of "customary phlegm" is best interpreted as meaning nothing more than that, in deciding whether psychiatric illness was reasonably foreseeable (and analogously to reasonable foreseeability in physical injury cases), one can take into account the robustness of the population at large to psychiatric illness ... We therefore recommend that although we do not think that legislation on the point is appropriate, while, in applying the test of reasonable foreseeability of psychiatric illness, it may be helpful to continue to assume that the plaintiff is a person of reasonable fortitude, that assumption should be regarded as merely an aspect of the standard approach to reasonable foreseeability that is applied in cases of physical injury'[1].

1   Law Com no 249.

B 'Eggshell personality'

4.24 However, once it is established that a person of normal phlegm would suffer psychiatric injury, then the fact that the victim has suffered unusually badly because of previous vulnerability means that the normal 'eggshell skull' or 'thin skull' rule of remoteness of damage applies, so that the susceptible plaintiff may recover for the full extent of the illness (known as the 'egg-shell personality'). But in respect of establishing the causation and extent of damage (as opposed to establishing liability for injury) there may still be issues as to apportionment and acceleration (see Chapter 7).

C 'Hindsight'

4.25 Foreseeability of the psychiatric illness is considered after the event in the light of all that has happened as, unless hindsight is used:

'... the question ceases to be whether it is foreseeable that a reasonably robust person would have suffered psychiatric illness as a result of what actually happened and becomes instead whether it is foreseeable that such a person would have suffered psychiatric illness as a result of what might have happened but did not in fact do so'[1].

1   *Page v Smith* [1996] AC 155, [1995] 2 All ER 736 at 750j.

4.26   In applying the test of reasonable foreseeability, the standard is that of the reasonable man. As Lord Bridge noted in *McLoughlin v O'Brian*:

'relying on his own opinion of the operation of cause and effect in psychiatric medicine, as fairly representative of that of the educated layman, [the judge] should treat himself as the reasonable man and form his own view from the primary facts as to whether the proven chain of cause and effect was reasonably foreseeable'[1].

1   [1983] 1 AC 410, [1982] 2 All ER at 312c.

4.27   The Law Commission commented that they agreed that the wrongdoer should not be liable for a psychiatric illness that is only foreseeable as a consequence of an accident to an immediate victim, if the accident to the immediate victim, albeit foreseeable, does not actually occur:

'So, for example, where a mother suffers psychiatric illness as a result of thinking about a potential accident which might have injured her son, but which in fact was avoided, the courts should assess the foreseeability of her illness on the basis that she is aware that the accident did not actually happen'[1].

But they were concerned that hindsight ought not to applied so that:

'... a defendant might be held liable for a psychiatric illness that was only foreseeable on the assumption that the defendant already had in mind an (otherwise unforeseeable) accident to the immediate victim. So for example, if a mother suffers psychiatric illness as a result of an injury to her son caused by the defendant in an accident that the defendant could not reasonably have foreseen, the courts should recognise that similarly the defendant could not reasonably have foreseen the consequential illness of the mother'.

However, they did not consider that legislation was required to clarify this point.

1   Law Com no 249.

D   The requirement for 'shock'

4.28   Lord Oliver held that there was a requirement for 'shock', namely:

'... an assault upon the nervous system of the plaintiff through witnessing or taking part in an event—and that they will, on account of this factor, provide a single common test for the circumstances which give rise to a duty of care'[1].

He used this principle to justify his judgment that those who were not physically present but viewed events on television could not suffer 'shock' in the same way as those who were physically present:

'... the shock in each case arose not from the original impact of the transmitted image which did not, as has been pointed out, depict the suffering of recognisable individuals. These images provided no doubt the matrix for imagined consequences giving rise to grave concern and worry, followed by a dawning consciousness over an extended period that the imagined consequence had occurred, finally confirmed by news of the death and, in some cases, subsequent visual identification of the victim. The trauma is created in part by such confirmation and in part by the linking in the mind of the plaintiff of that confirmation to the previously absorbed image. To extend the notion of proximity in cases of immediately created nervous shock to this more elongated and, to some extent, retrospective process may seem a logical analogical development. But, as I shall endeavour to show, the law in this area is not wholly logical and whilst having every sympathy with the appellants, whose suffering is not in doubt and is not to be underrated, I cannot for my part see any pressing reason of policy for taking this further step along a road which must ultimately lead to virtually limitless liability'[2].

1 [1992] 1 AC 310, [1991] 4 All ER 907 at 923a.
2 [1991] 4 All ER 907 at 931d.

4.29 Lord Keith agreed. However, the Law Commission stated that:

'The requirement for a shock was not explicitly referred to in the English case law until the decision in *Alcock v Chief Constable of South Yorkshire Police*',

and set out the comments made to them during consultation by medical practitioners on this aspect:

'The consultees with medical experience emphasised the difficulties that the shock test causes from a medical point of view. The Royal College of Psychiatrists Mental Health Law Group wrote:

"For psychiatrists the 'shock-induced' requirement causes serious problems. The term is vague, has no psychiatric meaning and is emotively misleading. The requirement should be abandoned. Psychiatric evidence should require demonstration, or not, of a psychiatric disorder distinct from a normal mental reaction and, if present, its relationship with the index event. This is usually possible. The requirement to fit the evidence around the concept of whether or not the disorder is 'shock-induced' has no scientific or clinical merit. It is simply playing with words"'[1].

1 Law Com no 249.

4.30 The Law Commission therefore concluded that the requirement for 'shock' introduced in *Alcock v Chief Constable of South Yorkshire Police* should be abandoned:

'While we recognise the force of the arguments for retaining the shock test, we have come to the conclusion that it should be abandoned. We believe that it is possible to counter all the arguments raised in favour of retaining the shock requirement. First, abandoning the requirement would not open the floodgates in its central meaning of a proliferation of claims arising out of a single event. The risk of a flood of claims is felt most strongly in the case of plaintiffs who suffer psychiatric illness as a result of the injury or imperilment of another. But provided the general requirement of a close tie of love and affection between the plaintiff and the immediate victim is maintained, the potential number of claims would be sensibly controlled. Secondly, we do not think that the courts will be unable to cope with the difficult issues of causation that might arise. The courts currently deal with similar problems which arise in relation to physical injury cases where a variety of factors may have contributed to an injury or disease ... Accordingly, we recommend that our proposed legislation should ensure that it shall no longer be a condition of liability for a recognisable psychiatric illness that the psychiatric illness was induced by shock'[1].

1   Law Com no 249.

4.31   As the Law Commission recommendations were not taken forward, *Alcock* remains good law in requiring a shocking event so as to establish liability for psychiatric injury for secondary victims. However, as may be seen (para **4.63** below), the courts have subsequently taken a more flexible interpretation of what might constitute a shocking event. If the issue returns to the Supreme Court in future, this aspect of the decision in *Alcock* is perhaps likely to be vulnerable to review.

E   Close ties of love and affection

4.32   Secondary victims have to establish that there is a close tie of love and affection between them and any primary victim (the person placed in danger by the negligence of the wrongdoer). This is not a requirement which affects a primary victim. Note the successful claims for the psychiatric injury suffered by the rescuer Mr Chadwick in *Chadwick v British Railways Board*[1], after he assisted a victim of the train crash who was unrelated to him, and similarly by the 'involuntary participant' Mr Dooley, the crane driver in *Dooley v Cammell Laird & Co Ltd*[2] as a result of his fear for the safety of his workmates (see Chapter 2).

1   [1967] 1 WLR 912.
2   [1951] 1 Lloyd's Rep 271.

4.33   In *Alcock* Lord Jauncey pointed out that at that time:

'The present position in relation to recognisable claims is that parents and spouses have been held entitled to recover for shock caused by fear for the safety of their children or the other spouse. No remoter relative has successfully claimed in the United Kingdom'[1].

1   [1992] 1 AC 310, [1991] 4 All ER 907 at 933j.

4.34   Lord Oliver pointed out that the law has always restricted the rights of those not directly affected by a tort to claim for the effect upon them:

'The infliction of injury on an individual, whether through carelessness or deliberation, necessarily produces consequences beyond those to the immediate victim. Inevitably the impact of the event and its aftermath, whether immediate or prolonged, is going to be felt in greater or lesser degree by those with whom the victim is connected whether by ties of affection, of blood relationship, of duty or simply of business. In many cases those persons may suffer not only injured feelings or inconvenience but adverse financial consequences as, for instance, by the need to care for the victim or the interruption or non-performance of his contractual obligations to third parties. Nevertheless, except in those cases which were based upon some ancient and now outmoded concepts of the quasi-proprietorial rights of husbands over their wives, parents over their children or employers over their menial servants, the common law has, in general, declined to entertain claims for such consequential injuries from third parties save possibly where loss has arisen from the necessary performance of a legal duty imposed on such party by the injury to the victim. Even the apparent exceptions to this, the old actions for loss of a husband's right to consortium and for loss of servitium of a child or menial servant, were abolished by the Administration of Justice Act 1982'[1].

Lord Ackner declined to allow the claim of a brother where no evidence was adduced to suggest that the bond between the brothers was exceptionally close:

'Only one of the plaintiffs, who succeeded before Hidden J, namely Brian Henderson, was at the ground. His relatives who died were his two brothers. The quality of brotherly love is well known to differ widely—from Cain and Abel to David and Jonathan. I assume that Mr Henderson's relationship with his brothers was not an abnormal one. His claim was not presented upon the basis that there was such a close and intimate relationship between them, as gave rise to that very special bond of affection which would make his shock-induced psychiatric illness reasonably foreseeable by the Chief Constable'[2].

[1] [1992] 1 AC 310, [1991] 4 All ER 907 at 924c.
[2] [1991] 4 All ER 907 at 921h.

4.35 However, Lord Oliver saw:

'... no logic and no virtue in seeking to lay down as a matter of "policy" categories of relationship within which claims may succeed and without which they are doomed to failure in limine. So rigid an approach would, I think, work great injustice and cannot be rationally justified. Obviously a claim for damages for psychiatric injury by a remote relative of the primary victim will factually require most cautious scrutiny and faces considerable evidentiary difficulties. Equally obviously, the foreseeability of such injury to such a person will be more difficult to establish than similar injury to a spouse or parent of the primary victim. But these are factual difficulties and I can see no logic and no policy reason for excluding claims by more remote relatives. Suppose, for instance, that the primary victim has lived with the plaintiff for 40 years, both being under the belief that they are lawfully married. Does she suffer less shock or grief because it is subsequently discovered that their marriage was invalid? The source of the shock and distress in all these cases is the affectionate relationship which existed between the plaintiff and the victim and the traumatic effect of the negligence is equally foreseeable, given that relationship, however the relationship arises'[1].

Lord Jauncey said:

'I would respectfully agree with Lord Wilberforce that cases involving less close relatives should be very carefully scrutinised. That, however, is not to say they must necessarily be excluded. The underlying logic of allowing claims of parents and spouses is that it can readily be foreseen by the tortfeasor that if they saw or were involved in the immediate aftermath of a serious accident or disaster they would, because of their close relationship of love and affection with the victim be likely to suffer nervous shock. There may, however, be others whose ties of relationship are as strong. I do not consider that it would be profitable to try and define who such others might be or to draw any dividing line between one degree of relationship and another. To draw such a line would necessarily be arbitrary and lacking in logic'[2].

[1] [1992] 1 AC 310, [1991] 4 All ER 907 at 930b.
[2] [1991] 4 All ER 907 at 935j.

4.36 The Law Commission considered that the House of Lords should have allowed the claim by a brother and therefore proposed that there should be a list of relationships that would statutorily satisfy the bond of close love and affection, whilst allowing for claims outside the list who could claim a similarly close relationship:

> 'We therefore recommend that the legislation should lay down a fixed list of relationships where a close tie of love and affection shall be deemed to exist, while allowing a plaintiff outside the list to prove that a close tie of love and affection existed between him or herself and the immediate victim...
>
> The fixed list of relationships where a close tie of love and affection is deemed to exist should consist of the following relationships:
>
> (a) spouse;
> (b) parent;
> (c) child;
> (d) brother or sister;
> (e) cohabitant, defined as being a person who, although not married to the immediate victim, had lived with him or her as man and wife (or, if of the same gender, in the equivalent relationship) for a period of at least two years'[1].

As these recommendations have not been taken forward, the test therefore remains as set out in *Alcock*, in other words a requirement to show a close tie of love and affection, as interpreted in subsequent decisions.

1   Law Com no 249.

4.37 Can a secondary victim who does not have close bond of love and affection (equivalent to a spouse for a spouse or a parent and child for each other), for example a mere bystander who cannot bring himself into the scope of a primary victim, ever claim compensation for psychiatric injury? Lord Ackner did not rule this out on principle:

> '... how do you explain why the duty is confined to the case of parent or guardian and child and does not extend to other relations of life also involving intimate associations: and why does it not eventually extend to bystanders? As regards the latter category, while it may be very difficult to envisage a case of a stranger, who is not actively and foreseeably involved in a disaster or its aftermath, other than in the role of rescuer, suffering shock-induced psychiatric injury by the mere observation of apprehended or actual injury of a third person in circumstances that could be considered reasonably foreseeable, I see no reason in principle why he should not, if in the circumstances, a reasonably strong-nerved person would have been so shocked. In the course of argument your Lordships were given, by way of an example, that of a petrol tanker careering out of control into a school in session and bursting into flames. I would not be prepared to rule out a potential claim by a passer-by so shocked by the scene as to suffer psychiatric illness'[1].

And Lord Oliver agreed:

> 'Equally, I would not exclude the possibility envisaged by my noble and learned friend, Lord Ackner, of a successful claim, given circumstances of such horror as would be likely to traumatise even the most phlegmatic spectator, by a mere bystander. That is not, of course, to say that the closeness of the relationship between plaintiff and primary

victim is irrelevant, for the likelihood or unlikelihood of a person in that relationship suffering shock of the degree claimed from the event must be a most material factor to be taken into account in determining whether that consequence was reasonably foreseeable. In general, for instance, it might be supposed that the likelihood of trauma of such a degree as to cause psychiatric illness would be less in the case of a friend or a brother-in-law than in that of a parent or fiancé'[2].

1 [1992] 1 AC 310, [1991] 4 All ER 907 at 919g.
2 [1991] 4 All ER 907 at 930e.

4.38 This would suggest that in the circumstances of an even more horrific accident than Hillsborough, a bystander who was not primary victim (by way of being a rescuer or an involuntary participant) could potentially claim. The Law Commission did, however, note that:

'… the Court of Appeal in *McFarlane v EE Caledonia Ltd* thought that as a matter of both principle and policy the court should not extend the duty of care to those who are mere bystanders or witnesses of horrific events. To extend liability to those who do not have a close tie of love and affection to an immediate victim would be to base the test of liability on foreseeability alone, something which was ruled out by the decision in *Alcock*. Moreover, there would be great practical problems in deciding which accidents were sufficiently horrific, since reactions to horrific events are entirely subjective'[1].

1 Law Com no 249.

F Proximity in time and space

4.39 In *McLoughlin v O'Brian*[1] the House of Lords extended the requirement for a secondary victim to be present at the scene of the accident to its 'immediate aftermath'. The claimant was two miles away at her home when a car carrying her husband and three of her children was involved in a crash caused by the defendant's negligence. One of the children died almost immediately and the other two were seriously injured. She was told of the accident about an hour later and went directly to the hospital. She saw her husband and two children there, still being treated for the effects of the accident. The House of Lords had held that she was sufficiently proximate to the events which made up the accident, Lord Wilberforce saying that it would be impractical and unjust to insist on direct and immediate sight or hearing of the accident itself.

1 [1983] 1 AC 410.

4.40 In *Alcock v Chief Constable of South Yorkshire Police* the House of Lords were not prepared to circumscribe the extent of the 'aftermath', Lord Ackner saying:

'It is accepted that the proximity to the accident must be close both in time and space. Direct and immediate sight or hearing of the accident is not required. It is reasonably foreseeable that injury by shock can be caused to a plaintiff, not only through the sight or hearing of the event, but of its immediate aftermath'[1].

1 [1992] 1 AC 310, [1991] 4 All ER 907 at 920j.

4.41 But, as Lord Jauncey stated, the House of Lords did not consider that this included seeing the dead in a mortuary hours after the disaster:

'My Lords what constitutes the immediate aftermath of an accident must necessarily depend upon the surrounding circumstances. To essay any comprehensive definition would be a fruitless exercise. In *McLoughlin v O'Brian* the immediate aftermath extended to a time somewhat over an hour after the accident and to the hospital in which the victims were waiting to be attended to. It appears that they were in very much the same condition as they would have been had the mother found them at the scene of the accident. In these appeals the visits to the mortuary were made no earlier than nine hours after the disaster and were made not for the purpose of rescuing or giving comfort to the victim but purely for the purpose of identification. This seems to me to be a very different situation from that in which a relative goes within a short time after an accident to rescue or comfort a victim. I consider that not only the purpose of the visits to the mortuary but also the times at which they were made take them outside the immediate aftermath of this disaster'[1].

1 [1992] 1 AC 310, [1991] 4 All ER 907 at 936j.

4.42 Once proximity in time and space is extended beyond the scene of the accident or disaster into the aftermath, any further imposition of such controls becomes necessarily artificial and the Law Commission said:

'We recommend that, where it is reasonably foreseeable that such a plaintiff might suffer psychiatric illness, the plaintiff's proximity to the scene of the "accident", and the manner by which he or she learns of it, should not be used as criteria to restrict the claim'[1].

1 Law Com no 249.

4.43 In the absence of implementation of the Law Commission report, the courts' interpretations of the requirement of proximity in time and space in subsequent cases are considered in paras **4.61–4.62**.

G Means by which events are perceived

4.44 In *McLoughlin v O'Brian*[1] the House of Lords had allowed the claim where the shock had come through direct sight or hearing the accident or its aftermath, but left open the question of whether an equivalent such as viewing it on simultaneous television would suffice, as a decision on this was not required on the facts of that case.

1 [1983] 1 AC 410.

4.45 In *Alcock*, a number of the claimants had not been physically present at the ground at the time of the disaster or its aftermath, but had viewed events on live television. Lord Ackner said:

'... it is common ground that it was clearly foreseeable by the Chief Constable that the scenes at Hillsborough would be broadcast live and that amongst those who would be watching would be parents and spouses and other relatives and friends of those in the pens behind the goal at the Leppings Lane end'[1].

1 [1992] 1 AC 310, [1991] 4 All ER 907 at 921c.

4.46 Lord Ackner placed great store on the broadcasting code:

'However he would also know of the code of ethics which the television authorities televising this event could be expected to follow, namely that they would not show pictures of suffering by recognisable individuals. Had they done so, Mr Hytner accepted that this would have been a "novus actus" breaking the chain of causation between the Chief Constable's alleged breach of duty and the psychiatric illness. As the Chief Constable was reasonably entitled to expect to be the case, there were no such pictures[1].'

1   [1992] 1 AC 310, [1991] 4 All ER 907 at 921d.

4.47 Lord Jauncey agreed:

'... although Lord Wilberforce in *McLoughlin v O'Brian* did not close the door to shock coming from the sight of simultaneous television I do not consider that a claimant who watches a normal television programme which displays events as they happen satisfies the test of proximity. In the first place a defendant could normally anticipate that in accordance with current television broadcasting guidelines shocking pictures of persons suffering and dying would not be transmitted. In the second place, a television programme such as that transmitted from Hillsborough involves cameras at different viewpoints showing scenes all of which no one individual would see, edited pictures and a commentary superimposed. I do not consider that such a programme is equivalent to actual sight or hearing at the accident or its aftermath'[1].

Lord Ackner commented:

'Although the television pictures certainly gave rise to feelings of the deepest anxiety and distress, in the circumstances of this case the simultaneous television broadcasts of what occurred cannot be equated with the "sight or hearing of the event or its immediate aftermath". Accordingly shocks sustained by reason of these broadcasts cannot found a claim'[2].

But he agreed with Nolan LJ in the Court of Appeal:

'... that simultaneous broadcasts of a disaster cannot in all cases be ruled out as providing the equivalent of the actual sight or hearing of the event or its immediate aftermath. The learned Lord Justice gave at p 122 an example of a situation where it was reasonable to anticipate that the television cameras, whilst filming and transmitting pictures of a special event of children travelling in a balloon, in which there was media interest, particularly amongst the parents, showed the balloon suddenly bursting into flames. Many other such situations could be imagined where the impact of the simultaneous television pictures would be as great, if not greater, than the actual sight of the accident'[3].

Lord Jauncey was, however, less impressed:

'I say nothing about the special circumstances envisaged by Nolan LJ in his judgment in this case (*Jones v Wright* [1991] 3 All ER 88 at p 122). If a claimant watching a simultaneous television broadcast does not satisfy the requirements of proximity it follows that a claimant who listens to the wireless or sees a subsequent television recording falls even shorter of the requirement'[4].

1   [1992] 1 AC 310, [1991] 4 All ER 907 at 936g.
2   At 921e.

76 *Secondary victims of negligence*

3   At 921f.
4   At 936h.

4.48   As discussed above, the Law Commission recommended that the requirement of proximity in time and space and the 'manner by which he or she learns of it' should no longer operate as controls restricting recovery by secondary victims. For the reasons set out in Chapter 10, technological changes since 1989 may mean that this control mechanism might be revisited in a subsequent case.

5   Excluded categories of secondary victim

4.49   Although not specifically raised on the facts of *Alcock*, a number of claims by secondary victims are also excluded.

A   Self-harm by defendant

4.50   In *Alcock v Chief Constable of South Yorkshire Police* Lord Ackner commented:

> 'As yet there is no authority establishing that there is liability on the part of the injured person, his or her estate, for mere psychiatric injury which was sustained by another by reason of shock, as a result of a self-inflicted death, injury or peril of the negligent person, in circumstances where the risk of such psychiatric injury was reasonably foreseeable. On the basis that there must be a limit at some reasonable point to the extent of the duty of care owed to third parties which rests upon everyone in all his actions, Lord Robertson, the Lord Ordinary, in his judgment in the *Bourhill* case 1941 SC 395 at 399, did not view with favour the suggestion that a negligent window-cleaner who loses his grip and falls from a height, impaling himself on spiked railings, would be liable for the shock-induced psychiatric illness occasioned to a pregnant woman looking out of the window of a house situated on the opposite side of the street'[1].

1   [1992] 1 AC 310, [1991] 4 All ER 907 at 917j.

4.51   And Lord Oliver referred to an Australian case:

> '... in *Jaensch v Coffey* 54 ALR 417, Deane J expressed the view that no claim could be entertained as a matter of law in a case where the primary victim is the negligent defendant himself and the shock to the plaintiff arises from witnessing the victim's self-inflicted injury. The question does not, fortunately, fall to be determined in the instant case, but I suspect that an English court would be likely to take a similar view...
>
> If, for instance, the primary victim is himself 75 per cent, responsible for the accident, it would be a curious and wholly unfair situation if the plaintiff were enabled to recover damages for his or her traumatic injury from the person responsible only in a minor degree whilst he in turn remained unable to recover any contribution from the person primarily responsible since the latter's negligence vis-à-vis the plaintiff would not even have been tortious'[1].

1   [1992] 1 AC 310, [1991] 4 All ER 907 at 932c.

4.52   However, the Law Commission felt that where the plaintiff's psychiatric illness is suffered as a result of another person's death, injury or imperilment, it should not be an absolute bar to recovery that that person is the defendant himself:

'... our proposed legislation should ensure that it shall not be a bar to liability for a recognisable psychiatric illness that the illness results from the death, injury or imperilment of the defendant, but that the courts should have scope to decide not to impose a duty of care where satisfied that its imposition would not be just and reasonable because the defendant chose to cause his or her death, injury or imperilment'[1].

1   Law Com no 249.

4.53 The facts have not yet arisen for a case to be decided on this point in England and Wales, so although it seems likely that the comments in *Alcock* will be persuasive to reject such a claim, that is not absolutely certain.

B   Recipients of news

4.54 The Law Commission pointed out that as a consequence of the statement of the proximity requirements of time and space and the direct perception of events in *Alcock*, claimants who suffer psychiatric illness after the communication of distressing news by a third party would not be able to recover:

> 'Following *Alcock* a plaintiff who suffers psychiatric illness after the communication of distressing news by a third party will not be able to recover'[1].

However, a person may potentially be liable for communicating untrue news or insensitively communicating true news. In *AB v Tameside and Glossop Health Authority*[2] where women were told by letter that a healthcare worker who treated them was HIV positive, the defendants admitted a breach of a duty of care not to communicate news in an insensitive manner.

1   Law Com no 249.
2   [1997] 8 Med LR 91, CA.

4.55 In *Alcock* the House of Lords doubted the correctness of the High Court decisions in *Hevican v Ruane*[1] and *Ravenscroft v Rederiaktiebølaget Transatlantic*[2]. In both cases the plaintiffs had suffered psychiatric illness after being told about the death of their child in an accident caused by the defendants' negligence. The decision in *Ravenscroft v Rederiaktiebølaget Transatlantic* was overruled by the Court of Appeal in *Frost v Chief Constable of South Yorkshire Police*[3], as being inconsistent with *Alcock*.

1   [1991] 3 All ER 65.
2   [1991] 3 All ER 73.
3   [1997] 3 WLR 1194 at 1202.

6   What did the Law Commission propose and was it necessary?

4.56 The Law Commission did not propose an entire statutory solution to the problems of psychiatric injury claims:

> 'We have no desire to restrict judicial activity in this area. We feel that it is important that the law should be able to develop incrementally as relevant experts learn more about

psychiatric illness and society further recognises its debilitating consequences. We do not think that medical knowledge has advanced to a sufficiently mature stage for the complete codification of liability for psychiatric illness to be a sensible option. We have therefore adopted an approach of minimalist intervention, proposing legislative reform only in those areas where the present law is clearly unsatisfactory, but in all other cases leaving the common law to develop'[1].

1   Law Com no 249.

4.57 The Law Commission made two recommendations generally in respect of psychiatric injury:

'First, the requirement that the psychiatric illness be induced by a shock should be abandoned. And secondly, where the plaintiff's psychiatric illness is suffered as a result of another person's death, injury or imperilment, it should not be an absolute bar to recovery that that person is the defendant him or herself'[1].

They concentrated most of their proposals for statutory intervention on secondary victims:

'... our recommendations for legislative reform deal primarily with one particular class of plaintiff: those who suffer psychiatric illness as a result of the death, injury or imperilment of a loved one. It is in relation to this class of plaintiff that most criticism of the current position has been made and that judges have called for legislative intervention. We recommend that, where it is reasonably foreseeable that such a plaintiff might suffer psychiatric illness, the plaintiff's proximity to the scene of the "accident", and the manner by which he or she learns of it, should not be used as criteria to restrict the claim'[2].

1   Law Com no 249.
2   Ibid.

4.58 The Law Commission said that these rules have been almost universally criticised as arbitrary and unfair and concluded:

'We believe that the imposition of all three proximity requirements is unduly restrictive, and that it is the last two limitations that have resulted in the most arbitrary decisions. How many hours after the accident the mother of an injured child manages to reach the hospital should not be the decisive factor in deciding whether the defendant may be liable for the mother's consequential psychiatric illness.

We consider that so long as special control mechanisms over and above foreseeability are required in order to limit the potential number of claimants, the most acceptable method of achieving this is to restrict the claimants by reference to their connection with the immediate victim. Provided that the requirement for a close tie of love and affection between the plaintiff and the immediate victim is retained, the main floodgates objection of the possibility of many claims arising from a single event is limited. Furthermore, the advice we received from medical consultees supports the view that where there is a close tie of love and affection between the plaintiff and the immediate victim, the plaintiff's proximity to the accident or its aftermath is not always a relevant factor in determining his or her reaction to it'[1].

1   Law Com no 249.

4.59 The fate of this report is traced in Chapter 10. It is now clear that the proposals will not be implemented by statute. The common law will be left to develop. The report, however, remains as a useful source of material for argument in future cases.

7 Subsequent case law

4.60 Following the decisions in *Alcock* and *Frost*, it has been clear that whether a secondary victim or bystander will meet the requirements set down is a question of fact that must invariably be decided on a case by case basis. This will require the courts to adopt a more flexible interpretation of differing factual scenarios and the categorisation of claimants within those scenarios.

A Interpretation of proximity

4.61 The need for flexibility was highlighted, for example, in *W v Essex County Council*[1], which looked at the question of immediate aftermath in the context of the foster parents of sexually abused children where the abuser had been fostered by them without knowing that he was a known sexual abuser. The House of Lords acknowledged that there were difficulties in the parents' claims in that they were not in sight or sound of the aftermath of the event which caused injury to their children but they also recognised that the categorisation of those claiming to be primary or secondary victims was not closed and the concept was still being developed in different factual situations. There were temporal and spatial limitations on persons who could claim to be secondary victims and therefore the concept of immediate aftermath of an incident had to be assessed in the particular factual situation. Lord Slynn suggested that parents learning of the sexual abuse of their children four weeks after the event may come within a 'flexible' concept of the immediate aftermath. Their Lordships did not make any ruling on the categorisation of the parents in this case but it is significant that they were prepared to adopt a more flexible attitude.

1   [2001] 2 AC 592.

4.62 Whilst the concept of immediate aftermath may have been stretched too far in the context of a four-week period, the courts have nevertheless been adopting more lenient interpretations of the concept of proximity in recent years. In *North Glamorgan NHS Trust v Ceri Ann Walters*[1], the court adopted a realistic view as to what constituted the index 'event' and allowed a mother to recover for psychiatric injury caused by the shock of witnessing the last distressing 36 hours of her baby son's life after his condition was negligently misdiagnosed and treated. Further, it was accepted in *Galli-Atkinson v Seghal*[2] that a mother who saw her daughter's badly burned body in a mortuary two hours after the accident was involved in its immediate aftermath. A mortuary visit could not be artificially separated from the accident itself, as the claimant's mortuary visit was not merely to identify the body but to complete the story as far as she was concerned, and the court accepted that a single event could be made up of components. This shows a much more liberal interpretation of the concept of proximity than the courts were prepared to adopt immediately after the *Alcock* decision, such as in *Taylorson v Shieldness Produce Ltd*[3] (see below).

1   [2002] EWCA Civ 1792.
2   [2003] EWCA Civ 697.
3   [1994] PIQR P329.

B Sudden, shocking event

4.63 *Alcock* required there to be an injury caused by a sudden, shocking event. The shock need only be the material, as opposed to the sole, cause of the injury[1]. However, where the illness grows out of a sequence of events that extend over an appreciable period of time, this is unlikely to qualify as a sudden, shocking event and will therefore be a complete bar to recovery. A good example is *Taylorson v Shieldness Produce Ltd*[2], where the claimant was told of his son's accident soon after the event and caught glimpses of him as he was taken in an ambulance to intensive care. He saw his son in hospital ten hours later and stayed with him for three days until his life support machine was turned off. Similarly in *Sion v Hampstead Health Authority*[3], a claimant who watched his son slowly deteriorate and die had not witnessed a shocking event.

1   *Vernon v Bosley (No 1)* [1997] 1 All ER 577.
2   [1994] PIQR P329.
3   [1994] 5 Med LR 170.

4.64 For practitioners dealing with post-traumatic stress disorder (PTSD) claims by secondary victims, one of the diagnostic criteria of the condition, namely that there has to be a shocking event of a particularly horrific nature, should not be overlooked as this could make the difference between the claim succeeding or failing. For example, in *Ward v Leeds Teaching Hospital NHS Trust*[1], it was held that the death of a loved one in hospital did not meet the diagnostic criteria for PTSD unless it was also accompanied by circumstances that were wholly exceptional in some way so as to shock or horrify. This may be an explanation for the disparity of approach between *Atkinson* and *Taylorson*.

1   [2004] EWHC 2106 (QB).

C Means of perception: broadcasters

4.65 There is inevitably a connection between the requirement for the claimant to have directly perceived the accident and the proximity in space and time, both of which require the victim to see or hear the accident or its aftermath, as opposed to the effects.

4.66 *Alcock* considered the possibility that direct perception of the accident through television could be sufficient to lead to a duty being owed, with particular reference to Nolan LJ's example of a televised hot air balloon fight where the balloon in which a parent's children were flying burst into flames. Given that live coverage of catastrophic events is now much more accessible via media such as YouTube, this begs the question as to whether the concept of perception needs to be re-evaluated, and the extent of any duty of care owed by broadcasters to viewers. Whilst broadcasters are able to show crowd scenes for major events such as the London Riots in August 2011 or the Libyan conflict, the Broadcasting Code should prevent broadcasters from focussing on the distress of an individual. Although the following terms are deemed 'practices to follow' as opposed to binding requirements, a breach of the same could follow if the broadcaster has been involved in an unnecessary infringement of privacy:

> 'Suffering and distress
>
> 8.16 Broadcasters should not take or broadcast footage or audio of people caught up in emergencies, victims of accidents or those suffering a personal tragedy, even in a public place, where that results in an infringement of privacy, unless it is warranted or the people concerned have given consent.
>
> 8.17 People in a state of distress should not be put under pressure to take part in a programme or provide interviews, unless it is warranted.
>
> 8.18 Broadcasters should take care not to reveal the identity of a person who has died or of victims of accidents or violent crimes, unless and until it is clear that the next of kin have been informed of the event or unless it is warranted.
>
> 8.19 Broadcasters should try to reduce the potential distress to victims and/or relatives when making or broadcasting programmes intended to examine past events that involve trauma to individuals (including crime) unless it is warranted to do otherwise. This applies to dramatic reconstructions and factual dramas, as well as factual programmes.
>
> - In particular, so far as is reasonably practicable, surviving victims and/or the immediate families of those whose experience is to feature in a programme, should be informed of the plans for the programme and its intended broadcast, even if the events or material to be broadcast have been in the public domain in the past'[1].

1 OFCOM's Broadcasting Code (February 2011).

4.67 However, the Code itself will not provide a civil remedy for damages to claimants and there is still a question as to whether a broadcaster, in breach of this Code, who insensitively broadcasts incorrect news relating to the injury or death of a loved one and thereby causes psychiatric injury, will be liable.

The development of new technologies post-Hillsborough might lead to a changed interpretation of the means of perception in an appropriate case. This is considered further in Chapter 10.

However, it does appear as if the courts are moving towards more flexible interpretations of 'proximity' and less restrictive interpretations of 'sudden shock' and it may be no coincidence that this has followed the Law Commission's criticism of the need for temporal proximity and sudden shock as limiting factors in such psychiatric injury claims.

D Liability of primary victims to secondary victims

4.68 In *Alcock*, Lord Oliver suggested that in cases where the defendant was the primary victim, a duty of care would be excluded on policy grounds given that it was the negligence of the loved one which caused the psychiatric injury to the claimant. His reservations have been shared by the courts subsequently, and particularly in *Greatorex v Greatorex*[1], where this very scenario arose. The defendant was the victim of a car crash and his father was a firefighter attending the scene, who suffered psychiatric injuries as a result of seeing his son in the crash. It was held by Cazalet J that it would be inappropriate to impose a duty of care on the son (or effectively his insurers) as it would unduly impose upon the defendant's right to determination, in that it would impose a duty on individuals to look after themselves simply in order to protect their loved ones from psychiatric injury. As a matter of policy, there was no duty of care owed by a primary victim of self-inflicted injuries towards a secondary party who suffered psychiatric illness as a result of those injuries, as it would open up a particularly undesirable type of litigation.

1   [2000] All ER (D) 677.

4.69   Lord Oliver also raised the point in *Alcock* as to whether the contributory negligence of the immediate victim can be imputed to a secondary victim in order to justify a reduction in damages for psychiatric injury. The concern was that the defendant would not be able to raise a claim in contribution against the contributory negligence of the immediate victim as his actions would not be tortious vis-à-vis the claimant. The Law Commission suggested that to impute the primary victim's contributory negligence would be unattractive as it runs counter to the imposition of a separate duty of care between the secondary victim and the defendant.

8   Secondary victims—a summary

A   Distinction between primary and secondary victims

4.70   There remains a distinction between primary victims and secondary victims. Primary victims include those 'directly involved' in an accident, including participants, rescuers and involuntary participants (see Chapter 2) or those directly affected in non-shock cases (see Chapter 3). It is important, but not always easy, to determine whether or not a claimant is a primary or secondary victim.

B   Reasonable foreseeability

4.71   Secondary victims need to establish that psychiatric injury was reasonably foreseeable by the wrongdoer (whereas primary victims, in shock cases only, need instead to show that a physical injury was reasonably foreseeable, even if it did not in fact transpire).

C   Controls

4.72   In addition, there are a number of additional controls on claims by secondary victims for public policy reasons to limit the number of potential claimants:
(1) the psychiatric injury must be caused by a 'shock', although this has been interpreted fairly widely by the courts;
(2) a requirement to show a close tie of love and affection to the actual or feared primary victim. Although there are no closed classes of victim, the courts have interpreted this very restrictively and it is difficult for anyone other than a spouse or a parent/child to succeed;

(3) the secondary victim must be 'proximate' to events in time and space. However, physical presence at the 'aftermath' will often suffice;
(4) the shocking event must be perceived directly and unaided by technology such as television.

D The future

4.73 See Chapter 10 for a discussion on likely future developments of the law relating to secondary victims.

5 Intentional acts and other liability

1 Assault and battery

5.1 It is important to note the distinction between battery and assault. Battery requires there to be physical contact either directly or through an intermediate item. In contrast, assault is focused on the apprehension of harm or unlawful force.

A Battery

Requirements of battery

5.2 The essential requirement for any battery is that there must be direct physical contact between the persons. 'Direct' touching does not only mean one person physically touching another but can also include a blow or touch that is inflicted through an intermediate item. It has been held that a battery can be constituted by the act of throwing water over someone[1], overturning a chair on which someone is sitting[2] and taking hold of a person's arm so that they continue to listen to you[3]. The question then arises as to how indirect the defendant's act must be to the actual contact or harm inflicted upon the victim and whether the defendant can be liable. For example, if they are not present at the location at which the harm takes place but are nevertheless responsible for the infliction of that harm (such as by use of a trap).

1 *R v Cotesworth* (1704) 6 Mod 172.
2 *Dodworth v Burford* (1670) 1 Mod 29.
3 *Collins v Wilcock* [1984] 1 WLR 1172.

5.3 Of course, not all forms of physical contact will constitute a battery. The leading test for what form of touching will constitute a battery is found in the speech of Lord Goff in *F v West Berkshire Health Authority*[1]. The threshold for establishing that a battery has occurred is not a particularly high one, as there is a general presumption that any touching of another person's body can potentially amount to a trespass. A claimant will succeed in establishing a battery where two essential requirements are established: first, that the touching has to be deliberate; and second, that the touching has to be in excess of that which is 'generally acceptable in everyday life'. Actions such as shaking a colleague's hand will normally be seen as generally acceptable.

1 [1990] 2 AC 1

B Assault

5.4 In order to commit an assault there must first be an act. Second, such act must cause another person to apprehend the infliction of immediate, unlawful force on his person and finally, such act must be capable of causing a battery to that person[1]. It is clear from this that words such as threats and abuse will not themselves amount to a tortious assault, although claimants may find alternative protection under the Protection from Harassment Act 1997 (provided other criteria are satisfied).

1   *Thomas v NUM* [1986] Ch 20.

5.5   When establishing whether conduct complained of is sufficiently threatening to constitute an assault, much of the case law in this area focuses on the immediacy of the threat. For example, it is an assault to aim a gun in a hostile manner within shooting distance, even if the gun is at half-cock, because cocking a firearm would only take a matter of seconds[1]. Further, it is an assault to run directly at a person and stop immediately before you are near enough to deal a blow, as this is sufficient to cause a reasonable apprehension of a battery[2]. However, passively standing in front of a person and refusing to move would not constitute an assault, given that such an act is not capable of causing a battery to another person.

1   *Osborn v Veitch* (1830) 1 F&F 317, 318.
2   *Stephens v Myers* (1830) 4 C & P 349.

5.6   A claimant need only establish causation of some injury once the assault has been proven. Problems could conceivably arise where the assault or battery is arguably minimal but the resulting injury is disproportionately serious. If the claimant has a pre-existing psychological vulnerability, then the egg-shell skull rule will apply and a defendant must compensate the claimant for the psychiatric consequences of the assault or battery, however disproportionate they may seem. There may be issues around the credibility of the claimant and whether there is any element of conscious or unconscious exaggeration of symptoms. Defendant practitioners should alert their medical experts to the possibility of exaggeration if there is a huge disparity between the tort and the injury, so that the expert can be vigilant to the particular signs and perform any appropriate test. However, caution would be advised against assuming that in every case of disproportionate responses there must be an element of exaggeration, as the detailed medical history of a claimant may reveal someone with an extensive pre-existing psychiatric history and a high probability of a psychiatric relapse in any event. There may be useful alternative arguments around acceleration of an inevitable relapse that could potentially confine compensation to the period of acceleration only.

5.7   It would seem that there is no separate causation requirement for psychiatric injury in assault. The test is simply causation of injury once the assault has been proved. There could be some potential problems with causation if the assault or battery is minimal and the resultant psychiatric injury is particularly grave.

C   Intentional infliction of harm

5.8   The essence of this tort is the defendant's intention to cause the harm which occurred. The origins of liability lie in the case of *Wilkinson v Downton*[1], which concerned a defendant who told the claimant, as a practical joke, that her husband had been seriously injured. The claimant suffered nervous shock and associated physical

86 Intentional acts and other liability

symptoms. Wright J held that the defendant was liable to the claimant on the basis that the defendant had wilfully performed an act calculated to cause harm or infringe a right to personal safety and that the act caused physical harm. Causes of action under this head are not common, especially given the difficulty in establishing that an act wilfully performed was calculated to cause harm. Claimants may be better off bringing a claim in negligence, where the threshold for establishing liability is lower and will not require a detailed examination of the defendant's motives and intentions.

1   [1897] 2 QB 57.

5.9   There is a lack of clarity as to what needs to be proven in order show the requisite intention and this may be an evidential hurdle which proves too difficult for many claimants to surmount. In *Wainwright v Home Office*[1] the Court of Appeal had held that this intention can be proved either by showing that the defendant subjectively intended to cause harm, or (as will more likely happen in practice) by imputing this intention to the defendant on the basis that the act was so egregious and done in circumstances where it was very likely that the harm would be incurred. However in the House of Lords, Lord Hoffmann was concerned that 'imputed' intention was not sufficient and it must be shown that the defendant actually intended to cause harm.

1   [2001] EWCA Civ 2081.

5.10   In practice, however, the difference between the Court of Appeal and the House of Lords approaches may be minimal, as courts can never know the subjective thoughts of defendants, and will invariably have to impute a mindset based on the objective evidence before them. Perhaps Lord Hoffmann's comments were advising the courts to exercise caution against going too far in imputing intention in this type of case. In practice the likelihood of the harm complained of actually occurring may allow the courts to impute the intention to cause such harm, which would be akin to the foreseeability test in negligence.

5.11   The cause of action under *Wilkinson v Downton* will only be made out when the damage results in physical harm or a recognised psychiatric illness. Severe emotional distress is not sufficient to found liability, so medical evidence will be needed confirming a diagnosis of psychiatric illness in this type of case[1]. Claimants who suffer from anxiety or emotional distress falling short of a medical diagnosis may be better off bringing a claim under the Protection from Harassment Act 1997 (PHA 1997), but will only be able to do so if the act occurred on more than one occasion. The further benefit of a PHA 1977 claim is that the claimant need not prove that the act was intentional, but simply that either the defendant knew their conduct amounted to harassment or ought reasonably to have known that it amounted to such harassment.

1   *Wong v Parkside Health NHS Trust* [2001] EWCA Civ 1721.

D   Criminal injuries

5.12   The Criminal Injuries Compensation Authority[1] is a government organisation that pays money to individuals who have been physically or mentally injured as a victim of a violent crime. The current CICA scheme applies to applications received by the Authority on or after 3 November 2008.

1   The CICA website can be found at www.justice.gov.uk/guidance/compensation-schemes/cica/index.htm (28 April 2011).

5.13 Under clause 6 of the scheme, compensation may be paid by the Authority to an applicant who sustained a criminal injury. The term 'criminal injury' is defined in clause 8 of the scheme as a personal injury sustained in and directly attributable to:

> 'a crime of violence (including arson, fire-raising or an act of poisoning; or an offence of trespass on a railway; or the apprehension or attempted apprehension of an offender or a suspected offender, the prevention or attempted prevention of an offence, or the giving of help to any constable who is engaged in any such activity'

occurring in Great Britain. However clause 10 makes it clear that 'it is not necessary for the assailant to have been convicted of a criminal offence in connection with the injury' and compensation may still be payable where the assailant cannot be convicted of an offence 'by reason of age, insanity or diplomatic immunity' if the conduct is capable of constituting a criminal act.

5.14 Clause 9 of the scheme states that personal injury includes 'mental injury (that is temporary mental anxiety; medically verified, or a disabling mental illness confirmed by psychiatric diagnosis)'. This definition is further refined in the notes to the Scheme tariff, which state:

> '8 Mental illness includes conditions attributed to post-traumatic stress disorder, depression and similar generic terms within which there may be:
>
> (a) such psychological symptoms as anxiety, tension, insomnia, irritability, loss of confidence, agoraphobia and preoccupation with thoughts of guilt or self-harm; and
> (b) related physical symptoms such as alopecia, asthma, eczema, enuresis and psoriasis.
>
> 9 "Medically verified" means that the mental anxiety has been diagnosed by a registered medical practitioner.
>
> 10 "Psychiatric diagnosis/prognosis" means that the disabling mental illness has been diagnosed or the prognosis made by a psychiatrist or clinical psychologist.
>
> 11 Mental anxiety or a mental illness is disabling if it significantly impairs a person's functioning in some important aspect of her/his life eg impaired work or school performance or significant adverse effects on social relationships or sexual dysfunction'.

5.15 The CICA scheme provision reflects the common law position on restrictions on recovery for mental injury by secondary victims, as clause 9 states that compensation will not be paid for mental injury in the absence of physical injury unless:

> 'the applicant was put in reasonable fear of immediate physical harm to his or her own person; or had a close relationship of love and affection with another person at the time when that person sustained physical and/or mental injury (including fatal injury) directly attributable to conduct within paragraph 8(a), (b) or (c), and that relationship still subsists (unless the victim has since died), and the applicant either witnessed and

was present on the occasion when the other person sustained the injury, or was closely involved in its immediate aftermath'.

Pursuant to clause 25, the injury must be sufficiently serious to qualify for the minimum compensation that can be awarded under the scheme, currently £1,000.

5.16 There is a two-year limitation period from the date of the incident for a claim to be received by CICA (clause 18). This time limit may be waived by a CICA officer only where they consider that: first, it is practicable for the application to be considered after the limitation period; and second, in the particular circumstances of the case, it would not have been reasonable to expect the applicant to have made an application within the two-year period.

5.17 The CICA scheme contains its own tariff of compensatory awards for general damages as a result of criminal injuries. A copy of the tariff for metal anxiety and both temporary and permanent psychiatric injuries is set out in Chapter 8.

5.18 Note 5 to the tariff sets out a number of principles to be used when calculating awards for damages which contain both a physical and mental element, namely:

> '5 When a person suffers both a physical injury and a mental injury, and the tariff amount for the physical injury is higher than that for the mental injury, the applicant will be entitled only to the tariff amount for the physical injury.
>
> When a person suffers both a physical injury and a mental injury, and the tariff amount for the mental injury is the same as or higher than that for the physical injury, the applicant will be entitled to awards for the separate injuries in accordance with paragraph 27 of the Scheme (the serious multiple injury formula).
>
> When a person is a victim of a sexual offence and also suffers a mental injury, the applicant will be entitled only to whichever is the higher of the two tariff amounts.'

The maximum award that CICA will make for any injury is £500,000 (clause 24).

5.19 However, under clause 13, CICA has the power to reduce the total award given to an applicant if it considers that the conduct of the applicant before, during or after the incident makes it inappropriate that a full, or any, award should be made.

E Contract

5.20 The advantage to the claimant of bringing an action in contract (assuming that such a cause of action is available) is that the claimant will not have to show that the defendant was negligent, merely that the contract was breached. Accordingly, the claimant will not have to address questions of breach of duty beyond the confines of contractual breach, nor does foresight of harm need to be established in order to succeed on liability. Another advantage for the claimant is that, assuming that there is only liability in contract and no concurrent claim exists in tort, the defendant cannot rely upon the Law Reform (Contributory Negligence) Act 1945 to reduce the claimant's damages because of their contributory negligence[1].

1   *Vesta v Butcher* [1989] AC 852, CA.

5.21 The claimant need only establish that the losses claimed are not too remote in order to recover damages. The test for remoteness, following the House of Lord decision in *Transfield Shipping v Mercator Shipping Inc ('The Achilleas')*[1] is that losses will only be recoverable if the type of losses were within the contemplation of the parties as not unlikely to result from the breach, and that the defendant can reasonably be regarded as having assumed responsibility for losses of the particular kind suffered. This is where the common law and contract law differ in respect of damages. Once negligence is established at common law, a claimant need not show that psychiatric harm was a foreseeable consequence of the negligence, but only needs to demonstrate that some type of harm was foreseeable, which could be physical or psychiatric. In contrast, a claimant claiming for psychiatric harm as a result of a breach of contract will need to show that the defendant has assumed responsibility for the psychiatric rather than general injury. The practical reality is that it will be in relatively rare cases that the claimant will successfully show a recognised psychiatric injury arising out of a breach of contract that was not too remote. In the event that this is established, the assessment of damages is often similar to that in tort.

1   [2008] UKHL 48.

5.22 Recovery is even more difficult for claims where there is no clinically diagnosed psychiatric condition but only general distress that has been suffered by the claimant. The general rule is that no damages are to be awarded for mental distress or anguish caused by a breach of contract[1]. However, *Heywood v Wellers*[2] illustrates the only exception to this rule, ie that recovery is permitted where the aim of the contract was to protect the claimant from distress. This was a claim against solicitors by their client for breach of retainer due to their failure to obtain an injunction against a man who had been abusive to her. The Court of Appeal, with Lord Denning MR giving the judgment, held that the claimant was entitled to recover an additional sum for the foreseeable annoyance that she had suffered, and would likely continue to suffer, as a result of the solicitors' negligence. *Hamilton-Jones v David & Snape (a firm)*[3] was a similar case against solicitors by their client, who was awarded damages in contract when the firm's failure allowed the claimant's husband to remove her children from the UK. Damages were awarded for the mental distress caused by the loss of the company of her children. It is only rare situations that will permit recovery for distress under contract law, and the above cases illustrate that the circumstances in which the courts are prepared to do so are very limited indeed.

1   *Johnson v Gore Wood & Co* [2002] 2 AC 1.
2   [1976] QB 446.
3   [2003] EWHC 3147 (Ch).

2 Statutory harassment

5.23 Under the Protection from Harassment Act 1997, s 1(1), 'a person must not pursue a course of conduct which amounts to harassment of another and which he knows or ought to know amounts to harassment of the other'. Section 3(1) of the Act creates a civil remedy for any actual or apprehended breach of s 1 for any person who is or may be the victim of the course of conduct in question.

5.24 The PHA 1997 encompasses harassment encountered in all manner of situations, including the workplace. It is not uncommon for an occupational stress claim in negligence to be brought concurrently with a harassment claim under the Act for bullying or victimisation by workplace colleagues. There are, however, four principal advantages of bringing a civil claim under the PHA 1997 when compared to an action in negligence:

(i) There is no requirement of foresight of harm (of either the type of harm or any harm at all) as a result of the harassment. Accordingly, once a course of conduct amounting to harassment has been established, a defendant will be required to compensate the claimant for all injuries and losses which result from that course of conduct. This was confirmed by the Court of Appeal in *Jones v Ruth*[1], where damages were sought for harassment by property owners for aggressive and intimidating conduct by adjoining property owners during the course of works to their property. It was confirmed that foresight of the injury or loss sustained by a claimant in a case of harassment was not an essential element in the cause of action as there was nothing in the statutory language to import an additional requirement of foreseeability, nor was foresight of damage the gist of the tort. Section 1 was concerned with deliberate conduct of a kind which the defendant knew or ought to have known would amount to harassment, and once that had been established the defendant would be liable in damages for all the injury and loss flowing from that conduct.

(ii) There is no need for the claimant to establish that they have suffered a recognised psychiatric disorder in order to be compensated under the PHA 1997. Under s 3(2), damages may be awarded for any anxiety caused by the harassment and any financial loss resulting from the harassment. Damages for emotional distress that is not of sufficient gravity to amount to a formally-diagnosable psychiatric illness can and are awarded under the PHA 1997. This is particularly useful where the condition the claimant complains of is 'stress' which is not of itself a formal psychiatric condition, nor can it be compensated in negligence, but which may attract an award under the PHA 1997.

(iii) There is a more generous limitation period for actions under the PHA 1997 than at common law. Under the Limitation Act 1980, s 11A (as inserted by the PHA 1997, s 6), the limitation period for actions under the PHA 1997 is six years as compared with three years for standard personal injury actions. It is of note, however, that unlike in personal injury claims in negligence where there is discretion under s 33 to disapply the limitation period, there is no such discretion under the PHA 1997.

(iv) In respect of harassment occurring in the workplace, there is no defence open to an employer that it took all reasonable steps to prevent the harassment from occurring.

1 [2011] EWCA Civ 804.

A Potential defendants

5.25 The PHA 1997 was primarily aimed at giving increased criminal and civil powers to deal with stalkers. The previous law had been deficient in dealing with stalkers, as many of the matters of complaint against them were for what would otherwise be lawful actions (for example standing in the street, sending gifts through the post, telephoning the stalked individual, sending numerous letters) rather than aggressive behaviour that could be dealt with under the common law of assault. It was therefore always clear that a harassed individual would have a civil claim directly against their harasser. However in *Thomas v News Group Newspapers Ltd*[1] it was conceded by the defendant that the PHA 1997 extended beyond the context of stalking.

1   [2001] EWCA Civ 1233.

5.26   Following the decision of the House of Lords in *Majrowski v Guys and & St Thomas NHS Trust*[1] an employer can be held vicariously liable for acts of harassment performed by employees during the course of their employment. This case involved an employee of the defendant trust alleging that they had been subjected to harassment, bullying and intimidation by their manager. It is not uncommon for claimants to bring concurrent claims in negligence and under the PHA 1997 where there has been bullying behaviour by colleagues that has resulted in psychiatric injury, especially given the advantages of not having to prove foresight of harm or a formal psychiatric disorder. Where practitioners are considering an occupational stress claim that has arisen out of the conduct of colleagues or managers, it is always worth considering whether there is a potential claim under the PHA 1997 subject to the other elements of harassment being present that would establish liability under the Act.

1   [2007] 1 AC 224.

B   Meaning of harassment

5.27   Establishing the definition of harassment has proven problematic for both claimants and judges alike, partly due to the limited guidance provided in the PHA 1997. 'Harassing a person' is defined simply at s 7(2) as including 'alarming the person or causing the person distress'. 'Conduct' within the meaning of the Act includes speech (s 7(4)), meaning that the PHA 1997 is not concerned solely with physical acts, unlike common law assault. There is clearly also a subjective element to harassment, as the courts are required to examine not only the state of mind of the victim in establishing whether alarm or distress has been caused, but also to look at the harasser's state of mind as to whether they knew or ought to have known that their actions caused or were likely to cause such harm.

5.28   The claimant will also be required to establish a course of conduct in order to qualify for protection under the PHA 1997. For a course of conduct to be found there must be harassing behaviour on at least two occasions, pursuant to s 7(3). This is an important requirement and one that is often overlooked in practice. Each of the separate occasions must of themselves amount to harassment within the meaning of the Act. There is no provision or mechanism by which conduct on separate occasions can be taken to cumulatively amount to harassment where it does not amount to such on each of those separate occasions.

5.29   Following the House of Lords decision in *Majrowski* the subsequent cases on the boundaries of harassment have focused on harassment in the occupational context. There are obvious issues as to the delineation of the boundary of harassment in the employment scenario because of the culture of 'banter' and teasing that is present in many workplaces. The law must tread a fine line between recognising the realities of the workplace and the personalities of employees and protecting the workers from potential abuse and harassment.

5.30 A useful summary for practitioners seeking to establish whether the necessary elements of a harassment claim are present under the PHA 1997 is contained in the judgment of HHJ Coulson QC in *Green v DB Group Services*[1], which concerned conduct within the workplace. It is important to remember that the claimant must first establish that the employer is vicariously liable for the actions of the employee and that such actions were either committed in the course of employment or were closely connected to the employment. It should not be assumed in every situation involving workplace harassment, that vicarious liability will automatically be established, although in reality it may be quite difficult for an employer to successfully defeat a claim on the ground that such conduct occurred outside the course of employment, especially where the events have physically occurred in the workplace. According to the checklist, there must be conduct which satisfies each of the following:

(i) it must occur on at least two occasions;
(ii) it is targeted at the claimant;
(iii) it is calculated in an objective sense to cause alarm or distress;
(iv) it is objectively judged to be oppressive and unreasonable.

1 [2006] EWHC 1898 (QB).

5.31 Whilst the above list is useful, it still begs the question as to what degree or severity of conduct is required in order to constitute harassment. The House of Lords provided guidance on this very issue in *Majrowski* in the following extracts:

> 'Courts are well able to recognise the boundary between conduct with is unattractive, even unreasonable, and conduct which is oppressive and unacceptable. To cross the boundary from the regrettable to the unacceptable the gravity of the misconduct must be of an order which would sustain criminal liability under section 2 [of the 1997 Act]'[1].

> 'A great deal is left to the wisdom of the courts to draw sensible lines between the ordinary banter and badinage of life and genuinely offensive and unacceptable behaviour'[2].

1 Lord Nicholls at [2007] 1 AC 224 at [30].
2 Baroness Hale at [66].

5.32 The threshold for establishing conduct amounting to harassment was clearly set very high following *Majrowski*. According to the judgment of Lord Nicholls, such conduct would effectively be required to be equivalent to criminal conduct, such that it would attract criminal liability under the same Act. However, it was arguable that in such cases, the individual concerned would have a possible remedy in criminal law, thereby reducing the effectiveness of extending liability to civil actions under the PHA 1997. The reality is that workplace conduct in the form of bullying, harassment or victimisation will rarely reach the level of criminal liability on more than one occasion, as one would expect some form of disciplinary or other action to be taken by the employer such that such conduct would be unlikely to be repeated. Not only would it be more difficult for claimants to establish that any one incident amounted to harassment, but also that there was a course of conduct of two or more incidents, each of such severity. It is possible that in seeking to recognise and preserve the practical reality of workplace banter, the burden of proof upon claimants was set too high.

5.33 *Conn v The Council of the City of Sunderland*[1] is a good example of how likening the alleged harassment to conduct that would attract criminal liability can operate to the detriment of a claimant even in circumstances where common sense and instinct would have expected a claim for harassment to succeed. This case involved alleged harassment by the claimant's supervisor who on one occasion had told the claimant that he was 'a little shit' and threatened to give him 'a good hiding'. On another occasion, the claimant's supervisor called him and two workmates into a portacabin and said that if they did not tell him who had been leaving work early he would punch in the windows. In respect of the former incident, the court found that this did constitute harassment. However, the claim failed overall as the claimant had failed to establish a course of conduct in that the second act was not found to have constituted an act of harassment. The reasoning of the Court of Appeal was that it did not constitute conduct which could be said to be unlawful as, even though it was unpleasant, there was no physical threat to persons and neither of the claimant's two workmates were themselves troubled by the event. The Court of Appeal focused upon whether the conduct of the alleged harasser would be sufficient to ground criminal liability. Gage LJ also considered that the context in which the conduct occurred could be relevant to whether it constituted harassment stating: '[w]hat might not be harassment on the factory floor or in the barrack room might well be harassment in the hospital ward or vice versa'. As only one act of harassment was found, the claimant was unable to show a course of conduct constituting harassment for the purposes of liability under the PHA 1997.

1   [2007] EWCA Civ 1492.

5.34 Perhaps recognising the difficulties imposed by the 'criminal liability' test, subsequent case law moved away from the analogy of criminal liability under the PHA 1997 and focused on the 'oppressive and unacceptable conduct' definition of harassment, as is markedly demonstrated in *Veakins v Kier Islington Ltd*[1]. The claimant claimed damages for harassment against her former employer based on conduct by her supervisor which resulted in her suffering from depression and going on extended sick leave from which she never returned. The claimant had stated in evidence that her supervisor had made her life hell and singled her out from fellow employees for no reason at all. Her evidence was not challenged and no evidence was called by her former employer. However, her claim was dismissed at first instance on the ground that the conduct complained of did not constitute harassment, given that no sensible prosecuting authority would pursue the allegations criminally or that if such a prosecution was brought, it would most likely be struck out as an abuse of process. On the face of it, it is difficult to see how any claimant could succeed in a workplace harassment claim given the application of the criminal standard as it will be rare occasions where the conduct of a colleague will be of such gravity as to attract criminal liability. It seems that the Court of Appeal shared this view as it retracted from sole reliance on the 'criminal liability' test and held that courts are to consider:

'whether the conduct complained of is "oppressive and unacceptable" as opposed to merely unattractive, unreasonable or regrettable ... albeit the court must keep in mind that it must be of an order which "would sustain criminal liability".'

The court reviewed the evidence given by the claimant (which had been accepted by the trial judge). This evidence included the allegations that the claimant's supervisor had sought to obtain information from the claimant's colleagues, including about her private life, in order to make her life more difficult at work; and the supervisor had torn up a letter of complaint without reading it. On the basis that the course of conduct adopted by her supervisor was sufficient to cause the claimant to deteriorate from a robust woman to suffering clinical depression within the space of two months, the court held that such conduct crossed the line into that which is oppressive and unacceptable.

1   [2009] EWCA Civ 1288.

5.35   A further example of workplace-related conduct that amounts to harassment can be seen in *Rayment v Ministry of Defence*[1]. It was held that the presence of pornographic pictures of women in a communal restroom constituted oppressive and unacceptable behaviour which could be said to be directed at the claimant, the only female employee. It was also held that the actions of a senior officer in using an administrative error to inform the claimant that she was without a job and would have to repay a month's salary constituted harassment, as it was conduct directed at getting rid of the claimant from her position. Further, the court held that giving the claimant a formal written warning and discharging her while she was off sick with appropriate medical certification constituted further acts of harassment. The claim in negligence did not succeed as it was found the acts complained of were deliberate and designed to end the claimant's employment, which did not fit easily with the concept of negligence given that each act was premeditated with a specific aim. In addition, foreseeability had not been established as the employer had taken steps to ensure the claimant's condition did not deteriorate following the first time she fell ill. Caution should be exercised in using *Rayment* as a precedent as it is arguable that the judgment may have set the bar too low as to what constitutes harassment.

1   [2010] EWHC 218 (QB).

5.36   The requirement for 'oppressive and unacceptable' conduct still presents a high threshold for claimants to overcome, and each of those elements must be established separately in order to constitute harassment. In *Dowson v Chief Constable of Northumbria Police*[1], it was held that instructions from a senior requiring police officers to act contrary to the law or incompatibly with professional standards; being blamed for the senior officer's shortcomings and vulgar abuse in front of subordinates did not constitute oppressive and unacceptable behaviour in the context of a generally dysfunctional group of police officers who were generally 'racked with division and backbiting'. Mr Justice Simon concluded that:

'although this was more than simply a clash of personalities, it was not conduct calculated to cause distress and, although it was unacceptable, it was not oppressive in the sense described in the cases.'

1   [2010] EWHC 2612 (QB).

C Harassment outside the workplace

5.37 It appears that in the context of harassment occurring outside the workplace, the courts have more readily recognised certain forms of conduct as constituting harassment. In *Esther Thomas v News Group Newspapers Ltd and Simon Hughes*[1], the claim arose out of the publication of an article by The Sun newspaper recounting the story of three police officers who had been disciplined and demoted for remarks made about an asylum-seeker. The remarks were made in the presence of a desk clerk. The article in the newspaper referred to a complaint made by a 'black clerk' about a private joke which prompted an outcry of angry letters from the public, some of whom blamed the clerk for the punishment of the officers. A follow-up article again referred to 'the black clerk'. The claimant alleged that the articles had caused distress and anxiety and that the act of naming her and her place of work coupled with the 'black clerk' reference amounted to racism and harassment. The newspaper's application to strike the claim out at first instance was unsuccessful. The Court of Appeal dismissed the newspaper's appeal. In attempting to define harassment, it was held that it was not the conduct that made up an offence of tort or harassment but rather the effect of that conduct and it was for the claimant to establish clear facts that alleged harassment and for the defendant to show that the motive for their conduct was reasonable, which is essentially what the test would turn on. In para 30 of the judgment, Lord Philips MR described harassment as:

> 'a word which has a meaning which is generally understood. It describes conduct targeted at an individual which is calculated to produce the consequences described in section 7 and which is oppressive and unreasonable'.

It is interesting that whilst in the context of workplace harassment claims, it is unacceptable as opposed to unreasonable conduct that would constitute harassment; *Thomas* would suggest that the threshold is slightly lower in claims outside the workplace.

1   [2001] EWCA Civ 1233.

5.38 However, the test was redefined by the Court of Appeal in *Allen v London Borough of Southwark*[1] to conduct that is 'oppressive and unacceptable'. In this case, the defendant local authority had issued five sets of unsuccessful proceedings against the claimant for possession on the grounds of non-payment of rent. The claimant held that the final set of proceedings constituted harassment. On the claimant's appeal against his claim being struck out at first instance, the Court of Appeal held that the claim had reasonable prospects of success. In doing so Longmore LJ held that the test for whether conduct constitutes harassment under the PHA 1997 is whether it is 'oppressive and unacceptable'.

1   [2008] EWCA Civ 1478.

5.39 The courts further synchronised the approach to harassment in the employment context when the matter came before the Court of Appeal again in *Ferguson v British Gas Trading Ltd*[1]. The court cited *Majrowski* and *Conn*, suggesting that the tests developed in the employment cases were applicable in other contexts. The court went on to say that it was at least strongly arguable that a company repeatedly sending unjustified threatening letters to cut off a parson's gas supply or to report her to credit agencies (thereby preventing her business from being able to access credit) was suitably grave to constitute a harassing course of conduct.

1   [2009] EWCA Civ 46.

5.40 Further clarification has been provided in case law as to the precise definition of conduct amounting to harassment. For example in *Oxford University v Broughton*[1] it was held that the protests of animal rights activists outside a university graduation ceremony did not constitute harassment. Treacy J held that although the protests, which could be heard during the ceremony, were allegedly 'irritating and distasteful' they did not cause the audience 'to be alarmed, distressed, threatened or frightened' by the protest. The judge decided that the protestors' conduct did not constitute harassment as:

> '[n]ot only is there an absence of evidence to show alarm, fear or distress, but the demeanour of those present at the ceremony did not appear to bear out the assertion that they were people undergoing harassment'.

Further clarification was provided in *Ferguson*, where it was held that 'a course of conduct must be grave before the offence or tort of harassment is proved ... [a]nd that ... the only real difference between the crime of section 2 and the tort of section 3 is standard of proof' and that the conduct must go beyond the 'merely annoying or aggravating matters of everyday life'.

1   [2008] EWHC 75 (QB).

5.41 It seems that the test for harassment is now fairly well established in the context of both workplace and non-workplace claims as being 'oppressive and unacceptable' conduct, although ultimately whether the conduct in questions satisfies that test will be a question of fact, evidence and subjectivity. The requirement for an analogy with criminal liability is not defunct, however, and it may be that such a comparison will assist in distinguishing between conduct that is unreasonable and conduct which is unacceptable.

D   Checklist for harassment claims under the PHA 1997

5.42 The following checklist should be used by both claimant and defendant practitioners alike when either contemplating or faced with a claim under the PHA 1997 to alert them to the potential pitfalls or defences to a claim:

- ensure that there is a course of conduct of at least two separate acts. Analyse the acts carefully to ensure they are truly separate and that one is not simply the continuation of an earlier act. For example, if a harasser uses threatening language against a claimant, leaves the room, then returns a few minutes later and uses further threatening language, that is unlikely to constitute two separate acts of harassment and will be viewed as part of a single act continuing over several minutes;
- ensure that the conduct was aimed at the claimant themselves. So, for example, in the context of the workplace, if potentially harassing comments or conduct

are made generally, either to a group of people or about some other persons and are not aimed at the claimant in particular, the claimant is unlikely to establish harassment against themselves personally;
- check that each of the acts complained of would individually meet the standard of 'oppressive and unacceptable' conduct. Remember that conduct must go beyond what is simply 'unreasonable' and the analogy of the act with criminal liability may assist in making this distinction;
- the act must be calculated in an objective sense to cause alarm or distress but be mindful of the circumstances and environment in which the comments were made. This is particularly important in cases of harassment in the workplace, in the context of workplace banter;
- in workplace harassment claims, can the employer be held vicariously liable in the circumstances for the harasser's conduct or was the harasser acting outside the scope of employment, even where the offending events may have occurred within the workplace?

3 Statutory discrimination

5.43 The legislation on discrimination has recently been consolidated and reformed within the Equality Act 2010 (EqA 2010) which came into effect in October 2010. The aim of the EqA 2010 is to synchronise and clarify discrimination law and assist courts, tribunals and litigants by applying a universal piece of legislation to all manner of discrimination claims. Whilst the majority of the EqA 2010 is now in force, it is important to note that s 14, which provided for protection against combined discrimination, will not be coming into force, as announced by the Government Equalities Office on 23 March 2011. In so far as any discrimination claims may relate to employment, the Code of Practice on Employment was issued on 6 April 2011 by the Employment and Human Rights Commission, and both courts and tribunal must take into account any part of the Code which may be relevant to issues which arise during the course of proceedings.

A Protected characteristics

5.44 The EqA 2010 makes it unlawful, in various circumstances, to discriminate because of the protected characteristics of:

(i) **Age**: there are two different aspects of age discrimination that are dealt with, namely discrimination against a person of a particular age or of a particular age group. So, for example, in respect of a person who is 51, the protected characteristic covers both the age of 51 and the age group of people in their fifties;

(ii) **Disability**: where a person has a physical or mental impairment that has a substantial and long-term adverse effect on that person's ability to carry out normal day-to-day activities. This definition is further explained within the EqA 2010, Sch 1 and there is much case law on the meaning of 'disability' under the substantially identical definition under the Disability Discrimination Act 1995. Practitioners should also refer to the Guidance Notes on the Meaning of Disability, which have been issued under the EqA 2010, s 6(1) by the Office

98 Intentional acts and other liability

for Disability Issues[1]. They provide specific and illustrative examples of what can and cannot constitute a disability;

(iii) **Gender reassignment**: where a person is proposing to undergo, is undergoing, or has undergone a process, or part of a process, for the purpose of reassigning the person's sex by changing psychological or other attributes of sex, this is protected. This is a broad definition of what gender reassignment means and the courts' and tribunals' attention may focus upon the *purpose* of any 'process' undergone in order to draw a distinction between transsexuals and transvestites;

(iv) **Marriage and civil partnership**;

(v) **Race**: includes colour of skin, nationality and ethnic or national origins. These concepts have been explained in the Explanatory Note to the EqA 2010, which provides the following examples: (a) colour includes being black or white; (b) nationality includes being a British, Australian or Swiss citizen; (c) ethnic or national origins include being from a Roma background or of Chinese heritage; (b) a racial group could be 'black Britons' which would encompass people who are both black and are British citizens;

(vi) **Religion or belief**: this includes: (a) religion; (b) a religious belief; and (c) a philosophical belief. Section 10 of the EqA 2010 expressly includes those who lack a belief. The Explanatory Note to the EqA 2010 provides that beliefs such as humanism and atheism would be beliefs for the purposes of the provision but adherence to a particular football team would not be. The requirement for a philosophical belief has been considered by Burton J in *Grainger v Nicholson*[2] under the provisions of the previous legislation. Burton J held that a philosophical belief: (a) must be genuinely held; (b) must be a belief as opposed to an opinion or viewpoint based on the present state of information available; (c) must go to a weighty and substantial aspect of human life and behaviour; (d) must attain a certain level of cogency, coherence and importance; and (e) must be worthy of respect in a democratic society and not conflict with human dignity or the fundamental rights of others. In *Granger* itself, it was held that a belief in man-made climate change, and the resulting moral obligation to act, where the claimant made substantial lifestyle changes as to the way he lived, travelled and even ate, was capable of amounting to a philosophical belief;

(vii) **Sex**: the status of being a man or a woman;

(viii) **Sexual orientation**: a person's sexual orientation towards persons of the other sex, the same sex or both sexes.

1   These Guidance Notes can be found on the Office's website at www.odi.gov.uk/equalityact.
2   [2010] ICR 360, EAT.

5.45 The EqA 2010 makes it unlawful to perform certain types of discriminatory actions in a number of contexts. Whilst the most familiar context is in the employment field, the Act also applies to: the provision of services to the public or a section of the public, whether for payment or gratuitously[1]; the disposal of premises; education and the membership of associations and transport.

1   EqA 2010, s 29.

B Disability and psychiatric injury

5.46 Prior to 2005, the law relating to disability discrimination adopted the same test as the common law in respect of psychiatric injury cases, namely that in order for a mental illness to qualify as a disability, it had to be a 'clinically well-recognised' illness. This requirement was repealed from 5 December 2005 under the Disability Discrimination Act 2005, s 18(2). However, certain other analogies with the common law remain. To qualify as a disability, the condition must go beyond mere stress and anxiety, which of themselves are not recognised as disabilities. In *Morgan v Staffordshire University*[1], it was held that occasional use of terms like 'anxiety' and 'stress' and 'depression' even by GPs was not proof of a mental impairment within the meaning of the Disability Discrimination Act 1995. Further, in *J v DLA Piper UK LLP*[2], the EAT affirmed that a distinction needs to be made between anxiety or stress suffered as a result of an adverse reaction to a life event and a clinical condition such as depression. Practitioners should be cautious against placing too much reliance on literal wordings such as 'stress' and 'depression' used by medical professionals such as GPs when writing sick notes, or occupational health physicians when compiling reports. Ultimately, the decision as to whether the claimant has a disability within the meaning of the legislation will be a question of fact for the tribunal to determine and the burden of proof will be on the claimant to prove that they satisfy all the individual elements of the test.

1   [2002] IRLR 190.
2   [2010] UKEAT/0263/09.

5.47 Under the Disability Discrimination Act 1995, Sch 1, para 4(1), an impairment was taken to have an effect on a person's ability to carry out normal day-to-day activities if it affected a person's mobility; manual dexterity; physical co-ordination; continence; the ability to lift, carry or otherwise move everyday objects; speech, hearing eyesight; memory or ability to concentrate, learn and understand; or perception of the risk of physical danger. Whilst this checklist is not included within the EqA 2010, tribunals still find the checklist to be a useful indicator of the existence of an impairment and it is of great use to practitioners alike. The tribunal will focus on what the claimant cannot do, rather than what the claimant can do with difficulty. Further, in the case of a claimant who is on medication for their disability, the tribunal will assess impairment on the basis of what the claimant cannot do when they are not on their medication, rather than what they can do when taking it.

5.48 There will also be a requirement that the injury has a long-term effect, which means that it has lasted or is likely to last at least 12 months; it is likely to recur if in remission; or alternatively it is likely to last for the remainder of the person's life. It is also important to note that where a claimant is making claims of a single or numerous acts of discrimination under the EqA 2010, they will have to satisfy the court or the tribunal that they had a disability within the meaning of the Act at the time of the acts complained of. A potential defence is available if the defendant or respondent (as they are named in the employment tribunal) did not know, nor could they reasonably have been expected to know, that the claimant had the disability at the time of the acts complained of. A useful point to note is that it will be an error of

100 Intentional acts and other liability

law if a tribunal makes a finding as to whether a claimant has a disability based on the way in which they physically present and give their evidence at the hearing itself, given that disability needs to be established at the time of the act complained of.

C Direct discrimination

5.49 Under the EqA 2010, s 13 direct discrimination occurs where there has been less favourable treatment of a person because of a protected characteristic. This is a two-stage test that requires the claimant to establish: first, that they have been less favourably treated than a person without the protected characteristic was or would have been treated; and second, that the less favourable treatment was because of the protected characteristic as opposed to some other reason. Once the primary test has been satisfied, the burden of proof shifts to the respondent under the EqA 2010, s 136 to prove the actual reason for the treatment, where it is asserted that it was something other than the protected characteristic.

5.50 Therefore, direct discrimination claims necessarily involve a two-stage process, namely:

(i) the claimant must show the existence of facts from which a court could draw the inference that, in the absence of any other explanation, a discriminatory act has been committed. Note that there are two things a claimant must establish: that he has received less favourable treatment, and that such treatment was on the protected ground;

(ii) the burden of proof will move to the respondent to provide a clear non-discriminatory explanation for the treatment of the claimant which must be supported by evidence[1].

1   *Igen v Wong* [2005] ICR 931.

5.51 Defences to a direct discrimination claim would be limitation, ie the claim has been brought outside the applicable time limit, or lack of knowledge, ie that the defendant did not know of the disability at the material time.

D Indirect discrimination

5.52 Indirect discrimination occurs where a person imposes a provision, criterion or practice (PCP) that applies to both those with and without the protected characteristic but that PCP places the claimant and those with whom the claimant shares a protected characteristic at a particular disadvantage when compared with those who do not share the protected characteristic. It is unlawful to indirectly discriminate against a person in relation to any protected characteristic (except pregnancy and maternity) unless the PCP can be shown to be a proportionate means of achieving a legitimate aim (otherwise known as the justification defence).

5.53 Following the EqA 2010, s 136 and *Nelson v Carillion Services*[1] the burden of proof is on the claimant to show the existence of the PCP and that it placed both themselves and those with whom they shared a protected characteristic at a particular disadvantage. The burden of proof then shifts to the respondent to show that the PCP could be justified as a proportionate means of achieving a legitimate aim.

1   [2003] IRLR 428.

E   Discrimination arising from a disability

5.54   By the EqA 2010, s 15 it is unlawful for a person to treat another unfavourably because of something arising in consequence of that other person's disability, unless the treatment can be shown to be a proportionate means of achieving a legitimate aim. The effect of s 15 is to overturn the House of Lords decision in *London Borough of Lewisham v Malcolm*[1] and to prevent disabled people being discriminated against due to matters arising out of a person's disability (ie an absence from work) as opposed to the disability itself. Section 15(2) will give a discriminator a defence to this claim if it can be shown that they did not know, nor could reasonably have been expected to know, that the claimant had a disability.

1   [2008] UKHL 43

F   Perceived and association discrimination

5.55   The EqA 2010 has now formalised two further types of discrimination: perceived discrimination and associative discrimination. Perception discrimination occurs where a person is perceived to have a disability and discriminated against on that basis, although they do not actually have the disability. An important limitation exists – the claimant must prove that the discriminator's perception of disability meets the criteria for establishing a disability, ie that the discriminator thought the relevant person had a physical or mental impairment that lasted or was likely to last for at least 12 months and which had a substantial adverse effect on normal day-to-day activities. In practice, it will be quite difficult for a claimant to establish that in the mind of the respondent, all these criteria had been met at the material time.

5.56   Associative discrimination arises where a person is discriminated against for their association with a disabled person. This sort of discrimination could arise for example, in the context of carers of disabled persons.

5.57   An interesting question arises as to whether there could ever be perceived, associative discrimination, ie that someone is discriminated against because they are associated with someone who is mistakenly perceived to have a disability. Whilst in theory, there is nothing within the EqA 2010 that would preclude a claim for such discrimination, in practice it would be extremely difficult to prove that in the discriminator's mind, the person with whom the claimant was associated met all the criteria for a disability within the legal meaning, and accordingly, such claims will be unlikely to succeed.

G   Practical considerations in a disability discrimination claim

5.58   The time limits for bringing a discrimination claim in the employment tribunal are far more restrictive than those in the county courts. A complaint must be presented

102 *Intentional acts and other liability*

to the tribunal before the end of the period of three months commencing when the act complained of was done[1]. Time limits are strictly enforced and if proceedings are issued outside of this period, the tribunal will not have jurisdiction to hear the claim and it will stand struck out.

1   EqA 2010, s 123(1)

5.59   There is, however a residual and very limited discretion afforded to the tribunal to extend time where it is just and equitable to do so. The tribunal will only extend time in the most exceptional of cases and the burden of proof is upon the claimant to show that those exceptional circumstances are present. Some of the factors which go to establishing what is 'just and equitable' are similar to the checklist contained in the Limitation Act 1980, s 33(3), such as the reasons for delay, the conduct of the parties and the nature of any disability of the claimant. Whilst an employment tribunal is not obliged to go through the s 33 checklist, it may constitute an error of law if a relevant factor is omitted from their consideration[1].

1   *Chohan v Derby Law Centre* [2004] IRLR 685.

5.60   If there is a series of acts of discrimination complained of, the time limit will begin to run from the date of the last act complained of in the series of acts. However, the claimant must establish that there is a continuing course of conduct rather than a series of isolated and unrelated acts. Further, a distinction needs to be made between a continuing act, policy, scheme or regime, and a single act that has continuing consequences[1]. In respect of the latter, time will start to run from the date of that act.

1   *Sougrin v Haringey Health Authority* [1992] ICR 650.

5.61   From a procedural point of view, if there is a dispute as to whether a claimant is disabled within the meaning of the EA 2010, or whether a claim has been issued within time, the parties can usually request a Pre-Hearing Review, similar to a preliminary issue hearing in the county court, where the tribunal can consider the narrow issues and whether the claim will proceed. It is important to consider having a PHR for two principal reasons: first, in terms of the jurisdiction of the tribunal; and second, in terms of costs.

5.62   Unlike in the county court, where the judge will have wide case-management powers and can strike out a claim in all manner of interlocutory hearings, the employment tribunal will only have the power to strike out a claim at a Pre-Hearing Review. Where case management discussions are held to set down directions, the judge does not have the jurisdiction to strike out all or any part of a claim: this can only be done at a PHR or a full merits hearing.

5.63   In terms of costs, the employment tribunal is generally a no-costs jurisdiction, so that each party will bear their own costs of litigation. Costs orders can be made in very limited circumstances, predominantly where there has been some unreasonable behaviour on the part of a party in bringing or defending the claim. Generally speaking, it is rare for the tribunal to make a costs order. Disability discrimination claims are often lengthy, factually complex and require multi-day hearings, are document-heavy and require hours of preparation. If a party wished to save the costs of proceeding to a full trial, particularly in circumstances where there is little or no prospect of recovering costs from the opposing side, a Pre-Hearing Review is often a sensible and proportionate means of dealing with or disposing of claims at a preliminary stage before the majority of costs have been incurred.

H Damages generally

5.64 Pursuant to the EqA 2010, s 119(2), the courts (and under EqA 2010, s 124, the employment tribunals) can grant any remedy which could be granted by the High Court in proceedings in tort. This means that damages for personal injury arising out of statutory discrimination can be awarded as in a negligence action. Further, EqA 2010, s 119(4) provides that an award of damages under the Act may include compensation for injured feelings, whether or not it includes compensation on any other basis. Thus, compensation may be available in the absence of a medically-recognised psychiatric illness, where generalised anxiety and distress has occurred.

I Injury to feelings

5.65 The general principles behind the size of awards for injury to feelings were set out by Smith J in *Armitage, Marsden and HM Prison Service v Johnson*[1]. Smith J stated that the awards should be compensatory and not punitive and should have a broad similarity to the range of awards in personal injury cases.

1   [1997] ICR 275.

5.66 The Court of Appeal in *Vento v Chief Constable of West Yorkshire Police*[1] gave more detailed guidance as to the size of awards to be given for injury to feelings, splitting the awards into three distinct bands, commonly referred to as lower, middle and upper bands. The bands have recently been subject to an RPI uplift in *Da'Bell v NSPCC*[2] and now stand as:

(i) £750–£6,000 for less serious cases, normally where the unlawful act is an isolated event. A bottom limit was given in *Vento* as negligible awards 'risk being regarded as so low as not to be a proper recognition of injury to feelings';
(ii) a middle band of £6,000–£18,000. This is for cases that are serious yet do not merit an award in the top band;
(iii) an upper band of £18,000–£30,000 for the most serious cases. This will normally involve a lengthy campaign of discriminatory harassment. In *Vento* it was held that it would take an exceptional case for the top of this band to be reached.

1   [2003] ICR 318.
2   [2010] IRLR 19.

5.67 It is clear from the case law (including *Da'Bell*) that although the *Vento* guidelines provide a relatively specific range of awards, they should not be treated as a statutory scheme. This means that awards made in the first instance cannot be challenged unless they are wrong in law or otherwise perverse[1].

1   See *Gilbank v Miles* [2006] IRLR 538.

J Psychiatric injury

5.68 Damages for psychiatric injury will be assessed in precisely the same way as in a tortious action, by use of the Judicial Studies Board Guidelines and medical evidence.

In *Essa v Liang*[1] the Court of Appeal held that the requirement of reasonable foreseeability for recovery in negligence did not automatically apply to the statutory tort of discriminatory harassment. The extent of the *Essa* exception is unclear and, in particular, it is not known whether the requirement of reasonable foreseeability of psychiatric injury applies in all discrimination cases, as the reasoning in *Essa* was concerned primarily with the intentional nature of the behaviour in that case.

1 [2004] ICR 746.

6 The illness

1 Recognised psychiatric conditions, and diagnosis

6.1 A psychiatric condition is 'recognisable' when a mental health professional (usually a psychiatrist or a psychologist) determines that there is a sufficient range and severity of symptoms and signs to satisfy the criteria for a particular disorder as defined in the psychiatric literature.

6.2 When a psychologist or psychiatrist determines that such a threshold is met they make a 'diagnosis'. Unlike some physical disorders, there is usually no identifiable pathogen associated with the diagnosis (for example the mycobacterium bacillus in tuberculosis). A diagnosis is therefore essentially a clinical opinion made by a combination of 'symptoms' described by the claimant and 'signs' observed at interview. Further information can be obtained from third parties and information contained in medical and occupation records. There are a number of psychometric instruments which are semi-structured interview schedules which produce a diagnosis (for example Structured Clinical Interview for DSM Disorders (Revised) SCID-R[1] or OPCRIT[2]). These are not widely used in medico-legal settings. Some are simple screening instruments used in, say, primary care which indicate a diagnosis might be present (eg PHQ for depression).

1 www.scid4.org.
2 sgdp.iop.kcl.ac.uk/opcritplus.

6.3 There are two major psychiatric classification systems in use:

(1) the International Classification of Diseases, Version 10 of the World Health Organisation (ICD 10)[1];
(2) the Diagnostic and Statistical Manual of Mental Disorders, 4th edn, Text Revision of the American Psychiatric Association (DSM-IV-TR)[2].

1 *ICD-10: The ICD-10 Classification of Mental and Behavioural Disorders: Clinical Descriptions and Diagnostic Guidelines* (World Health Organisation, 1992).
2 *DSM-IV-TR: Diagnostic and Statistical Manual of Mental Disorders* (Diagnostic & Statistical Manual of Mental Disorders) (American Psychiatric Association, 2000).

6.4 Both ICD 10 and DSM-IV-TR are due to be replaced in time by the next versions (ICD 11 and DSM-V). ICD 10 is used in the UK and Europe and DSM-IV in the United States and Canada.

Post-traumatic stress disorder was first described in DSM-III and not in ICD 9 and therefore for historical reasons some UK psychiatrists use DSM when describing psychiatric injuries.

106 *The illness*

Some conditions can be 'recognised' by a substantial group of clinicians but may not have found their way into either of the two main classification systems (for example sex addiction).

6.5 DSM-IV-TR uses a multi-axial system of five axes each of which refers to a different domain. Axis I consists of clinical disorders whilst Axis II includes personality disorder or mental retardation. Therefore an individual might be diagnosed as having a major depressive disorder (Axis I) and an antisocial personality disorder (Axis II). The term 'Axis II disorder' is therefore sometimes used as a euphemism for personality disorder. Axis III refers to general medical conditions, Axis IV to psychosocial and environmental problems and finally Axis V to a global assessment of functioning.

2 Types of injury

A Post-traumatic stress disorder

6.6 Post-traumatic stress disorder (PTSD) is a popular diagnosis in medico-legal practice because it is one of the few diagnoses which require the presence of an external event to make the diagnosis; there has to have been a trauma of sufficient severity as one of the diagnostic criteria. This can reduce any argument about the causation.

6.7 PTSD was first described only in 1980, following research into veterans of the Vietnam war and the survivors of a number of civilian disasters. It was first described in DSM III. However, looking back in history, it has long been known that psychiatric disorders arise in response to traumatic events such as war, assaults and disasters. Railway accidents, the American Civil War and subsequent World Wars were all associated with such conditions. The First World War was important in increasing the understanding of the effects of trauma on psychiatric disorders[1].

1   E Jones and S Wessley *Shell Shock to PTSD: Military Psychiatry from 1900 to the Gulf War* (Maudsley Monographs, 2005).

6.8 PTSD can be diagnosed in both ICD 10 and DSM-IV-TR and the definitions in each are broadly similar. The criteria for DSM-IV-TR are more clearly defined than those in ICD 10 and therefore are often preferred by both medical experts and lawyers. However, it is illogical to argue that PTSD is present using one classification system and not the other.

(a) Criteria A

6.9 Criteria A in DSM-IV-TR specifies that:

(a) the person experienced, witnessed, or was confronted with an event or events that involved actual or threatened death or serious injury, or a threat to the physical integrity of self or others;
(b) the person's response involved intense fear, helplessness, or horror. Note: in children, this may be expressed instead by disorganised or agitated behaviour.

6.10 Interestingly it is likely that in DSM-V and ICD 11 the necessity to have experienced an event of sufficient severity may well be reduced. It is important to note that it is often the perception of the individual of the severity or potential severity of the event which is important. For example a road traffic accident may cause little material damage but if the driver involved considered that there was a serious threat to his or her life it could still cause PTSD.

6.11 The symptoms of PTSD in DSM-IV-TR are grouped into three criteria, which require differing numbers of symptoms to be present (at least one from B, three from C and two from D). To make a diagnosis there must be sufficient symptoms in B, C and D.

(b) Criteria B: re-experiencing symptoms

6.12 The traumatic event is persistently re-experienced in one (or more) of the following ways:

(1) recurrent and intrusive distressing recollections of the event, including images, thoughts, or perceptions. Note: in young children repetitive play may occur in which themes or aspects of the trauma are expressed;
(2) recurrent distressing dreams of the event. Note: in young children, there may be frightening dreams without recognisable content;
(3) acting or feeling as if the traumatic event were recurring (includes a sense of reliving the experience, illusions, hallucinations and dissociative flashback episodes, including those that occur on awakening or when intoxicated). Note: in young children, trauma-specific re-enactment may occur;
(4) intense psychological distress at exposure to internal or external cues that symbolise or resemble an aspect of the traumatic event;
(5) physiological reactivity on exposure to internal or external cues that symbolise or resemble an aspect of the traumatic event.

(c) Criteria C: avoidance/numbing

6.13 Persistent avoidance of stimuli associated with the trauma and numbing of general responsiveness (not present before the trauma), as indicated by three (or more) of the following:

(1) efforts to avoid thoughts, feelings, or conversations associated with the trauma;
(2) efforts to avoid activities, places, or people that arouse recollections of the trauma;
(3) inability to recall an important aspect of the trauma;
(4) markedly diminished interest or participation in significant activities;
(5) feelings of detachment or estrangement from others;
(6) restricted range of affect (eg unable to have loving feelings);
(7) sense of a foreshortened future (eg does not expect to have a career, marriage, children, or a normal life span).

(d) Criteria D: hyper-arousal

6.14 Persistent symptoms of increased arousal (not present before the trauma), as indicated by two (or more) of the following:

108 *The illness*

(1) difficulty falling or staying asleep;
(2) irritability or outbursts of anger;
(3) difficulty concentrating;
(4) hypervigilance;
(5) exaggerated startle response.

The symptoms have to result in impairment of occupational and/or social functioning and have to be present for at least one month.

6.15 The ICD 10 definition is similar to the one in DSM-IV-TR, although there is less clarity in the number of symptoms required:

> 'This arises as a delayed and/or protracted response to a stressful event or situation (either short- or long-lasting) of an exceptionally threatening or catastrophic nature, which is likely to cause pervasive distress in almost anyone (eg natural or man-made disaster, combat, serious accident, witnessing the violent death of others, or being the victim of torture, terrorism, rape, or other crime). Predisposing factors such as personality traits (eg compulsive, asthenic) or previous history of neurotic illness may lower the threshold for the development of the syndrome or aggravate its course, but they are neither necessary nor sufficient to explain its occurrence. Typical symptoms include episodes of repeated reliving of the trauma in intrusive memories ("flashbacks") or dreams, occurring against the persisting background of a sense of "numbness" and emotional blunting, detachment from other people, unresponsiveness to surroundings, anhedonia, and avoidance of activities and situations reminiscent of the trauma. Commonly there is fear and avoidance of cues that remind the sufferer of the original trauma. Rarely, there may be dramatic, acute bursts of fear, panic or aggression, triggered by stimuli arousing a sudden recollection and/or re-enactment of the trauma or of the original reaction to it. There is usually a state of autonomic hyperarousal with hypervigilance, an enhanced startle reaction, and insomnia. Anxiety and depression are commonly associated with the above symptoms and signs, and suicidal ideation is not infrequent. Excessive use of alcohol or drugs may be a complicating factor. The onset follows the trauma with a latency period which may range from a few weeks to months (but rarely exceeds six months). The course is fluctuating but recovery can be expected in the majority of cases. In a small proportion of patients the condition may show a chronic course over many years and a transition to an enduring personality change'.

6.16 The natural course of PTSD is slow and gradual recovery and approximately one third of cases become chronic. The presence of another psychiatric disorder and lack of social support are poor prognostic factors. The symptoms of PTSD vary in severity with time in response to other life events.

6.17 PTSD is more likely following a trauma in females, those with previous psychiatric problems, low educational achievement, previous PTSD, family history of PTSD. The percentage of survivors of a traumatic event who go onto develop PTSD ranges from 30%–70%. PTSD is more common in events which have a human cause rather than a natural disaster

6.18 Some individuals have symptoms whose range and severity are insufficient to achieve diagnostic significance for PTSD. Some use the term 'partial PTSD'. In ICD 10 the term adjustment disorder F43.2 and in DSM-IV-TR adjustment disorder

309 can be used in such cases. The commonest cluster in which there are insufficient symptoms is Criteria C.

6.19 It is considered that there is an interaction between an individual's resilience and the severity of trauma required to develop PTSD. Someone who is vulnerable would develop PTSD with lesser trauma than someone of average resilience.

Over 80% of individuals with PTSD satisfy the diagnostic criteria for other disorders, such as a depressive episode, panic disorder, or substance misuse disorder.

6.20 PTSD can be delayed so that symptoms develop six months or more after the traumatic event. In some occasions the symptoms develop within six months but the individual does not present for medical attention until six months after the traumatic event. In some cases the development of depression or of a bereavement reaction in someone previously traumatized can 'release' PTSD type symptoms. This is common in, for example, prisoners of war from World War II who first present in later life after developing depression.

6.21 PTSD has more recently been classified into simple or complex. Simple occurs typically after a single traumatic event. Complex occurs after multiple events and is often associated with childhood trauma including childhood sexual abuse. There is a significant overlap between the symptoms of PTSD and those of a personality disorder.

6.22 PTSD is not usually seen if there is a concurrent head injury with unconsciousness because the victim has no memory of the material event.

B   Anxieties and phobias

6.23   Anxiety is a useful human emotion. It is thought to have evolved as a human response to danger, activating the 'flight or fight' mechanisms and is associated with avoidance of dangerous situations (phobic avoidance). An anxiety state is an unhelpful condition in which psychological and physiological manifestations of anxiety interfere with day-to-day life. Anxiety states can occur all the time (a generalised anxiety disorder) or in specific situations (a specific phobic anxiety). They can also be associated with episodes of acute anxiety (panic disorder). Agoraphobia can occur with or without episodes of panic. Obsessive compulsive disorder is classified as an anxiety disorder.

6.24   Travel anxiety is a type of a specific phobic anxiety consisting of symptoms of anxiety associated with driving in a car/riding a bike together with avoidance of travelling by the relevant means. This is a common psychiatric injury which develops after a road traffic accident. The avoidance can be partial or total. Individuals usually are more comfortable driving rather than being a passenger in a car (because they feel in greater control).

6.25   Travel anxiety can occur together with another disorder such as PTSD, an adjustment disorder or as the only psychiatric reaction. In ICD 10 it is classified as an isolated or specific phobia F40.2. In DSM-IV-TR the category is 300.29.

6.26 It is, on occasion, difficult to separate what is avoidance due to anxiety from a rational, conscious decision that, for example, riding a bicycle again is too dangerous. It can also be difficult to diagnose if the physical injury itself makes it difficult to ride the bike or drive the car and therefore the degree of avoidance cannot be easily tested.

6.27 Agoraphobia originally means fear of open spaces or the market place. Individuals with agoraphobia as a clinical condition have a fear of crowded places such as supermarkets.

6.28 Panic attacks can become associated with particular situations. Sufferers then avoid such situations. Panic attacks can occur with or without agoraphobia. If there is no associated agoraphobia the DSM-IV-TR diagnostic term used is panic disorder without agoraphobia 300.01 (and with agoraphobia, 300.21). ICD 10 describes agoraphobia F40.0 and panic disorder F41.0.

6.29 Panic attacks insufficient to reach the diagnostic threshold for a separate panic disorder diagnosis are common psychological reactions to a traumatic event and can be a component of PTSD, adjustment disorders and depression.

6.30 Obsessive compulsive symptoms can be found following trauma. Obsessive compulsive disorder (OCD) is an anxiety disorder characterised by symptoms including intrusive thoughts that produce anxiety, by repetitive behaviours aimed at reducing anxiety, or by combinations of such thoughts (obsessions) and behaviours (F42 in ICD 10 and 300.3 in DSM-IV-TR). OCD usually begins in early adult life and runs a chronic course, often waxing and waning in severity in response to particular life events. Therefore it would be unusual for a traumatic event to cause OCD but it might cause either a relapse or an exacerbation in severity. It is estimated that 1% of women and men over 16 have OCD at any one time.

6.31 Obsessional thoughts are usually of themes such as contamination with dirt, or sexual or religious themes. The sufferer recognises these thoughts as being irrational but belonging to themselves (in contrast to sufferers from schizophrenia who can experience such thoughts as being alien to them). Obsessional symptoms can occur as part of a depressive disorder and can occur in cases of PTSD.

6.32 Obsessional traits are common in the general population and can pre-dispose to the development of a depressive disorder.

6.33 Social phobia is an anxiety disorder associated with anxiety and avoidance of social situations. Such fears can be triggered by perceived or real scrutiny from others. It can occur in situations such as public speaking. The diagnosis is only appropriate if the anxious anticipation of the social or performance situation interferes significantly with the person's day-to-day life. The categories used are F40.1 in ICD 10 and 300.23 in DSM-IV-TR.

C Depression

6.34 Depression is one of the commonest diagnoses in psychiatry; it is estimated that half of all women and a quarter of men will be affected by depression at some time in their life and 15% experience a disabling depression. 10% of new mothers suffer from postnatal depression. Some individuals who experience depression also develop episodes of elevated mood (mania or hypomania) and this is classified as bipolar affective disorder or manic depression. Bipolar affective disorder is not thought to be caused by a traumatic event, although an episode might be triggered by one.

6.35 The typical symptoms of depression include low mood, lack of pleasure in life (anhedonia), negative thoughts, poor concentration, guilt, disturbed sleep, reduced appetite, loss of interest in sex, feeling tired and experiencing suicidal thoughts. The symptoms disrupt normal occupational and social functioning. Some sufferers complain of physical symptoms (bodily pain, fatigue etc). Sleep disturbance can be difficulty getting to sleep (initial insomnia) or waking early (early morning wakening). Appetite is normally reduced and associated with weight loss, although it can be in rarer cases increased, as can sleep. Mood is worse in the morning (diurnal variation in mood). The combination of early morning wakening, diurnal variation in mood and sleep and appetite disturbance is referred to as 'somatic' symptoms in ICD 10.

6.36 Depression has a life-time prevalence of 17–20%. The cause is thought to be multi-factorial, with causative factors including genetic pre-disposition, early childhood experiences and adverse life events, including traumatic events in later life. Some factors, such as having a close confiding relationship, may be protective.

6.37 If there have been more than two discrete episodes of depression in a life time, the term recurrent depressive disorder is used. After one episode of depression the risk of a further lifetime event is increased to 40–50% and after two previous episodes to 60%.

6.38 DSM-IV-TR uses the term major depressive disorder 296, which can be mild, moderate or severe. ICD 10 uses the term mild, moderate or severe depressive episode F32. Some very severe depression can have so-called psychotic features (delusions and hallucinations).

6.39 Anti-depressant medication is an effective treatment for depression, especially those in the moderate to severe categories but can take several weeks of treatment before a response is experienced. Once the symptoms of depression have improved anti-depressant medication is continued for least six months. At this point the depression is said to be in remission. After a suitable period the medication can be stopped and if no symptoms reoccur the disorder is said to have recovered.

6.40 An effective but rarely used treatment for depression is electro-convulsive therapy. It is used in particular for severe depression with psychotic features. In some cases it can have a very rapid response and if someone has stopped eating and drinking it can be a life saver.

6.41 Depression used to be considered to be 'reactive' or 'endogenous'. Reactive depression was thought to occur in response to a particular event whereas endogenous depression was thought to occur 'out of the blue' in relation to alternation to biological factors. Research, however, demonstrated that those with endogenous depression had as many or more life events as those with reactive depression. It is therefore now not used as a classification system, although such concepts still can be found in medical notes and reports. Endogenous depression is associated with the so-called somatic symptoms. Some cases that might have been diagnosed as reactive depression might now be classified as an adjustment disorder or PTSD. Mixed anxiety and depression

6.42 There are some psychological reactions which are a mixture of symptoms of anxiety and depression but with neither being sufficient to reach a separate diagnosis for anxiety or depression. ICD 10 defines mixed anxiety and depressive disorder F41.2 as:

> '… when symptoms of anxiety and depression are both present, but neither is clearly predominant, and neither type of symptom is present to the extent that justifies a diagnosis if considered separately. When both anxiety and depressive symptoms are present and severe enough to justify individual diagnoses, both diagnoses should be recorded and this category should not be used'.

6.43 Approximately 11% of women and 7% of men over 16 have mixed anxiety and depressive disorder at any one time. In DSM-IV-TR this category would be classified as 'anxiety disorder not otherwise specified' 300.00.

There is a considerable overlap between the diagnostic categories of an adjustment disorder and those of a mixed anxiety and depressive disorder.

D Adjustment disorders

6.44 An adjustment disorder (F43.2 in ICD 10 and 309 in DSM-IV-TR) is a syndrome consisting of a mixture of symptoms of anxiety and depression in response to a life event including trauma. It can be used to describe responses to trauma which fall short of the full diagnostic criteria for PTSD. The symptoms of either anxiety or depression are not of sufficient range or severity to achieve an individual diagnosis of anxiety or depression

6.45 The symptoms of an adjustment disorder do not usually last for more than six months (24 months in the case of a prolonged depressive reaction). However if the stressor is a continuing event this can explain a prolongation of the syndrome.

E Somatisation and somatoform disorders

6.46 'Somatisation' is a term which refers to the process of expressing psychological distress in terms of physical symptoms.

A somatisation disorder (F45.0 in ICD 10 or 300.81 in DSM-IV-TR) is a specific disorder which is applied to patients who persistently complain of varied physical symptoms that have no identifiable physical origin. The disorder begins before the age of 30 years, resulting to either medical seeking behaviour or significant treatment. Individuals who are liable to somatisation and who suffer some form of physical injury are more likely to complain of chronic physical symptoms than those who are not somatisers. Those with a specific somatisation disorder may complain of physical problems after an accident but perusal of their previous medical records may indicate that the frequency of complaint after an accident is not greater than that which pertained before.

There is a variety of other disorders which are included in somatoform disorders, including chronic pain syndromes (see below), dissociative disorders and fatigue syndromes.

6.47 Hysterical conversion disorder is now properly termed a dissociative disorder (F44.4–F44.7 in ICD 10 and 300.11 in DSM-IV-TR). Essentially the idea is that the individual presents with symptoms of physical illness, which are believed to be attributable to underlying unconscious psychological conflict. The definition of this in ICD 10 is as follows:

> 'There is a loss of or alteration in functioning of movements, or of sensations (usually cutaneous). The movements or sensations are changed or lost so that the patient presents as having a physical disorder, but one cannot be found that can explain the symptoms. The symptoms can often be seen to represent the patient's concept of physical disorder, which may be at variance with physiological or anatomical principles. In addition, the assessment of the patient's mental state and social situation usually suggest that the disability resulting from the loss of functions is helping the patient to escape from an unpleasant conflict, or to express dependency or resentment indirectly. Although problems or conflicts may be evident to others, the patient often denies their presence, and attributes any distress to the symptoms or the resulting disability. The degree of disability resulting from all types of these symptoms may vary from occasion to occasion, depending upon the number and type of other persons present, and upon the emotional state of the patient; in other words, a variable amount of attention-seeking behaviour may be present in addition to a central and unvarying core of loss of movement or sensation which is not under voluntary control. In some patients the symptoms usually develop in close relationship to psychological stress, but in others this link does not emerge. Calm acceptance ("belle indifference") of serious disability may be striking, but is not universal; it is also found in well-adjusted individuals facing obvious serious physical illness. The diagnosis should be made with great caution in the presence of physical disorders of the nervous system, or in an individual previously well adjusted and with normal family and social relationships. For a definite diagnosis, (i) evidence of physical disorder should be absent, and (ii) sufficient must be known about the psychological and social setting and personal relationships of the patient to allow a convincing formulation to be made of the reasons for the appearance of the disorder. The diagnosis should remain probable or provisional if there is any doubt about the contribution of existing or possible physical disorders, or if it is impossible to achieve an understanding of why the disorder has developed. In cases which are puzzling or not clear-cut, the possibility of the later appearance of serious physical or psychiatric disorders should always be kept in mind.'

This is similar to a somatoform disorder and is an unconscious process but thought to be related (according to psychodynamic theory) to issues related to unresolved childhood anxieties.

6.48 Chronic fatigue syndrome (CFS) or myalgic encephalopathy (ME) is a collection of disorders characterised by persistent fatigue, widespread muscle and joint pain, cognitive difficulties, muscle weakness, hypersensitivity, digestive disturbances, depression, and cardiac and respiratory problems. There is a strong association between symptoms of chronic fatigue and various chronic pain syndromes.

6.49 The cause of CFS is poorly understood. There are various immunological theories, partly because some cases seem to be related to viral infection (post viral fatigue). There is no good explanation as to why a traumatic event should cause CFS. However it is accepted that a traumatic event can cause a relapse of CFS via 'nervous shock' (*Page v Smith*[1]).

1   *Page v Smith* [1996] 1 AC 155.

6.50 There is good evidence that cognitive behavioural psychotherapy, including a particular type known as 'pacing', is effective in CFS/ME. However there are some patient groups associated with CFS/ME who do not accept that there might be a psychological explanation for the disorder.

6.51 In a medico-legal setting it is possible for there to be experts from a very different background (for example an infectious diseases consultant and a psychiatrist) reporting for opposite sides on a claimant with CFS/ME, which makes it difficult for the court.

F Chronic pain

6.52 Chronic pain can simply mean pain that has lasted beyond a certain period, such as six months. However, in practice it has a variety of meanings, including pain that has persisted for a month beyond the usual course of an acute illness or a reasonable duration for an injury to heal, pain that is related to a chronic pathological process, and pain that recurs at intervals for an extended time. In medico-legal settings the usual issue is when pain has persisted for longer than expected or can be easily explained by the underlying physical pathology.

6.53 There are some specific pain syndromes associated with other particular signs and symptoms such as complex regional pain syndromes and myofascial pain. There is considerable overlap between chronic pain syndromes and other somatoform disorders such as chronic fatigue. Pain syndromes are often labelled according to where the pain is situated, eg chronic pelvic pain, atypical facial pain, etc.

The cause of such chronic pain syndromes are poorly understood, with both physical and psychological factors implicated.

6.54 They can be considered as a somatoform disorder, ie an individual who experiences physical symptoms for psychological reasons. This is termed a persistent somatoform pain disorder (categories F45.4 in ICD 10 and 307 in DSM-IV-TR). This is the term used for patients who experience chronic pain thought to be of psychological rather than physical causation. It is defined as:

> 'The predominant complaint is of persistent, severe and distressing pain, which cannot be explained fully by a physiological process or a physical disorder and which occurs in association with emotional conflict or psycho-social problems that are sufficient to allow the conclusion that they are the main causative influences. The result is usually a marked increase in support and attention, either personal or medical. The commonest problem is to differentiate this disorder from the histrionic elaboration of organically

caused pain. Patients with organic pain for whom a definite physical diagnosis has not yet been reached may easily become frightened or resentful, with resulting attention-seeking behaviour. A variety of aches and pains are common in somatisation disorders, but without being so persistent or so dominant over the other complaints'.

6.55 Another explanation of chronic pain is the interaction between depression and physical pain/disability, ie pain makes depression worse and depression makes the perception of pain worse. This is a simple and easily-understood explanation.

6.56 Another way of explaining chronic pain (or other symptoms without obvious physical cause) is the concept of abnormal illness behaviour. In this explanation, individuals obtain unconscious reward for adopting the sick role, ie if being ill avoids unpleasant activity (eg doing a job one does not enjoy), the state of illness is rewarded and may continue.

6.57 Of course, a claimant may deliberately and consciously complain of pain and other physical symptoms, which he does not experience, for his gain. This is malingering.

6.58 Factitious disorder is when an individual presents to hospital complaining of symptoms he or she does not have, not for financial gain but for the psychological reward of receiving medical attention. This is also known as Munchausen's syndrome. There is an overlap here with types of personality disorder.

6.59 Complex regional pain syndrome is a chronic progressive disease characterised by severe pain, swelling and changes in the skin. CRPS is divided into two types based on the presence of nerve lesion following the injury. Type I, formerly known as reflex sympathetic dystrophy (RSD), Sudeck's atrophy, reflex neurovascular dystrophy (RND) or algoneurodystrophy, does not have demonstrable nerve lesions. Type II, formerly known as causalgia, has evidence of obvious nerve damage.

6.60 Myofascial pain syndrome (MPS), also known as chronic myofascial pain (CMP), is a condition characterised by chronic, and in some cases severe, pain. It is associated primarily with painful lumps in muscles.

The cause of these syndromes is currently unknown.

G Exacerbation of existing conditions (eg psychosis or bipolar disorder)

6.61 In addition to pre-disposing factors, individuals may have had either an existing or previous psychiatric disorder. Some disorders are recurrent (such as bipolar affective or recurrent depressive disorder) and can be said to be in remission (ie not currently active) or have relapsed. It can be difficult in a medico-legal setting to know whether someone has suffered a relapse of a pre-existing recurrent disorder because of a traumatic event or because of the natural course of the illness. In some cases the relapse is of greater severity than would be expected from the natural course of the disorder because of the relevant event or events.

6.62 Others conditions are chronic and therefore a nature of the psychiatric injury is of an increase in the severity of the disorder. Examples of this include personality disorder, and chronic psychotic disorders such as schizophrenia.

6.63 A personality disorder is defined as 'an enduring pattern of inner experience and behaviour that deviates markedly from the expectations of the culture of the individual who exhibits it'. It is usually present from late adolescence. It is not, therefore, something that is caused by a traumatic event but the presence of a personality disorder may either complicate or worsen the outcome of a psychological reaction to such an event or be mistaken for a psychological reaction.

6.64 Personality disorder is classified in a categorical way. DSM-IV-TR divides personality disorder into 'clusters'. Cluster A includes paranoid, schizoid and schizotypal personality disorders. Cluster B includes antisocial, borderline, histrionic, and narcissistic personality disorder. Cluster C includes avoidant, dependant and obsessive compulsive personality disorder. ICD 10 uses slightly different terms: emotionally unstable personality disorder rather than borderline, anankastic rather than obsessive compulsive and discoed rather than anti-social. Emotionally unstable personality disorder (borderline type) is a common personality disorder typically associated with adverse childhood experiences such as childhood sexual abuse. Paranoid personality disorder can be found in individuals characterised by paranoia and a pervasive, long-standing suspiciousness and generalised mistrust of others. Such individuals may get involved with litigation more than average. In some cases they may perceive ill-treatment and discrimination which others would not experience. In many cases individuals may have aspects of their personality which are abnormal but not in a sufficiently defined way to constitute a specific psychiatric disorder.

(Individuals who suffer from severe chronic PTSD may experience a permanent change to their personality and there is a category of enduring personality change in ICD 10. This is found in cases of severe complex trauma, for example prolonged incarceration in a concentration camp.)

H   Psychotic disorders

6.65 Psychosis means literally 'beyond the mind' and it is a general term to describe those who have lost their normal rational judgment. It is typically associated with hallucinations, delusions and disorders of form and content of thought. The major categories of psychotic illness are schizophrenia (F20 and 295) and bipolar affective disorder (manic depression) (F31 in ICD 10 and 296 in DSM-IV-TR). There is an argument whether these are two very different disorders or are on a continuum. It is estimated that between 0.5% and 1% of the population have a serious (psychotic) mental health problem.

6.66 Schizophrenia is diagnosed if a mixture of characteristic signs and symptoms are present for a significant portion of time in a one month period with some symptoms persisting for at least six months. Characteristic symptoms are divided into positive and negative symptoms. The former include delusions, hallucinations, disordered language and thought processes and disorganised behaviour. The negative symptoms include restrictions in the range and intensity of emotional expression, in the fluency and productivity of emotional expression in the productivity of thought and speech and in the initiation of goal-directed behaviour. Schizophrenia is thought to have some genetic cause as well as environmental and social factors. It tends to run a chronic course and is associated with a decline in occupational and social functioning. It is not normally considered to be caused by an event (such as an accident of relevance to a medico-legal case). However, an accident might trigger a relapse in someone at risk of developing schizophrenia.

6.67 Bipolar affective disorder is a mood disorder in which an individual has episodes of both depression and mania (or hypomania). The episodes of depression are similar to those which occur in so-called unipolar depression. However the episodes of hypomania include the opposite of depression, ie elevated mood, increased activity, grandiose thinking and irritability. There may be psychotic features but these are said to be 'mood congruent', ie any delusion or hallucination experienced is in keeping with the individual's prevailing mood. Bipolar affective disorder, like schizophrenia, is not normally considered to be caused by an event (such as an accident of relevance to a medico-legal case). However, an accident might trigger a relapse in someone at risk of developing bipolar affective disorder.

I Alcohol and substance misuse problems

6.68 Misuse and dependence on alcohol and other drugs is extremely common and places a huge burden on the individual and society. The prevalence of alcohol dependence in 2007 was 5.9% (8.7% in men and 3.3% in women). 24% of the adult population have a hazardous pattern of drinking. Co-morbidity of alcohol and substance misuse with other psychiatric disorder is common. For example 80% of people receiving treatment for alcohol misuse also experience anxiety and depression. Up to half of people with mental health problems may misuse alcohol or drugs.

6.69 Substance misuse problems are classified as mental disorders and can themselves cause other mental disorders. ICD 10 uses a system of classifying the different substances F 1x.0/1/2 and whether there is intoxication 0, harmful use 1 or dependence 2. So for example harmful use of alcohol is F10.1 and cannabis dependence F11.2. Harmful use is divided into physical psychological and social damage. Dependence is a syndrome in which individuals continue to take the substance despite evidence of harm, they require increasing amounts (tolerance), there are significant withdrawal symptoms and a narrowing of repertoire (that is a reduction in range and types of situation in which they use the substance). DSM-IV-TR divides the disorders up into substance misuse disorders and disorders caused by the substance.

6.70 Cannabis can cause psychosis, although there is disagreement whether it can actually cause schizophrenia or whether it triggers the disorder in someone with pre-existing vulnerability. Cocaine can lead to mood disturbance and paranoid thinking. Chronic alcohol use can lead amongst other things, to depression.

6.71 Alcohol and substance misuse is a common consequence of PTSD, as victims self medicate to help them sleep and reduce their anxiety levels. Unfortunately, as the blood alcohol levels fall individuals suffer an increased 'rebound anxiety'. Excessive drinking of alcohol disturbs the pattern of sleep and can increase the quantity and frequency of dreams.

6.72 Some other behaviours (such as gambling and sex) have been described as if they were identical to harmful use/dependence related to chemical substances.

6.73 In general, within addiction research there is an argument as to the relative importance of social and biological factors. Some adhere to a 'disease model' and take a particular (12 step) approach to abstinence. Others cite the importance of the social environment in maintaining substance misuse.

3 Head injuries – overlap with structural brain injury

6.74 Psychiatric injury (usually a depressive syndrome) is common after a head injury (research indicates a prevalence of between 25–50%). However the there are difficulties separating out cognitive problems from depression. Some cases of depression are similar to normal depressive episodes in that they may occur in response to external stresses and loss, (ie a psychological reaction to an event) and may be pre-disposed to by some inherited vulnerability. Other cases of depression following head injury may differ, in that they are caused by physical damage to those parts of the brain, which are relevant to emotions and mood. Such cases caused by a physical injury may be less responsive to normal psychiatric interventions.

6.75 In addition to depressive disorder caused by physical brain damage, some effects of brain damage cause symptoms which can be confused with depression. This is because some of the signs and symptoms of physical brain damage, such as the dysexecutive syndrome which can occur after an injury to the frontal lobes, including symptoms of lack of drive, irritability, disturbed sleep and disturbed concentration, are similar symptoms to those of a depressive illness. As a result some individuals who do not have a depressive episode are mis-classified as having one because of confusingly similar, but qualitatively different, symptoms caused by the brain damage.

6.76 A further complication is that the neuropsychological assessment to determine the degree of any cognitive damage is affected by the presence of co-morbid depression due to the effects of the latter on concentration and attention.

One way to attempt to tease out the relative importance of depression versus cognitive damage is to have a trial of treatment with anti-depressant medication.

4 Whiplash etc – overlap with physical injury

6.77 There is a strong association between whiplash and psychiatric injury, especially anxiety and depression. The majority of those with a whiplash injury recover within three months but a substantial minority run a chronic course. There is evidence of an increased association with psychiatric disorder in the latter group in particular. It is uncertain whether the psychological distress precedes and causes the chronic pain, or, conversely, the psychological distress is a consequence of chronic pain. Recent research[1] has suggested that those with pre-existing anxiety and depression are more likely to develop chronic whiplash after an injury. Examining the medical records in whose who have developed a chronic whiplash injury often reveals evidence of previous somatoform symptoms.

1   Mykletun A, Glozier N, Wenzel HG, Overland S, Harvey SB, Wessely S, Hotopf M (2011) Reverse causality in the association between whiplash and symptoms of anxiety and depression; the HUNT study; Spine Aug 1; 36(17):1380–6.

5   Pre-existing vulnerability

6.78   There are a variety of factors which make someone more vulnerable to developing a psychiatric disorder if exposed to a traumatic event.

A common way of classifying vulnerability (often described as pre-disposing factors) is to divide them into biological, social and psychological.

6.79   Some individuals have a genetic vulnerability, as evidenced by a family history of psychiatric disorder. These are almost always not a single gene effect but the presence of multiple genes that increase the vulnerability to develop a psychiatric disorder. Brain injuries, either through trauma in adult life or at birth can cause psychiatric disorder by disrupting brain function and development. Exposure to toxic substances during development interutero can lead to psychiatric disorder, as can levels of hormones and the general functioning of the neuroendocrine system.

6.80   Social factors and social deprivation are associated with increased rates of mental illness[1]. Factors found to be relevant include a lack of social cohesion. This is common in immigrant populations where there is separation from extended family and other means of social support. Housing is very important, with various factors such as a lack of space and excessive noise; as well as homelessness being associated with increased levels of mental illness[2]. Poverty and social deprivation in general (people in the lowest 20% of household income have increased rate of mental disorder compared with those in the top 20%[3]) and racial or sexual discrimination are associated with increased rates of mental illness.

1   Marmot Review 2010 *Fair Society, Healthy Lives: A Strategic Review of Health Inequalities in England Post–2010* (www.ucl.ac.uk\gheg\marmotreview).
2   Mental Health Foundation, 2002.
3   McManus S, Meltzer H, Brugha T, Bebbington P, Jenkins R (2009) *Adult Psychiatric Morbidity in England, 2007: results of a household survey* (National Centre for Social Research).

6.81   In addition to biological and social factors, the psychological environment in which people are brought up is extremely important. This includes poor or absent parenting[1]. Sexual and physical abuse as a child too is very potent and common cause of mental illness in childhood and adult life[2]. Bullying and harassment, both at school and in the work place is important. Research has shown too that some factors may be protective, such as the presence of an emotionally confiding relationship.

Bereavement, unemployment and the loss of a relationship can all lead to mental illness. There is an increased prevalence of psychiatric disorder.

1   Meltzer H, Gatward R, Corbin T et al *Persistence, onset, risk factors and outcomes of childhood mental disorders* (The Stationery Office, 2003).
2   Collishaw S, Pickles A, Messer J et al *Resilience to adult psychopathology following childhood maltreatment: evidence from a community sample* (2007) Child Abuse & Neglect 31(3) 211–229.

6.82 Another important cause of vulnerability is the presence of a personality disorder. A personality disorder is defined as 'an enduring pattern of inner experience and behaviour that deviates markedly from the expectations of the culture of the individual who exhibits it'. It is usually present from late adolescence. It is not, therefore, something that is caused by a traumatic event but the presence of a personality disorder may either complicate or worsen the outcome of a psychological reaction to such an event or be mistaken for a psychological reaction.

6 Psychiatric treatments

6.83 Most psychiatric disorders of relevance in a medico-legal setting are treated with either medication (anti-depressants, mood stabilizers, anti-psychotic or hypnotic medication) or various forms of cognitive behavioural psychotherapy (CBT). Treatment with medication is best supervised by a consultant psychiatrist but can be prescribed by a general practitioner.

6.84 Medication can be administered by mouth or in some cases (some anti-psychotic medication) by long acting (depot) injections. If possible it is better for individuals to only take one medication but in some cases people are prescribed combinations of medication.

6.85 CBT is best administered by a clinical psychologist. CBT for PTSD is often referred to as 'trauma focused PTSD'. Eye movement desensitisation and re-processing is a particular type of CBT in which the subject follows with their eyes a moving object at a particular frequency, at the same time as on focusing on recalling memories of a traumatic event. It is a recommended treatment for PTSD and found in the National Institute of Clinical Excellence guidelines.

6.86 Other therapists, such as counsellors, may deliver CBT, but clinical psychologists, cognitive behavioural psychotherapists or trained psychiatrists are to be preferred. There are other forms of psychotherapy, such as analytical or psychodynamic, mindfulness, cognitive analytical therapy, etc which may have specific indications. Treatments that are recommended in the NICE guidelines are to be preferred to treatments that are not.

6.87 CBT is usually delivered in weekly treatments (which may be spaced out as the treatment progresses). It usually is delivered in a course of 12–20 treatments. There is a principle of diminishing returns with psychotherapy such that beyond a certain point one would not expect much in the way of improvement. Some patients find such sessions supportive but it would be hard to sustain an argument for long-term supportive psychotherapy.

6.88 CBT is usually administered on a one-to-one basis, although it can sometimes be delivered in a group setting on a particular theme, for example anger or anxiety management. There is also some evidence to suggest that online therapy can have some efficacy. There are particular reasons to see some patients with either their partner (couple therapy) or family (family therapy).

6.89 CBT is often difficult to obtain on the NHS, although a recent Department of Health Programme, Improving Access to Psychological Therapies (IAPT), has improved this. However, it is not uncommon for those involved in litigation to be refused access to treatment from the NHS, either because it is known they could fund therapy privately from the litigation or alternatively because it is considered that the process of litigation will interfere with the therapeutic process.

6.90 The majority of treatment for psychiatric disorders is given on an out-patient basis. There are occasionally reasons for in-patient care (for example co-morbid alcohol or substance misuse which cannot be managed as an out-patient) but this is rare.

6.91 The National Institute of Clinical Excellence[1] undertakes research into what is cost effective treatment and usually represents the 'gold standard' for what constitutes appropriate treatment.

1   www.nice.org.uk.

7   Children

6.92 Psychiatric disorders in children and young people can be divided into similar disorders to those found in adult life and those specific to children. The presentation of typical adult mental disorders (eg depression, anxiety, psychotic illness) is uncommon before adolescence. Children may express symptoms differently, ie in play and drawings rather than in verbalised expressions of distress.

6.93 Childhood sexual abuse is common. Studies in the US have shown that approximately 15%–25% of women and 5%–15% of men were sexually abused when they were children. The prevalence varies depending on the definition of abuse used. Such abuse can cause both emotional distress at the time as well as predispose to developing a variety of psychiatric disorders in adult life.

6.94 Autistic disorder and associated autistic spectrum disorder is recognised in children and adolescence and there is an overlap with mental disability.

6.95 Traumatic events in childhood may interfere with normal emotional and educational development as well as cause specific psychiatric disorders.

6.96 Attention deficit and hyperactivity disorder (ADHD) is a relatively recently recognised disorder which is most often detected in childhood but then goes on into adult life. It is associated with conduct disorder and educational under-achievement. It is estimated that 2% of children aged 5–16 have hyperkinetic disorder.

6.97 Some psychiatrists and psychologists specialise in children and adolescents and therefore in a medico-legal setting it is important to use an appropriate expert.

122 *The illness*

There is some discretion where the subject is aged around 17–18, where an adult expert may feel qualified to report.

8 Psychiatric experts

6.98 Mental health can be a difficult field to navigate. It is important to understand the various professionals involved so that one can make a judgment on both expert and professional evidence.

A Psychiatrists and psychologists

6.99 Psychiatrists are registered medical practitioners (ie medical doctors) who specialise in psychiatry (as opposed to general medicine surgery, general practice etc). Psychiatrists follow the usual route of training to reach the consultant grade. The training grades used to be Senior House Officer (3–4 years) and then Senior Registrar (3–4 years). These have been replaced by either Core Trainee (CT) or Specialist Trainee (ST) 1–6. An ST 6 is a trainee in their 6th grade. Once training is completed, doctors apply for and are appointed to consultant posts. There is a parallel clinical academic route and a lecturer is equivalent to a senior registrar and a senior lecturer a consultant (as is a Professor). To become consultants, psychiatrists need to pass examinations to become a member of the Royal College of Psychiatrists (MRCPsych). More senior consultants can be elected a Fellow (FRCPsych). There are non-training grade doctors (Staff Grades, Associate Specialists or Specialist doctors), who may or may not have their MRCPsych qualification. Doctors may study for various academic degrees including PhD, MD and DPhil. If a consultant has retired they may have an honorary title (emeritus consultant). If not in a substantive post they are locums. For an expert report, it is appropriate to use a consultant psychiatrist rather than a training grade or staff grade/specialist doctor. When reviewing the medical records, it is important to consider the grade of the doctor when weighing up the significance of different entries. To use the Mental Health Act 1983, psychiatrists have to be approved clinicians and hold s 12(2) approval. There are a variety of sub-specialists, including:

— child and adolescent;
— general adult;
— forensic;
— addictions;
— learning disabilities;
— liaison;
— rehabilitation and social psychiatry; and
— old-age psychiatry.

Liaison psychiatrists work in acute hospitals and deal with both emergencies presenting to Accident and Emergency departments and mental disorders in patients with physical problems. They are experienced in somatoform and chronic pain. Neuropsychiatry is not a subspecialty recognised by the Royal College, although some general adult psychiatrists specialise in it. The Diploma in Psychological Medicine (DPM) is an old-fashioned qualification, which indicates a psychiatrist who has had a free bus pass for many years.

6.100 Psychologists have completed an undergraduate psychology degree and then undertaken further training to be a chartered psychologist in one of nine areas:

— clinical;
— occupational;
— counselling;
— educational;
— forensic;
— health;
— sports and exercise;
— teaching; and
— neuropsychological.

Many complete a doctorate, so have the title Dr but are not medically qualified, which can add to the confusion. Others are plain Mr (as, of course, are medically qualified consultant surgeons). There are occasionally issues if one side instructs a psychologist and the other a psychiatrist. Psychiatrists have greater expertise in prescribing and understanding physical illness or injury. Psychologists usually have greater experience in psychotherapy and cognitive behavioural psychotherapy in particular. In practice it is possible in many cases to instruct either a psychologist or psychiatrist, although there are some who consider that greater weight is ultimately given to psychiatric opinion. Psychologists also may undertake cognitive testing (usually neuropsychologists) and often use various psychometric tests to assist in their assessments. For most purposes a clinical psychologist would be the appropriately qualified expert to instruct, unless there is a specific educational, forensic, neuropsychological or occupational issue.

6.101 In addition to psychologists, other mental health practitioners include:

— psychotherapists;
— medical psychotherapists;
— counsellors;
— cognitive behavioural psychotherapists;
— EMDR therapists.

Psychotherapists train in a variety of modalities of psychotherapy (for example Freudian, Jungian etc). Medical psychotherapists are psychiatrists who specialise in psychotherapy. Counsellors usually have a counselling diploma and training in a specific model of psychotherapy. Cognitive behavioural psychotherapists come from a variety of backgrounds but have done specific training in CBT and an EMDR therapist a specific training in EMDR. Consultant psychiatrists also can undertake CBT and other forms of psychotherapy.

B Psychometric tests

6.102 There are a large number of psychometric tests which can be administered. They can be designed for a variety of purposes, including diagnosis, intensity of symptoms, personality traits, cognitive abilities, and exaggeration of symptoms. Some tests are only valid if the person administering it has had appropriate training (for example the Minnesota Multiphasic Personality Inventory (MMPI)). Many are subject to copyright and require royalties. Very few have been designed or validated in a forensic setting. Results of such tests are usually more useful if they have been used in a clinical setting prior to the commencement of litigation. In a medico-legal context, claimants wishing to exaggerate would have no problem in knowing which response to pick. There are no simple tests to reliably detect exaggeration or lying.

6.103 Neuropsychologists use a complex battery of tests to measure various aspects of cognitive functioning. Unfortunately many are confounded by the presence of depression and anxiety as well as lack of effort. Given that depression and anxiety are common co-morbid conditions found in head injury cases, it can be very difficult to tease out the relative contributions of an organic brain injury and an anxiety or depressive disorder.

C Understanding medical notes and reports

6.104 It is useful to understand reports from non-mental health experts so as to know when it is useful to commission a report and whom to ask. 'Organic' usually means caused by physical factors (such as an *organic* brain injury). In contrast 'functional' means caused by psychological factors. There are other terms used such as 'supratentorial' (which also indicates not caused by physical factors). The tentorium is a membrane of the brain. 'Idiopathic' or 'atypical' are also terms which can indicate that the author does not consider that a clear physical cause will be found. 'Non-anatomical sensory loss' implies that the pattern of sensory loss does not correspond with the known innervation pattern of the body.

6.105 General practice records are always important to review in psychiatric cases, because the presence of previous episodes of mental health problems is important in determining vulnerability. It is also relevant if there is evidence of psychiatric disorder at the time of the material event. The number of consultations may indicate evidence of, for example, somatisation disorder. Data from the NHS information centre indicated that the overall crude consultation rate rose from 3.9 consultations per patient-year in 1995 to 5.3 consultations per patient-year in 2006.

6.106 Consultation rates varied markedly by age and sex; in 2006, the highest overall consultation rates occurred in the age band 85–89 years for both sexes (males 12.9 consultations per person-year, females 12.6 consultations per person-year). Consultation rates for females tended to be higher than those for males in general although the consultation rates for the extremes of age (ie the very young and the very elderly) were quite similar for males and females.

6.107 Almost all GP notes are computerised. This makes them more legible but in some ways more difficult to navigate. Some separate out different problems by date and others separate by medication and investigations. In some systems letters from hospital consultants are summarised and included in the GP record. It is important to make sure that such a summary is accurate as it is possible for the summary to miss out important issues of relevance to the case. Handwritten records (on Lloyd George Cards) are often difficult to read but can contain more revealing comments about the claimant.

6.108 Counselling records can be problematic in a medico-legal setting. In the first instance many counsellors either appear not to keep records, or are very reluctant to release them. If they are made available they often include psychological speculation and interpretations which need to be treated with some reservation.

6.109 A psychiatric report is usually divided into standard sections (family history, personal history, psychiatric history, pre-morbid personality, mental state examination and opinion). As in all reports, it is helpful to separate out evidence, sources of such evidence and the opinion. Some experts produce very lengthy reports which appear to have been dictated virtually as a transcript of the interview, which is often not helpful. The mental state examination traditionally includes a brief description of the dress and appearance of the claimant. There are useful comments about behaviour during the interview. Then there should be reference to the mood. This is divided into objective (what the person's mood seemed to be from the psychiatrist's perspective) and subjective (how the claimant described their mood). This can be supported by, for example, whether they cried (and at what point of the interview). 'Responsive' means that although for example depressed they were able to smile at times. There are comments about the form and content of thought. There can be mention of abnormal perceptions (eg hallucinations) or abnormal ideas (eg delusions). A delusion is a fixed false unshakeable belief. An 'over valued idea' is a partial delusion. There may also be reference to orientation (ie does the person know where they are, who they are and what time it is). Finally there may be mention of insight (ie what does the claimant think is the problem). In cases of, for example, PTSD, it can be very useful to know if the claimant demonstrated objective anxiety when describing the traumatic event. It is not uncommon, for example, for a claimant to give a history of sweating, palpitations and great anxiety when thinking about the index trauma and yet appear completely calm when being interviewed by the expert.

D Miscellaneous difficulties with obtaining a psychiatric report

6.110 Psychiatrists arguably obtain more detailed and potentially sensitive information about a claimant than any other expert. This can include issues which are of potential relevance to a psychiatric disorder developing as result of the issue of relevance to the litigation, such as childhood sexual abuse. The claimant may be reluctant to disclose such information and if they do, ask for it to be removed from the report. It is clearly up to the discretion of the expert, but uncomfortable as it might be, if it is of potential relevance, it should be mentioned.

6.111 Some claimants are suspicious and can be paranoid. Some may ask to record or tape the interview. Others may tape or record the interview without asking permission. Claimants often ask for a friend or family member to accompany them into the interview room. The presence and identity of such a person should be mentioned in the report. The expert should ensure that the presence of such a person does not interfere with the interview. Some experts refuse to allow the presence of a third party at all. Most experts would not allow the presence of the claimant's lawyer in the interview.

6.112 It is always preferable to instruct an expert who is able to converse in the claimant's first language. If this is not possible, care must be taken with interpreters, as it can sometimes be difficult to distinguish how much a response is accurate. It is not ideal to have a family member or close friend to interpret because of the potentially sensitive nature of the material discussed. In some cases the claimant might underplay symptoms of say suicidality in the presence of a member of their family.

6.113 Some individuals involved in litigation can be threatening and intimidate experts. There have been cases of experts being referred to their governing body, for example the GMC by disgruntled claimants.

6.114 There can be difficulties when psychiatrists or psychologists find themselves opposing an expert from another field, for example an anaesthetist dealing with chronic pain or a rheumatologist in a chronic fatigue case. This normally occurs with disorders in which there is a dispute as to how much of the causation of the disorder is related to psychological factors and how much to (often unknown) physical processes.

7 Compensation

1 Background

7.1 In order to recover compensation for psychiatric injury the claimant must establish that he has suffered both a recognised psychiatric illness and that he falls within one of the groups of people entitled to claim. Once that is established, the 'usual' rules concerning quantifying the case follow.

7.2 As usual, the burden of proof is upon the claimant. The claim must be supported evidentially, and so far as the nature and extent of the psychiatric injury is concerned this will be with expert medical evidence. Certainly a psychiatric report will be required and possibly a report from a neuropsychologist (especially if there is a need to either establish or rule out cognitive brain injury where there has been an injury to the head).

7.3 The issue of psychiatric damage, more so than in many areas of personal injury litigation, is dependant upon the credibility of the claimant, the acceptance by the court of what the claimant says, and the evaluation of that by the respective experts instructed, in order to make an award of compensation:

> 'a consequence of the fact that diagnosis in a psychiatric case depends upon assessment of what is reported by the patient is the necessity for the psychiatrist confronted by a patient to consider whether or not to accept at face value what the patient reports. Inevitably there is a disposition on the part of the psychiatrist to take as genuine what the patient reports, because otherwise it is difficult to consider the issue of diagnosis'[1].

1   His Honour Judge Seymour QC in *Turner, Turner & Jordan v IB* [2010] EWHC 1508 (QB).

7.4 The development of the law concerning who can claim and who cannot is discussed out in other chapters. Briefly, those entitled to recover are expounded in the case of *Alcock v Chief Constable of South Yorkshire Police*[1] where Lord Oliver set out two 'types' of victims: those who are actually involved in the accident (the primary victim) and those who witness the event (the secondary victim).

1   [1992] 1 AC 310.

7.5 The primary victims are eligible for compensation because they have been directly affected by the events that led to the injury. They may have been physically injured and develop a psychiatric injury as an adjunct to the physical injury at a later date or they may develop (in the absence of any actual physical injury) psychiatric illness following the accident, but because they were 'part' of the accident they are always entitled (provided they can satisfy the other qualifying hurdles) to claim.

7.6 The secondary victim is a person who is eligible for compensation because, although they have not been directly affected, they are 'secondary victims' to the incident/accident/or events that led to the injury. The secondary victim can recover compensation provided they can fit the necessary criteria to satisfy the court that they are eligible (see Chapter 4 for more detail).

7.7 There have been difficulties in establishing what sort of 'psychiatric conditions' fall to be compensated. What constitutes psychiatric illness? Can the less 'robust' person be compensated for emotionally 'falling apart' where somebody else would just carry on? And what about the client who presents with an unusual set of odd and weird symptoms that do not fit into any 'organic' description of injury? Can the person who has taken to a wheelchair, who will not or says they cannot walk, recover compensation in the absence of any medical evidence that there is any physical damage to account for the ongoing symptoms?

7.8 Prior to *Page v Smith*[1], where a minor car crash caused the flare up of the claimant's ME, a primary victim suffering psychiatric damage had to show that it was reasonably foreseeable that they would suffer psychiatric harm as a result of the incident. *Page* went to the House of Lords, who ultimately said that provided it was established that there was a duty of care to the claimant and that duty was breached, it did not matter whether the injury suffered was physical, or psychiatric, or a mixture of both. Even if psychiatric injury was not foreseen provided that physical injury was, then the claimant could recover damages. *Page v Smith* was decided in 1996 and still holds good. It opened up the category of claimant who can recover for psychiatric injury sufficiently to include those who claim for what can be seen as the psychiatric consequences of even very minor damage.

1   [1996] AC 155.

7.9 Working from the principle that judges have a substantial degree of humanity in their approach to their decision-making, it is not difficult to see that that a claimant who suffers a significant psychiatric reaction to a horrific event is 'worthy of compensation'. It is more difficult to see that the claimant who becomes bedbound, with a psycho-somatoform disorder as a result of a minor whiplash injury should recover substantial compensation, especially if there is factual evidence to show that they were a 'strange' type of person before the accident and there is psychiatric expert evidence saying that they may have developed problems of a psychiatric nature in later life in any event. If a debilitating condition 'may' have occurred at a later date, can they claim?

7.10 As the law currently stands, the claimant is entitled to claim but such cases require greater consideration and preparation by virtue of their complexity, and it is not enough to state that 'this happened because of the accident, therefore I am entitled to be compensated'. In order to achieve the hurdle of fitting into the category of a person who can be compensated, there has to be a 'recognised psychiatric illness' and there has been some struggle over the years to define what that means. The development of a codification of psychiatric illness by both the English and American psychiatric Establishments provides a framework to 'fit' an illness to and therefore justify it as recognisable. The two current manuals are ICD 10 *Classification of*

Mental and Behavioural Disorders; Clinical Description and Diagnostic Guidelines 1992 published by the World Health Organisation (known for short as ICD10 and referred to as such in most psychiatric reports) and the *Diagnostic and Statistical Manual of Mental Disorders 1994* (DSM-IV), published by the American Psychiatric Association.

7.11 Whilst both manuals caution against an over-reliance or exhaustive attempt to get the illness to fit the description (rather like Gilbert and Sullivan asking for the punishment to fit the crime), whatever is felt about the ease with which mental classifications can fit into 'brackets', the fact is that without a label that is recognisable, a claimant is likely to have an uphill struggle to achieve compensation without a psychiatric condition that will fit within one, or more, of the diagnostic descriptions. The inclusion of an illness within the diagnostic criterion will not, in its own right, merit an award of compensation (for example pathological grief, whilst being a recognised clinical diagnosis in day-to-day psychiatry, is not found as a separate entitled condition within the ICD 10 or DSM-IV, yet it is clear from the case law that such will fall to be compensated). However, that the Law Commission in its Consultation Paper No 137 following Hillsborough recognised pathological grief reaction certainly helped. Often, in order to fit the diagnostic descriptions, the claimant practitioner will scrabble around to get the instructed psychiatrist to find other diagnoses that will. However desirable it is to 'fit within the brackets' it is not entirely necessary, but a caution should be given to practitioners who rely on reported cases that were not heard before the courts but merely the product of a negotiated settlement: minor anxieties or simple 'psychological injury' without more may well not stand up as a compensatable head if the case were actually tried by a judge.

7.12 The manuals themselves are fascinating reading and the categories of illness described are certainly worth reviewing. Any lawyer preparing a case for—or against—a claimant with a major claim arising out of a predominately psychiatric illness ought to give the manual at least one read through especially if they are not familiar with the diverse types of mental illness and sometimes difficult (and odd) presentation of clients and their symptoms. This can be particularly important when choosing which specialist to instruct to advise in the claim.

2   General damages: pain, suffering and loss of amenity (PSLA)

7.13 If there is a difficulty in establishing how damaged a client is when dealing with a psychiatric injury it is in the very fact of attempting to assess what you cannot see, save in a subjective way ('I think he is depressed because he looks depressed', or perhaps 'he ought to get better—he just will not'). The remainder is based on what the client and those around him report and what is observed (sometimes over an extended period of time). It is not so long ago that declaring a prior bout of psychiatric illness almost certainly guaranteed the loss of a job offer at interview, and the stigma of psychiatric problems—whilst having reduced over the years—certainly still prevails. Insurers are generally much more wary of claimants with 'prior history' of such psychological problems, quirks, oddities and generally 'out of the ordinary' behaviour. In addition, there are cultural issues to be taken into account: sexual abuse, whilst abhorrent in any culture, may well carry more taboos in one than another whilst there is little more abhorrent (and emotive) to our society than sexual abuse of minors or vulnerable adults. In the development of the decisions over how much such victims should be awarded, there are moral overtones of how to categorise severity, with abuse by those in positions of trust or close familial relationships attracting higher awards. Such criteria appear to be absent from psychiatric injury arising out of, say, a particularly dreadful road traffic accident where a claimant may be rendered tetraplegic and paralysed: utterly irreversible life changing injuries. It is the victim's response to the injury that determines the level of general damages rather than their age or status.

7.14 Actually working out what 'something is worth' can be problematic, especially when there is an unusual presentation of symptoms, or a client is reluctant to talk about their difficulties. Rather like chronic pain (which interestingly is put within the chapter on psychiatric injury within the Judicial Studies Board Guidelines for the Assessment of General Damages in Personal Injury Cases (JSB guidelines)), assessing the nature and extent of a psychological response to an incident is skilled work. But even with the most well-prepared case and the most supportive psychiatric and witness evidence, as with physical injury, there are finite amounts that will be awarded, however devastating the damage.

7.15 The main reference books and resource material for quantification of damages contain substantial references to awards for psychiatric injury (even if most are 'by agreement' rather than by order of a judge). Historically it was difficult to divide the quantum for such from the physical but judges now tend to separate awards from the global, setting out what they award for each type of injury, amalgamating the award and then discounting the same for overlap.

7.16 Over the years JSB guidelines have set out—and expanded—the section on the level of awards for psychiatric injury. Published by the Oxford University Press and available both in hard copy and online, it is an essential tool for assessing the baseline value of a claim both at the onset of the case (where information from the book can be given to the client both as information and a tool for managing expectation) and of course when a more formal valuation of the claim is made once medical and other evidence is available. Final assessment of the value of a claim should not be done on the JSB guidelines alone, but in conjunction with a research of case law, but the JSB has now become an essential, along with 'Facts and Figures'[1] when assessing the quantum of a claim.

1   *Facts and figures 2010/11: tables for the calculation of damages* (Sweet & Maxwell).

7.17 The JSB guidelines are a distillation of what levels of compensation have been awarded by judges (and decided by agreement, where such agreement is published) up and down the country within the recent past. In the introduction Mr Justice Mackay makes it quite clear that the guidelines take account of what judges do, and then reflect that within the book (rather then the other way around):

> 'We do not attempt to prescribe what levels of damages ought to be awarded, but instead set out what we consider to the be the current level of awards and settlements adjusted

where necessary for inflation. A judge wrote to the JSB in the last year to say that he disagreed with one of our suggested brackets. The answer to that is that he should therefore ignore it/exercise his judgment and say what the figure ought to be. We would then hope to catch and reflect that award in the next edition'.

7.18 The JSB guidelines are the starting point for advising clients on the likely value of their claim. Both in the early stages of a case when asked about possible values, and after gathering evidence and being relatively certain of the prognosis, they are invaluable. The chapter on the value of psychiatric damage is divided into three sections:

A   psychiatric damage generally;
B   post-traumatic street disorder; and
C   chronic pain, which is a bit of a rag bag of conditions.

7.19 Sections A and B are sub-divided, for the purpose of valuation, into severe, moderately severe, moderate and minor; section C into chronic pain syndrome (severe and moderate), fibromyalgia, chronic fatigue syndrome, reflex sympathetic dystrophy (or complex regional pain syndrome), severe and moderate and, lastly, somatoform disorder. The inclusion and format of section C and the quantification of these conditions as 'psychiatric injury' is interesting in itself and in the preamble to the section the justification given for the inclusion of this group in the section is stated to be:

'while the conditions ... do not necessarily arise out of psychiatric injury, they are dealt with here partly because they almost always include an element of psychological damage and partly for the convenience of users of the Guidelines because symptoms caused by these conditions can affect a variety of areas of an injured person's anatomy'.

7.20 Sexual assaults do not have their own bracket, but are dealt within the main brackets, reference to the same being made in the pre-amble to the chapter:

'where cases arise out of sexual and/or physical abuse in breach of parental, family or other trust, involving victims who are young and/or vulnerable, awards will tend to be at the upper end of the relevant bracket to take into account'.

The reason for this may be because (aside from claims for institutionalised abuse) such cases tend to fall within the remit of the CICA tariff (see below).

A   General psychiatric damage

7.21 There are four brackets for general psychiatric damage: severe, moderately severe, moderate and minor. It is envisaged that any award within section A of this bracket includes an element of post-traumatic stress disorder and that if there is such an element then the awarded figures should be towards the upper end of the bracket. The guidelines set out factors to be taken into account when valuing the claim. These include the claimant's ongoing capacity to deal with life and work; the effect of the injury on their relationship with their family and those they come into contact with; the extent to which treatment would be effective; their future vulnerability; their prognosis for the future and whether medical help has been sought; whether the injury results from sexual and/or physical abuse, and/or breach of trust and if so the nature of the relationship between victim and abuser, the nature of the abuse, its duration and the symptoms caused by it. The brackets are artificial: there will be a variation between one psychiatrist's view and another, and often awards are made 'between the brackets', eg moderate to severe. Psychological injury caused by stress in the workplace will generally fall within the bracket of general psychiatric injury.

Severe: £36,000–£76,000

7.22 The guidelines specify that in cases that merit an award of this amount there will be 'marked problems' associated with the claimant's ability to cope with day-to-day life and working, with their relationships with family and others and that the prognosis for recovery is very poor. To obtain an award within this bracket the claimant must have suffered, and continue to suffer, very life changing effects.

7.23 *Reed v Sunderland Health Authority*[1] was a clinical negligence claim which involved the failure to diagnose a twisted and herniated small intestine (an excruciatingly painful condition) in a girl just short of her 18th birthday. She spent three days in hospital in terrible pain, without seeing a consultant and with the nursing staff not believing her symptoms. She was discharged without treatment and readmitted three days later, when she underwent surgery during which a substantial piece of necrotic (dead) intestine was removed. From being an outgoing and sociable teenager she turned into a withdrawn depressive unable to control her temper. She also made two suicide attempts. She had continuing bowel symptoms but the predominant ongoing problems were the continuing psychological problems; a mixed affective disorder, depression and mood swings. These stopped her taking her 'A' levels, going on to University and—essentially—caused her to lose her ability to take up a career. Her condition must have been very damaged because it was found that she would be unlikely to take up gainful employment. At first instance, she was awarded PSLA of £35,000[2], although this was reduced to £27,500 (updated to £41,018.48) on appeal by the defendants to the Court of Appeal.

1 [1998] All ER (D) 447.
2 Updated today to £51,611.29.

7.24 Most of the cases in this bracket that have been reported involve sexual assault, where the PSLA award is generally 'only' for psychiatric damage (ie there is no actual physical harm to take into the equation).

7.25 *BJM v Eyre*[1] involved a 12-year-old boy (born 1989) who suffered sexual and physical abuse. He was 12 years old when the abuse started; he was 'managed' by the three defendants and essentially he was 'sold' to the second defendant for the sexual gratification of the second defendant's male adult clients. Prior to this he was deliberately exposed—for the purpose of grooming him—to activities of a sexual nature. He was described as having been used as chattel to be bought sold and used sexually for financial gain.

The Swift J said:

> 'the JSB guidelines provide only limited assistance in cases of sexual abuse. In assessing damages for pain, suffering and loss of amenity in such cases, it is also necessary to take into account, not only the very significant psychiatric effect of the abuse on the claimant, but also the immediate effects of the abuse at the time it was perpetrated'.

She found that the defendants' conduct warranted an award for aggravated damages in the sum of £20,000 plus PSLA of £70,000.

1   [2010] EWHC 2856 (QB).

Moderately severe: £12,500–£36,000

7.26 The guidelines specify that in cases that merit an award of this amount there will be significant factors associated with the claimant's ability to cope with day-to-day life and working, that there will be a serious effect on the claimant's relationships with family and others and that if treatment is successful there will be a future vulnerability but that the prognosis is more optimistic than for the 'severe' bracket. Cases where there is likely to be a future vulnerability fit into this bracket.

7.27 *Jones v Royal Devon and Exeter NHS Foundation Trust*[1]: A mother was entitled to recover general damages of £20,000 in respect of her prolonged pathological grief reaction to the death of her daughter which was occasioned through the negligence of the defendant NHS Trust.

There was, as there often is, conflicting evidence from the opposing psychiatric experts about the nature and extent of damage and in the course of his judgment the King J said:

> 'I leave aside for the moment the diagnostic label to put on this symptomotology but I have no doubt that the independent evidence of the lay witnesses is that the claimant did become a changed person in the way described and one particular operating feature was the traumatic effect upon her of the effects of the labour, the loss (including that ... as the particularly harrowing effect of the decision to turn off the life support machine) and the inquest, and her perception that she was being held to blame and the engendered feeling of guilt'.

> 'I find the psychiatric injury in all the circumstances of my findings does fall into the moderately severe category bracket described at A(b) of the current Guidelines'.

He assessed general damages at £20,000 (updated to £22,178.22).

1   [2008] EWHC 558, [2008] 101 BMLR 154.

Moderate: £3,875–£12,500

7.28 To fit within this bracket, the guidelines specify that whilst there will have been problems similar to those required to merit an award under the above brackets in the first years after the incident that caused the problems, by the time the claimant comes to settlement or trial, they will be markedly improved with a good prognosis for full or almost full recovery.

7.29 In *Kirk v Plotzer*[1] the claimant suffered a whiplash injury when his vehicle was hit by another and spun into a lamp-post. He took a few weeks off work and had some ongoing physical symptoms from his injury, but the most serious problem was psychological. He talked excessively about the accident, he became a nervous passenger and driver and drove only a few times after the accident. He became so concerned about what could have happened to his girlfriend that their relationship broke down. He suffered nightmares and became isolated and depressed and nervous in crowded places. He left his job within the year and moved out of the family home because of arguments with his father about his condition. The medical experts felt that he would recover, with appropriate treatment, 6–12 months after the trial.

This case is, like so many others, interesting in that there is a 'prediction' about when a claimant, whose life is significantly affected by what has happened to them, will recover with treatment. The psychological injury was found by the judge to fall within the moderate to severe bracket 3(A)(b) and awarded (at 2008 rates) the sum of £13,000. An award of £5,000 was made for the whiplash and the total award was discounted for overlap.

1 (3 March 2008, unreported), Hull County Court.

7.30 *F (a child) v Virgin Holidays*[1]: a girl aged 11 at age of injury and 13 at date of trial was awarded £9,000 (updated to £9,428.95) as a result of developing an anxiety and a phobic reaction to lifts as a result of being trapped in a lift. She was trapped in the lift with her parents, and had to wait for 20 minutes before somebody heard their calls for help, during which time she became tearful, upset and vomited in reaction to her anxiety. This was an approved case, and the experience she suffered had not stopped her enjoyment of her subsequent holiday. She had had some cognitive behaviour treatment (CBT) without much effect. She continued to be reluctant to use lifts but it was felt that her symptoms would resolve without further treatment and that she would make a full recovery by age 20.

1 (20 August 2010, unreported), Leeds County Court.

Minor: £1,000–£3,875

7.31 This bracket deals with transitory psychiatric injuries, typically periods of psychological problems that have resolved within months of the incident itself. Indicators for an award within this bracket are the length of time of the period of disability, and the extent to which daily activities were affected. There is specific reference to whether or not sleep was affected during the time of disability.

7.32 The guidelines state that awards have been made below this bracket in cases of temporary 'anxiety'. Typically, within reported cases there is often mention of 'travel anxiety', which is normally associated with minor physical damage such as a mild whiplash injury as falling below the minor bracket.

7.33 *R (a child) v Hibbert*[1]: a 3-year-old child suffered trauma to his forehead and abdomen and shock and distress when he was restrained in a child seat in the front of a vehicle hit by another. He suffered insomnia, and an acute anxiety separation disorder which became chronic; he was excessively fearful or reluctant to be without his father. He had 12 sessions of CBT which resulted in improvement and 28 months after the accident his psychological problems had resolved. It was found that his psychological injury fell within JSB 3(A)(d) minor psychiatric damages and he was awarded £3,750 (updated £3,944.54).

1 (28 July 2010, unreported), Cambridge County Court.

7.34 In *Cook v Sherwood*[1] the claimant suffered psychological upset after a road traffic accident: she had marked anxiety, apprehensiveness as a passenger, episodes of sweating and palpitations and her normal sleep pattern was disturbed for around six months. Her prognosis for psychological recovery within 15–18 months of settlement was said to be good. Her physical injuries were bruising to her shoulder and upper right pectoral area for about a month and muscular discomfort which settled within two months of the accident. She was awarded £2,500 (updated to £3,052.96) for all her injuries.

1 [2006] CLY 3086.

B Post-traumatic stress disorder

7.35 Again, there are four brackets in this category: severe, moderately severe, moderate and minor. To fall within this section a claimant must have a 'specific diagnosis' of PTSD. The guidelines were compiled by reference to cases which variously reflect the criteria established in the DSM-IV-TR. To fit within this bracket a claimant must have a psychiatric report which supports the diagnosis.

Severe: £40,000–£66,000

7.36 To fit within this bracket the injury must have—in part at least—permanent effects. A claimant with a severe PTSD will be unable to work by virtue of the ongoing psychological trauma.

7.37 In *Re TP*[1] the board made an award of £65,000 in damages, to include loss of congenial employment to a female teacher following a rape. She was 26 years old when raped but the matter was not heard until she was 53; this was a further award made after re-application. A particularly terrible rape left her unable to sustain a relationship and as a result of her emotional trauma she lost her opportunity to have children. She was unable to travel by public transport, was fearful of strangers and society and remained withdrawn and isolated. She managed to work as a teacher for 17 years with increasing difficulties, eventually retraining as a data processing clerk so that she could work from home. She was diagnosed as suffering severe PTSD and having an enduring personality change after a catastrophic experience.

1 (2008, unreported), CICB, London.

Moderately severe: £15,250–£40,000

7.38 In *Bucanan v Broadleigh Developments Ltd*[1] a 24-year-old woman suffered a puncture wound to her breast 5mm long when she slipped and impaled herself on metal wiring. The wound itself was not serious but she suffered a moderate to severe clinical depression and moderately severe PTSD. It was found that she was unusually vulnerable psychologically. By trial she had made an almost full recovery and it was found that with professional help she would fully recover. She was awarded £17,500 (updated to £22,034.26) for the psychiatric component of the injury.

1 (8 July 2004, unreported), Sheffield County Court.

Moderate: £5,400–£15,250

7.39 *Moore v Ministry of Justice*[1] involved a 54-year-old male prison officer, who suffered moderate PTSD that was likely to become chronic and was awarded £17,000 (updated to £18,511.11) (the court found it was at the top of the JSB 3BC) following an assault at work. He suffered flashbacks, sleeplessness, sweating, nausea, loss of confidence and motivation. Treatment did not help, he tried to return to work without success, and was medically retired finding alternative work elsewhere.

1 (22 October 2009, unreported), Plymouth County Court.

Minor: £2,600–£5,400

7.40 In *Spencer v First West Yorkshire Ltd*[1] a 42-year-old male bus driver (43 at date of trial) who suffered a PTSD when he suffered a whiplash injury in a road traffic accident was awarded a PSLA of £6,000 split £3,000 for the neck injury and £3,000 (updated to £3715.64) for the psychological injury. He suffered distressing dreams of the accident for around eight months and flashbacks for around nine months. He had bouts of irritability and anger and difficulty in managing in his job. He was also depressed for months. Prognosis was of recovery from the PTSD within 21–24 months of the accident.

1 (9 December 2004, unreported), Leeds County Court.

C Problematic medical/psychological conditions

7.41 Section 3(C)(a)–(e) in the JSB guidelines deals with a collection of what are often regarded by practitioners as 'problematic medical/psychological conditions': chronic pain syndromes, fibromyalgia, chronic fatigue syndrome, reflex sympathetic dystrophy (sometimes known as complex regional pain syndrome) and the group of somatoform disorders.

7.42 The preamble to section C acknowledges that these conditions do not 'necessarily arise out of psychiatric injury'. The reason that they are placed within the psychiatric damage bracket is because they 'almost always include an element of psychological damage and partly for the convenience of users of the Guidelines, because the symptoms caused by these conditions can affect a variety of areas of an injured person's anatomy'. So mostly these conditions are within this section for convenience. The conditions in section C to some extent overlap with one that is certainly properly placed within the Chapter; that of somatoform disorder, where the bracket for an award for this condition is 'in the region of £30,000'.

7.43 Would a claimant who was wheelchair bound with such a condition merit an award comparable with that of a true spinal cord injured claimant? In such circumstances the guidelines are only the guidelines, and if the evidence is that the claimant with a somatoform disorder has such a poor prognosis that they are not going to ever walk again, then the judge must surely be constrained to deal with the case on the basis that the award should be comparable to that of an organic spinal cord injury.

7.44 The bracket of somatoform disorder is worth a little extra attention, in part because clients with this disorder can cause havoc in the solicitor's office. This is a complicated psychiatric condition where psychiatric illness manifests itself in physical symptoms sometimes in a very florid manner. For example, the claimant who has a minor injury who develops unexplained and often inconsistent physical problems that cannot be explained by medical tests.

7.45 Such claimants can present as very difficult to handle and often very resistant to accept that their condition is psychiatric in origin. ICD 10 lists somatoform disorders within the 'neurotic and stress-related' bracket:

> 'the main feature of somatoform disorders is repeated presentation of physical symptoms, together with persistent requests for medical investigations, in spite of repeated negative findings and reassurances by doctors that the symptoms have no physical basis. If any physical disorders are present, they do not explain the nature and extent of the symptoms or the distress and preoccupation of the patient. Even when the onset and continuation of the symptoms bear a close relationship with unpleasant life events or with difficulties or conflicts, the patient usually resists attempts to discuss the possibility of psychological causation; this may even be the case in the presence of obvious depressive and anxiety symptoms'.

7.46 In *Turner, Turner & Jordan v IB*[1] HHJ Seymour QC said:

> 'in essence a conversion disorder is a psychological condition in which a person genuinely experiences symptoms suggestive of a neurological or other general medical condition for which there is no physical cause'.

In that case there was a dispute over what had caused the significant conversion disorder complained off by the claimant. Was it the effects of a relatively minor car accident or the finding of and surgery upon a right inguinal hernia three days later? It was clear from the judgment that—at least by the time of the trial—the judge was unimpressed with the claimant's arguments. The claimant was acting in person, which may reflect the difficulty that solicitors have in dealing with such claimants.

1 [2010] EWHC 1508 (QB).

7.47 There is little doubt that the development of any, but in particular a serious, somatoform disorder can be life altering and extremely difficult to deal with, not only for the claimant but for all involved with them: both the treating doctors—such claimants often have had a battery of medical tests (often quite invasive ones too) and copious medical notes—who often have gone through exhaustive medical testing to finally come to the view that the claimant suffers from no or no substantive physical problem, and the solicitor who not only has to deal on a day-to-day basis with the claimant but also has to ensure that the way the case is presented is approved by their client. It is not unusual for such clients to come to the office in a wheelchair or on crutches complaining that they are unable to walk properly. The solicitor may then obtain a raft of apparently relevant (and expensive) medical opinions all of whom state that there is nothing physically wrong with the client and that a psychiatric opinion should be sought. Such clients are often highly-charged emotionally, and resistant to the idea that they have a psychological problem. The solicitor is then left to try to persuade the client to accept that he or she may be suffering from a psychological problem. Such clients are often distressed and behave in a difficult way with the solicitor and his or her staff. They may shout, cry and complain and it is not unusual for such clients to attempt to move from solicitor to solicitor for 'better' advice, which can present a significant problem to a solicitor who by this time will probably have invested a substantial amount of time and money in advising to date. Such clients, difficult as they may be, are mentally unwell. But there are differential diagnoses and with a client who can take up, literally, hours of a solicitor's time each and every week, a sympathetic and knowledgeable psychiatric opinion, properly instructed (with full records and witness statements) is required to get a supportive opinion.

7.48 More so than in any other area of personal injury litigation the medical evidence in the claim contains statements of whether or not these claimants are 'telling the truth'. Reports on such awards are littered with video evidence to try to discredit the claimant. Judgments are full of comments on 'whether or not the claimant has exaggerated the true extent of a genuine injury and its symptoms or, at worst, that his claim is essentially false'[1].

1   Sir Robert Nelson in *Darg v Commissioner of Police for the Metropolis* [2009] EWHC 684 (QB).

7.49 One of the issues in dealing with cases involving psychiatric problems is that of proving what the claimant states is 'true'. This need to 'test' the evidence of the principal character is the responsibility—mostly—of the expert(s) and in practice usually that of the psychiatrist. Generally, showing that a claimant is 'not telling the truth' is not as simple as, for example, the claimant who says that they cannot lift their arm as a result of a fracture who is shown on video to be lying or exaggerating their assertions. If that is so in straightforward cases of psychiatric injury, the matter becomes much more complicated in cases involving somatisation and its related condition. The diagnosis is often dependant upon the interweaving of other experts such as rheumatologists, pain experts and others related to the 'type' of problems that the claimant complains off. More so than any other type of claim for psychiatric injury, such claims must be carefully researched and prepared if they are to be properly supported and compensated. Such claims are amongst the most difficult, not only to understand, but also in terms of the presentation of the client and his or her demands.

3   CICA and the tariff scheme

7.50 A substantial body of the reported claims on psychiatric injury involve cases before the Criminal Injuries Compensation Authority (CICA).

This of course is now a 'tariff scheme'. Within the CICA the tariff distinguishes between medically recognised illnesses/conditions that are not mental illness and those that are 'mental illness and temporary mental anxiety'.

7.51 Mental illness includes conditions attributed to PTSD, depression and similar generic terms within which there may be:

(a) such psychological symptoms as anxiety, tension, insomnia, irritability, loss of confidence, agoraphobia and preoccupation with thoughts of guilt or self-harm; and
(b) related physical symptoms such as alopecia, asthma, eczema, enuresis and psoriasis.

7.52 'Medically verified' means that the mental anxiety has been diagnosed by a registered medical practitioner. 'Psychiatric diagnosis/prognosis' means that the disabling mental illness has been diagnosed or the prognosis made by a psychiatrist or clinical psychologist.

7.53 Mental anxiety or a mental illness is disabling if it significantly impairs a person's functioning in some important aspect of her/his life, eg impaired work or school performance or significant adverse effects on social relationships or sexual dysfunction.

7.54 There is no real scope for expanding the award; the tariff is the tariff here and the figures are set out below.

Disabling but temporary mental anxiety lasing more than 6 weeks, medically verified	1	1,000
Disabling mental illness, confirmed by psychiatric diagnosis:		
lasting up to 28 weeks	6	2,500
lasting over 28 weeks to 2 years	9	4,400
lasting 2 years to 5 years	12	8,200
lasting over 5 years but not permanent	14	13,500
Permanent mental illness, confirmed by psychiatric prognosis:		
moderately disabling	16	19,000
seriously disabling	18	27,000

4 Special damages

7.55 For the most part special damages follow the usual rules in respect of personal injury claims. For example, a claimant who is psychiatrically unwell, and who cannot work as a result of this will have a claim for loss of earnings in the traditional way, based on the usual principles and evidence in the usual way for personal injury claims. Consideration must be given to setting up a personal injury trust in the early stages of the claim to protect the claimant from claw-back of means tests benefits. Evidence should be kept to ensure that claims can be supported and so on. Practitioners have traditionally looked at these types of claims, in the absence of serious physical injury, as general damage alone claims apart from a small amount of cognitive counselling.

But this can be doing a disservice to the more seriously unwell psychiatrically injured client, especially where the client is reluctant to accept any intervention or help. It is possible to attempt to rehabilitate, or help and improve the quality of life for such clients with a case management and care package. The issues of Individual Needs Assessments (INAs) and other protocol issues are dealt with in the chapter on practical steps. But prior to spending substantial sums on such care and treatments before settlement, consideration should be given to the issues of whether or not the sums are potentially recoverable on a 100% basis and prior to putting the costs as a future loss whether or not they form part of a recognisable claim (for example such claims may well be unsuccessful as part of a claim to the CICA).

A Case managers/carers/buddies

7.56 The traditional view of the need to input case management, care and help is based on the claimant who is not capable of doing a task because of physical disability. It is not difficult to see why an amputee may need help with, for example, household decorating whereas it takes a little more thought to understand why a claimant who is depressed or paranoid or obsessive may need help around the home, or just some sort of companionship to stop their condition deteriorating and to improve the quality of their life. A depressed person living on their own may not bother to clean their house, or shop, or cook for themselves. Such a person may need somebody to help with these tasks whether on a short or long-term basis.

7.57 The need for case management, help and companionship is evidence-based and this requires the solicitor and the experts to actually take note of what is happening in the claimant's life. This in itself may be easy if the claimant has loving and considerate family who can tell the expert/solicitor what is happening in the claimant's life, but is more challenging if the claimant lives alone, or does not speak much English, or is hostile or too ill to communicate properly. Consideration should always be given to home visits to such clients. The client may say that they are doing well, when consideration of their home environment may lead to a surprising discovery of weeks of dishes in the kitchen sink, bed linen not changed for months and a pile of unopened post in the hallway. Sometimes the first that the solicitor hears of problems is by way of final demand notices (or worse) on the client for non-payment of bills. Some clients will not come to the office because they cannot (in particular the agoraphobic), some will not come because they cannot be bothered (the depressed) and some are too paranoid or obsessive to get out of the home. Some just need to be visited to see their home circumstances. In dealing with these issues the solicitor (and the experts involved) should properly assess the risk of visiting the client at home alone before doing so. Taking an assistant or trainee is normally advised.

7.58 It is vital that the instructed care expert is experienced and used to dealing with clients with psychological illness. Often care experts are occupational therapists; they may or may not have dealt with mentally-ill people and their CVs should be carefully perused before instructions and the providing agency asked to ensure that a suitably qualified person is instructed. Speaking with the care expert can provide the solicitor with a good idea about whether or not they are likely to be sympathetic and understanding with a difficult client. It is easier to do this before sending them in as money will have been spent by that time if the client refuses them as an expert. An expert has to make the recommendations for a carer and if the psychiatrist does not, either because they are not experienced or simply do not understand that a carer can be claimed for, then the care expert must pick this up. That leaves the case manager and/or the care expert.

7.59 Mentally ill clients are often poorly served by inexperienced experts who simply do not understand mental illness or who are not sympathetic to it. A care expert who understands psychological illness will recognise the need and recommend the input of an experienced case manager and carer/buddy for a number of hours a week to help the client help themselves, to encourage the client to socialise (perhaps by way of accompanying them shopping for example) or just to ensure that they are taken to the various appointments that they have. The need is of course case specific and can be quite life altering to the client.

7.60 The provision of care is usually reasonably urgent, and not catered for in the NHS/local authority sector, where such packages are usually skimpy and time-limited. The client is entitled to input such care with an interim payment and the benefit of doing this is that there is no greater way to show need than to spend money on it. The need can be assessed over a period of time and care input either increased or decreased as advised.

7.61 In an ideal world the case manager makes the treatment recommendation, the care is provided, and the care expert supports the package in their expert report. The package is already in place and (hopefully) working at the time of trial and a proper assessment of ongoing need made by the care expert and supported by the treating psychiatrist.

7.62 Such care packages are often very expensive. That is because specialist carers do not come cheap. The 'normal' care rates for home helps and carers[1] are often inappropriate. The rates are more akin to those required by the seriously head injured. The carer may need to have special skills in their own right and in these circumstances nurses with specialist mental health qualifications of staff with psychology degrees may well be appropriate, even though such care can be expensive and it is not unusual to have to pay £20 ph upwards. Normally such care will need to be accessed through an agency to ensure that the carers themselves get the necessary support, as working with the mentally ill can be very stressful.

1 *Facts and figures 2010/11: tables for the calculation of damages* (Sweet & Maxwell).

7.63 There is an additional difficulty in dealing with claimants who are psychologically unwell but who will by reason of this illness not accept help, or only accept help with 'strings attached'. Such individuals may, themselves, be quite abusive in their dealing with others and it can be difficult to persuade carers to work with them especially when the carer is expected to be with the client in the clients own home. There can be safety issues for the carer; there have been a string of high profile cases involving the violent mentally unwell and it takes a particular type of person to actually want to work with such a difficult client group. It is for this reason that an experienced and strong case manager is needed.

B Short term treatment interventions

Counselling and therapy

7.64 There are many types of therapies that can help clients who have psychological trauma. The standard ones are courses of cognitive or therapy with a behavioural approach and these will typically be recommended by the advising psychiatrist. Care should be taken to ensure that appropriate counselling for the illness is obtained.

7.65 Where there is a possibility of relapse, or the likely need for strategic intervention at periods of stress in the claimant's life, it is probable that there will be a recommendation for extra help/sessions at those times.

Outpatient facilities

7.66 This is a cheaper option and less likely to lead to institutionalisation or the possible development of overdependence of inpatient admission. Such facilities include the costs of day care, which is dependant upon the hours required, and counselling and associated costs. If the client has become dependant upon prescription (or non-prescription) drugs, which is a danger where there is a severe pain type syndrome, then a period of outpatient care may be necessary. Often clients who will not accept inpatient admission are happy to consent to either outpatient facilities or rehabilitation input within their own homes.

Inpatient psychological assessment and rehabilitation

7.67 Again these are proper heads of claim and should not be ignored. The client who is depressed or who has developed an obsessive type problem may need a period of admission to a private facility. It is very difficult to get effective treatment for such conditions within the NHS sector unless there are issues of self-harm or harm to others, and even where these issues are present the solicitor should not be shy of seeking treatment within the private sector.

7.68 Where there has been a development of a drug addiction as a result of medication or perhaps alcohol addiction then admission to a unit for substance withdrawal may be necessary. These admissions can be very expensive: a 12-week admission for dependency withdrawal can cost in excess of £50,000.

7.69 Where the client is aggressive, or requires a sectioning under the Mental Health Act, a more specialist unit may be required. There are limited places in the private sector for clients who have significant psychological symptoms. Most of these placements deal with the organically brain injured, however St Andrews Hospital in Northampton takes clients who are mentally unwell and has secure inpatient facilities (and the ability to keep a client under a Mental Health Act section, if necessary). Such placements are expensive. A private psychiatric inpatient facility for a non-violent client is likely to cost in excess of £3,000 per week at current rates depending where in the country the facility is. Such facilities are more expensive if the client is self-harming and suicidal or aggressive to others. But these costs are properly claimable if the need is supported by the psychiatric expert. Again, it is usual that, pre-discharge, the instructed case manager will work with the hospital and the client and set up a care regime at their home upon discharge.

5 Practical effect on financial loss claims

Mitigation

7.70 The claimant must take a reasonable approach to recovery of compensation from the wrongdoer; having established that they have a psychiatric condition that falls to be compensated that does not mean that they have 'carte blanch' to claim for what they wish. They have a duty to 'mitigate their loss'—terminology which confuses most claimants and which needs translating into clear English to be understood (and preferably backed up in written form so that it can be remembered). Explanations on the duty to mitigate their loss and the issues of mitigation are often poorly received by claimants, certainly in the early stages of their illness. Often claimants with psychiatric illnesses are very vulnerable, sometimes in a very emotional and sensitised condition, and explaining mitigation to such a client can be challenging in its own right.

7.71 Whilst the claimant has to be reasonable, and do all that they reasonably can to reduce the amount that the defendant pays out, the duty to show that the claimant has acted unreasonably falls on the defendant. If the defendant wishes to allege that the claimant has not mitigated their losses, they must clearly set this out.

7.72 Whether the claimant has mitigated their losses or not is a matter for the trial judge to decide. At the end of the day a claimant can take whatever action he wishes to take, but he cannot expect to recover compensation if the court finds that he failed to take appropriate steps to avoid the loss. So, for example, if the claimant states that he cannot work, and will not seek employment he cannot expect to recover a loss of earnings in the absence of expert evidence to confirm why he cannot work and the judge's acceptance of that evidence.

7.73 There is an obvious difficulty with the claimant who will not comply with treatment that is recommended by a medical expert. For example, what is to be done with the client who is so psychiatrically unwell that they will not attend a psychiatrist, despite the fact that treatment is recommended, or who will not take medication despite the fact that it is prescribed? Has that claimant failed to mitigate their loss by their failure to comply with treatment? Does the claimant who is recommended a stay in a psychiatric establishment but who will not go fail to mitigate their loss by (ostensibly) impeding their chances of recovery? When is it reasonable for a claimant to refuse treatment and expect this not to have an effect on his ultimate award where there is a chance that such treatment would have an effect on their prognosis? This can be a more difficult question in a case of psychiatric damage, where the claimant's conduct and decision-making abilities are often affected by the condition they suffer from. Most of the case law in this area deals with acceptance or otherwise of electro-convulsive therapies.

7.74 Each case will turn on its own facts and on its own particular evidence. The cases on whether or not a claimant who refuses surgery (or other such invasive) treatment are not necessarily helpful here, save that it is unlikely that the case of

Marcroft v Scrutton[1], where the judge thought it unreasonable of the claimant to refuse electro-convulsive therapy, would be decided in the same way today.

1   [1954] 1 Lloyd's Rep 395.

7.75 What about the claimant who requires, for example, expensive psychiatric care but who cannot afford to pay for the same? Will their failure to 'find' the money be held against them as their failure to mitigate their loss? The answer to that is no, although the claimant who obtained money by way of interim payment for rehabilitation and who fails, without good reason, to use their interim payment for that purpose, may well find themselves in a different and difficult position[1].

1   *Clark v Tull* [2003] UKHL 64.

7.76 The claimant is free to choose whether or not to use services provided by the NHS or local authority or whether or not to use such services provided in the private sector. He is not compelled to use the NHS if he chooses not to, but if he does use NHS facilities then he suffers no loss and so cannot make any claim for them. Section 2(4) of the Law Reform (Personal Injuries) Act 1948 states that there is a 'disregard in determining the reasonableness of any expenses, the possibility of avoiding those expenses or part of them by taking advantage of facilities available under the NHS'.

7.77 Certainly, within the life of an Initial Needs Assessment (INA) the insurers to a claim will require the INA provider to look at State provision before provision in the private sector, but once the claimant can establish that liability is not in dispute, he is in a position to apply for an interim payment to pay for the necessary treatment in the private sector. State provision for psychiatric care is often woefully inadequate, with only the most seriously disturbed being admitted to psychiatric units, pressure on beds being such that often very damaged patients are discharged too early and standard therapeutic care normally being severely time limited. Such treatment and rehabilitative care in the private sector is very expensive, and often such costs are balked at by the insurer.

6   Provisional damages

7.78 In every case there is a presumption that the court will make a final order in settlement of a claim.

The courts have the power to make an award of provisional damages under the Senior Courts Act 1981, s 32A. However, such an award can only be made where there is 'a chance that at some definite or indefinite time in the future the injured person will develop some serious disease or suffer some serious deterioration in his physical or mental condition'. Section 32A reads:

> '(1) This section applies to an action for damages for personal injuries in which there is proved or admitted to be a chance that at some definite or indefinite time in the future the injured person will, as a result of the act or omission which gave rise to the cause of action, develop some serious disease or suffer serious deterioration in his physical or mental condition.

Causation of damage: material contribution, apportionment and acceleration 145

(2) Subject to sub-section (4) below, as regards any action for damages to which this section applies in which a judgment is given in the High court, provision may be made by rules of court for enabling the court, in such circumstances as may be prescribed, to award the injured person—

(a) damages assessed on the assumption that the injured person will not develop the disease or suffer the deterioration in his condition; and
(b) further damages at a future date if he develops the disease or suffer the deterioration.'

7.79 If an award for provisional damages is to be made, then the claimant must plead for them in their particulars of claim.

7.80 It is difficult to see a situation in a claim for compensation for psychiatric injury, in the absence of physical injury, in which an award of provisional damages can be made, save for an increased risk of the development of epilepsy following a head injury. Whilst it is easy to see that a claimant whose mental health has deteriorated and who has suffered perhaps a serious breakdown is more likely to suffer a further breakdown in the future, an award of provisional damages is not designed to cater for this type of possibility and an award of provisional damages is subject to the court's discretion. So even if both parties agree to the making of an award it is technically possible (if unlikely) for the judge to make the order granting it.

7.81 If there is more then a chance that serious disease or a serious deterioration will arise, then an award is not appropriate and the correct approach is to value that within the claim at the point of settlement and for settlement to be final. The reason for that is that the judge is able to deal with a probability and attribute a value to the same.

7.82 Further, the word 'chance' is interpreted to mean something that is more then a mere possibility. It must be 'measurable rather then fanciful'[1] and the word 'measurable' is translated into percentage possibility (else how do you measure 'measurable'!). The issue of how to measure is left to the clinical expert.

The risk must be one of a serious disease or deterioration.

1   Scott Baker J in *Wilson v MOD* [1991] 1 All ER 638.

7 Causation of damage: material contribution, apportionment and acceleration

7.83 The development of a psychiatric illness is often a multi-factorial process. There may be more than one wrongdoer who each contributed to the development of the injury. There may be a number of other non-negligent stressors which contributed to the development and/or severity of the injury (eg problems in the claimant's personal life such as bereavement, divorce or other trauma). The claimant may have suffered from a psychiatric illness before and thus be more vulnerable than would generally be the case to further injury. These questions raise difficult questions of causation.

A Material contribution

7.84 Unless public policy requires otherwise[1], if there are a number of separate possible causes of the whole injury, but the claimant cannot establish that any one or more of them did so materially contribute to it, the claimant will usually fail to establish causation at all[2]. And if the claimant would have gone on to develop an illness at about the same time and of the same severity in any event, the claimant will not obtain compensation[3]. However, neither of these scenarios usually applies in the case of a psychiatric injury where the effects of the various causes are likely to be cumulative and are obviously contributory to the overall severity.

1   Eg *Fairchild v Glenhaven Funeral Services Ltd* [2002] UKHL 22.
2   *Wilsher v Essex Area Health Authority* [1988] AC 1074.
3   *Hotson v East Berkshire Area Health Authority* [1987] AC 750.

7.85 The claimant must, however, show that the 'breach of duty caused or materially contributed to the injury' and 'material' in this context meant more than negligible[1]. It is important that the medical experts understand the principle of material contribution, which here displaces the usual 'but for' test on the balance of probabilities. It is of course entirely possible that expert evidence might establish that on the balance of probabilities as a result of the breach of duty the claimant sustained injury. If so, the claimant will obviously succeed. However, it is not necessary to establish such a degree of probability. If the court determines that the breach of duty was a more than negligible contribution to the illness, the claimant will succeed.

1   *Bonnington Castings Ltd v Wardlaw* [1956] AC 613.

B Apportionment

7.86 The next question for the court is whether establishing material contribution means that the claimant recovers full compensation for the illness, notwithstanding other contributory causes, or whether the illness should be apportioned between the various contributory causes, so that the claimant only recovers part of the compensation in proportion to the relative contribution of the breach of duty. Much depends on whether the injury should be treated as 'divisible' or 'indivisible'.

7.87 If an indivisible injury is caused by two separate wrongdoers, but there is no other contributory factor, the claimant is entitled to compensation in full from either of the wrongdoers, with the court then being required to apportion the liability between the wrongdoers under the provisions of the Civil Liability (Contribution) Act 1978. In *Rahman v Arearose Ltd & University College London NHS Trust*[1] the claimant suffered a serious assault at work for which his employer was liable. The hospital was then negligent in his subsequent medical treatment. He suffered psychiatric injuries which were caused by a combination of the trauma of the assault and the trauma of the loss of vision in one eye as a result of the operation. The psychiatric injury was treated as an indivisible injury. In determining the apportionment under the 1978 Act, the court is required to attribute blame between the two wrongdoers (his employer and the NHS Trust). This apportionment of the relative 'blame' of each defendant which is required under the 1978 Act is quite different from the more usual situation where the injury was caused partly by a breach of duty and partly by factors that do not give rise to any liability.

1   [2001] QB 351.

7.88   Assuming that the claimant can establish that the breach of duty did materially contribute to the injury, the next question is whether the responsibility for the injury can be apportioned between the various potent causes. If the injury is divisible then an apportionment will be made. The most obvious examples of his are industrial deafness, where it is possible to measure the deterioration over a period of time[1], or some kinds of asbestos exposure[2]. However, with other illnesses an injury is not divisible, but rather the various causes are cumulative. In *Bailey v Ministry of Defence*[3] the claimant suffered brain damage as the result of a cardiac arrest suffered after she inhaled her own vomit. This was because she was in a weakened state contributed to by a negligent and a non-negligent cause. The Court of Appeal found that without the contribution of the breach of duty, she would not have been so weak. The breach was a material contribution and the claimant succeeded. The injury was seen as being indivisible and apportionment of the injury was not even argued at first instance or on appeal.

1   *Thompson v Smiths Ship Repairers (North Shields) Ltd* [1984] QB 405.
2   *Holtby v Brigham & Cowan (Hull) Ltd* [2000] PIQR Q293.
3   [2008] EWCA Civ 883.

7.89   In the case of psychiatric injury caused by workplace stress, in *Hatton v Sutherland*[1] the court held that the injury was divisible and needed to be 'apportioned', with the employer paying only for his share of the damage (*Hatton* Proposition 15). It should be noted that *Hatton* Proposition 15 is strictly speaking obiter as it did not fall to be decided in any of the appeals before the court. The Court of Appeal revisited this subject in *Dickins v O2 plc*[2]. The employer had appealed a first instance decision in favour of the employee's claim that she had suffered a nervous breakdown caused by overwork. The Court of Appeal rejected the appeal. However, the judge at first instance had allowed only 50% of the claimant's damages by way of apportionment in accordance with *Hatton* Proposition 15 between negligent and non-negligent causes. In *Dickins*, these included a prior irritable bowel syndrome which might have been stress related, relationship problems (which may have been exacerbated by the work stress) and a subsequent flood which had required her to live in a hotel for nine months and may have delayed her recovery. This apportionment finding was not appealed by either side. However, the Court of Appeal proceeded, obiter, as the point was not argued and was not therefore the subject of the appeal, to critique *Hatton* Proposition 15 on apportionment. Smith LJ revisited the question of whether psychiatric injury is in fact a 'divisible injury' allowing for apportionment saying:

> 'I am doubtful of the applicability of this type of approach to a case of psychiatric injury where there are multiple causes of the breakdown.'

1   [2002] EWCA Civ 76.
2   [2008] EWCA Civ 1144.

7.90   At first sight, it might be thought that *Hatton* Proposition 15 on apportionment would continue to be applied as it forms part of a judgment that has been approved by the House of Lords. However, whilst generally giving support for the propositions of Hale LJ, the House of Lords expressly declined in *Barber v Somerset County Council*[1] to endorse Hale LJ's approach on apportionment. So the issue of apportionment has been considered separately by two distinguished Lady Justices of Appeal with great experience in personal injury law. Both comments are obiter.

1   [2004] UKHL 13.

7.91   In *Thaine v London School of Economics*[1] Keith J sitting in the Employment Appeals Tribunal preferred the approach of Hale LJ and dismissed an appeal from an employment tribunal which had apportioned compensation for psychiatric injury in a discrimination claim between their assessment of the contribution of the discrimination and the contribution of other extraneous factors to the illness, on the basis:

> 'why should the LSE have to compensate Miss Thaine for her psychiatric ill health and its consequences in its entirety when the unlawful discrimination for which it was responsible, though materially contributing to her psychiatric ill-health, was just one of the many causes of it?'

1   [2010] ICR 1422, EAT.

7.92   However, this was discrimination which occurred and a psychiatric injury which developed over a long period. The answer might be different in the case of a psychiatric injury which results from a single shocking event. Keith J in *Thaine* did consider and distinguish the Court of Appeal decision in *The Environment Agency v Ellis*[1], a back injury case where three separate falls (one arising from negligence by employers, one a non-negligent fall at work and one arising from an accident at home) all contributed to the injury. In *Ellis* May LJ characterised the case as 'essentially a single accident case' and said that 'the *Holtby/Allen* principles' do not apply to single accident cases as distinct from cases of injury arising from successive exposures to harm.

1   [2009] PIQR P5.

7.93   The decision in *Thaine* is binding upon the county court, but will be of persuasive authority in the High Court. It would therefore seem likely that apportionment will now be applied in appropriate psychiatric injury claims (but perhaps not psychiatric injury arising from a single shocking event). But the issue is not entirely clear-cut and may have to be decided by the Court of Appeal in due course.

C   Acceleration

7.94   Although the starting point should be that if the claimant can establish that the breach of duty was a material contribution to an indivisible psychiatric injury he should recover full compensation, the court is still entitled to ask whether the compensation should still be reduced by reason of 'acceleration' rather than 'apportionment'. If, prior to the negligent breach of duty, the claimant had a history of psychiatric injury or a pre-existing vulnerability then the court may treat the breach not as the sole cause of the claimant's entire loss, but rather as the trigger which accelerates the onset of an illness that would have developed in any event (*Hatton* Proposition 16).

Causation of damage: material contribution, apportionment and acceleration 149

7.95 Dealing with an 'acceleration' of injury is common for personal injury lawyers (eg where a negligent act accelerates back problems which already exist, whether or not they are then symptomatic, through degenerative change, see *Kenth v Heimdale Hotel Investments Ltd*[1]). In *Dickins v O2*, whilst doubting *Hatton* Proposition 15 on apportionment of damages, Smith LJ stressed:

> 'It may well be appropriate to bear in mind that the claimant was psychiatrically vulnerable and might have suffered a breakdown at some time in the future even without the tort. There may then be a reduction in some heads of damage for future risks of non-tortious loss.'

There is therefore a complex interplay between 'apportionment' between different factors contributing to the injury and the assessment of the likelihood that the claimant would have become ill in any event ('acceleration'), but as Smith LJ points out:

> '... ultimately the result of a different approach might not have been very different'.

1   [2001] EWCA Civ 1283.

7.96 Whether acceleration should apply or not in a particular case is principally a question of expert medical evidence. Care should be taken to direct the experts to properly consider this question. In *MG v North Devon NHS Primary Care Trust*[1] the claimant succeeded in her claim for damages against her employer for mishandling her return to work following a breakdown, but the judge reduced her compensation by 20% 'to reflect the claimant's vulnerability following her [first] breakdown'. However, it is not inevitable in the case of a vulnerable employee that the damages will be reduced. In *Moore v Welwyn Components Ltd*[2], a conjoined appeal in *Hartman* the court declined to find 'acceleration' on the basis that previously the claimant had always quickly recovered from his psychiatric injury whereas this bullying had led to a disorder of an entirely different order. However, applying one discount for acceleration is more just than double-discounting for both apportionment and acceleration, which was often the practical effect of the *Hatton* approach.

1   [2006] EWHC 850 (QB).
2   [2005] EWCA Civ 6.

D   Summary of causation of damage issues in psychiatric injury claims

7.97 In psychiatric injury cases:

(a) provided that the contribution of the breach to the injury is more than negligible, the breach will be a 'material contribution' to the injury and thus satisfy the 'but for' test;
(b) if the injury is an 'indivisible' injury, and if there are no other contributory factors to the injury, compensation in full can be obtained from any of the wrongdoers;
(c) an injury arising from a single shocking event (for example, post-traumatic stress disorder arising after a car accident) is more likely to be held to be 'indivisible' than an injury developing over a longer period (for example, depression arising from stress at work);

(d) if the injury is held to be 'divisible' then with regard to apportionment of damages between different potent causes, some of which do not arise from the negligence (as in *Hatton* Proposition 15):
  (i) this was not endorsed by the House of Lords in *Barber;*
  (ii) it was doubted by Smith LJ in *Dickins*;
  (iii) the comments on apportionment in both *Hatton* and *Dickins* are obiter;
  (iv) the EAT (Keith J presiding) in *Thaine* preferred *Hatton*, at least in respect of an injury which develops over time;
(e) 'acceleration' of injury by reason of vulnerability (*Hatton* Proposition 16) can also apply whether or not the injury is 'indivisible', but consider the particular facts with care.

8 Practical steps

1 Instructions: identifying potential psychiatric injury

8.1 Most people who suffer significant injury in an accident will go on to develop symptoms of psychiatric injury. A substantial proportion of people who witness others suffering serious injury, or who feel threatened that they are going to suffer serious injury (even if they do not suffer such injury) will go on to develop symptoms of psychiatric injury. Psychiatric injuries can often arise out of serious physical injury, such as the person who is in unremitting and remorseless pain who develops a significant depressive condition. There are also conditions which arise out of psychiatric problems but which manifest themselves as physical problems, such as somatoform disorders where the client presents with a bewildering array of supposed physical complaints which, after careful investigation, have either no or only a tenuous physical basis.

8.2 Even if, at the beginning of taking instructions, psychiatric problems are not apparent, it would be wise for the practitioner to expect that a client has been affected psychologically by what has happened to them. If symptoms are not present in the early stages after an accident, they may develop in the future. By keeping observant, the practitioner will remain alert to the development of such potential problems. They will then neither be missed in terms of ensuring that help can be put in at an early stage to alleviate the symptoms, nor will they be missed in respect of medico-legal reporting.

8.3 On occasion, it can be difficult to 'spot' a secondary victim; the woman who develops a depressive disorder following the death of her child in a road traffic accident, or the sister who saw her brother dead in an A&E unit and who is now unable to sleep or work as a result of that event. Even when it is clear that there is some sort of psychiatric problem, it must 'fit' into the criteria for a recognised psychiatric condition and only a medical report from a psychiatrist well versed on what to look for, together with a consideration of the relevant law as it applies (see Chapter 6), will establish whether or not a valid claim can be brought.

8.4 In any event, when taking instructions in any personal injury claim, it is sensible to assume that there are problems, that early treatment could be of benefit and that there will be a need for a psychiatric report at some point in the future. Some clients feel very threatened by the idea of seeing a psychiatrist; some deny any psychiatric symptoms at all even in the face of what seems like an obvious psychiatric disorder. It can be very difficult to get a client with a significant psycho somatoform disorder to even consider seeing, let alone actually see, a psychiatrist. Sometimes persuasion is needed and on occasion subterfuge. The solicitor dealing extensively with clients with serious injury needs good client skills, and must get used to explaining that the client will probably need to be seen by a psychiatrist however reluctant the response is. By this means, all clients—especially those who feel uncomfortable, or awkward about the demand—will understand the probable necessity of such an appointment. It is of help to understand that clients often feel reassured to understand that psychiatric problems are 'normal' following significant trauma.

8.5 Most clients do not present with a 'psychiatric emergency'. The very seriously injured often spend months in hospital, where their problems are picked up by the psychiatric in-house services within the NHS. Often more serious physical injuries mask developing psychiatric problems; sometimes pain of itself will cause depression, and anxiety over life issues such as ongoing financial stresses can add to the problems. But there are clients who, during the life of the claim, will present with symptoms which can range across the psychological spectrum from being suicidal to floridly psychotic. Having in place a good network of support and treatment is essential for these vulnerable clients; and this begins with early intervention probably best accessed through good case management.

8.6 There can be a significant interplay between the physical and emotional issues that develop after serious injuries; this is exacerbated by, and often made more difficult both to identify and treat where there has been, a head injury. Some clients do better than others. Sometimes the most unlikely client remains psychiatrically well when the less-injured person becomes totally disabled by the situation in which they find themselves. Sometimes a small injury will cause what appears to be disproportionate and bewildering (for the lawyer and occasionally the surrounding professionals) symptoms. It is easier to understand that the client who faces a lifetime of paralysis, who knows he cannot return to his home or job, and who has suffered perhaps through no fault of his own a complete life changing incident, is quite likely to suffer at the very least a period of depression. Whereas the person who suffered a whiplash injury but who develops a full-blown psychosomatic disorder engenders a less sympathetic response even if the end effect (total disruption of their life) may be the same. As an extreme example; compensation is theoretically the same for the client who, as a result of a psycho-somatoform disorder, believes that they cannot walk again and is wheelchair bound as it is for the person who has suffered an actual spinal injury and cannot walk, although there would probably be substantial discounts given for the prospect of recovery in the first example. The fact is that the law as it stands does not and should not distinguish—neither as a moral nor practical statement—between the levels of compensation recoverable. The fact that the injury is psychiatric should not mean that a less robust approach be given to the investigation and proving of the case.

8.7 Sometimes this aspect of moral judgment can get in the way of the solicitor's (and their staff's) handling of the claim. If the client is not likeable, or their condition is less believable, it is easier to abandon the client, to under-settle the claim, to accept the first medical report—even if it is not a credible one in the circumstances. The client who screams and cries can find that the staff in the lawyer's office run out of sympathy. These clients can be amongst the most challenging clients that the personal injury lawyer will face. It is difficult to work happily for somebody whose phone call you dread, who complains vociferously about everything you and the experts do, even when the lawyer knows that the client is mentally unwell. To recover full and proper damages for such clients and for the lawyer to escape emotionally unscathed is a great challenge. Often the solicitor feels aggrieved at the amount of time that is being tied up dealing with such clients; extra phone calls, extra hours in explanations and re-explanation of the process and suchlike. Understanding that there is a provision for recovery of the extra costs incurred from dealing with clients who have suffered psychiatric injury (see below) helps.

8.8 Although likely, psychiatric problems in the seriously injured are not a certainty and those who regularly work with the seriously injured will confirm that a number of factors can help re-establish the client's physical and mental well-being; a return to work package, good affordable housing and a strong family relationship all mitigate against psychiatric breakdown.

8.9 There are two scenarios that can confound or assist the process. The first is the current practice to try liability issues ahead of quantum issues. In respect of legal costs control, and a more sound way of quantifying a claim (it is far easier to spend money properly quantifying a claim when you have an admission of liability or judgment in the claimant's favour) it is best practice to try the issues of liability ahead of quantum in nearly all cases. The problem here is in obtaining early and sufficient interim payments without admission of liability. Often, by the time the liability issues are resolved (whether with an allegation of contributory negligence or not) the psychological trauma that could have been averted with early interim payments is entrenched. The second, which if properly handled can work in a claimant's favour, is that of the rehabilitation protocol and an insurer's willingness to put in place some sort of rehabilitation support in the early stages after an incident.

2 Reviewing past medical history

8.10 The fact that a client has a significant (or any) pre-accident history of psychiatric illness does not mean that there is a bar on a claim for the occurrence, reoccurrence or increase of any ongoing psychiatric injury whether incurred or exacerbated by a negligent event (see Chapter 7). But it does mean that the practitioner has to be very careful to identify the nature and extent of any past problems, as the causation and extent of any injury caused may well become substantial issues in any claim.

8.11 It is essential in any claim where psychological damage is going to be a, or perhaps, the main head of the general damages claim, for the practitioner and the nominated experts to ensure that they are aware of any pre-injury history and/or vulnerability. Initial medical reports can then be properly prepared and the defendants and their experts made aware, from the outset of the claim, that the claimant's team know about pre-existing problems and have dealt with them in the evidence.

8.12 The nature and extent of any previous psychological problems must be dealt with both in the client's witness statement and, if possible, in the witness evidence of family and friends. There may be a simple explanation for a period of distress or depression; maybe a failed relationship or a family bereavement. It is not unusual for the client to forget, or not mention, such episodes; maybe they have genuinely put them out of their mind or they may sometimes think that they are not relevant. But it is unsafe to assume that what the client says about previous medical problems is accurate; the records must be checked.

8.13 The expert must be told about any previous problems and the existence of the same should be highlighted in the letter of instruction. In a claim where psychiatric injury is a significant component of the claim, if there is evidence of a substantial or series of pre-existing illnesses then the nominated expert should be given a full chronology of these events as that will help them to put them into life context. This chronology, taken initially from the medical records (all of them, not just the GP notes) and then added to by reading the other relevant records such as school records, work records and perhaps notes of previous accidents, will form a framework for drafting the client witness statement and act as an aide memoire to the client so that he can properly put in context previous problems. It will also be of great use when instructing counsel.

8.14 At the point of their instruction, all experts must also be given a full set of all of the medical and other relevant records. Not to provide the expert with the relevant information is a failure to properly prepare the case. At best, the expert will prepare an interim report and ask for the further information before a final report can be given and this is usually a waste of money. If the expert, in his second report, has had to correct their first report, and the first report has been disclosed, it can significantly undermine their evidence and credibility as a witness.

What records

8.15 Care should be taken to gather in all of the medical records. Sometimes this can turn into a forensic exercise. The first port of call will be the GPs notes, and consideration ought to be given as to whether there is a private as well as an NHS GP. Sometimes clients think that 'private' GP notes can be kept secret. This is not the case. All GP notes should be checked to ensure that there are no gaps in the history and that the entire file has been disclosed (including notes kept on the computer). If there are gaps, then the GP must be asked where the records have gone, and efforts made to locate them.

8.16 Reading the GP records will identify what other (if any) psychiatric problems there may have been. If time is of the essence, or if there are substantial numbers of records and the claim is one of significant value, then a good medical record sorting agency can assist in sorting the records into chronological order and preparing a numbered bundle. In clinical negligence cases it is usually good practice (and a demand on the first order on directions in the High Court) that a numbered bundle is prepared. A numbered bundle makes reference to particular instances very easy, and cross referencing to particular problems or issues in the notes easy in, for example, a conference with counsel. A good agency can prepare a medical chronology and include a note of references to past and current psychiatric problems. Particular note should be taken of any other attending hospitals, both past and present, and those notes should be obtained and read for ongoing clues.

8.17 A word of warning about obtaining records from the usual agencies which gather in records and hand them over to instructed experts: often such agencies will accept the production of records from a GP surgery or a hospital as the sum total of all the records that exist. If there are gaps in the notes, and/or the notes are not read, then there is the potential problem that the solicitor will be missing the whole picture. If the practitioner allows an agency to source and obtain the records then it is vital that they are checked to ensure that they are complete. In a complex case where there are contentious issues dealing with the causation of clinical symptoms, the medical experts should be instructed directly by the solicitor.

8.18 Not all claims may warrant careful forensic analysis, but where there are issues or allegations of pre-existing problems, it is well for the practitioner not to be taken by surprise by the defendant's experts, who will almost certainly subject the claim to careful analysis and raise a request for missing records. It is potentially embarrassing and certainly careless to miss these enquiries and to assert that there were no pre-existing problems if, for example, an entry in the handwritten GP notes clearly states that there are. A little medical knowledge will help.

8.19 For example, the following entry in the GP's handwritten notes, where there is an issue of depression and suicidal feelings, following an accident in 2010:

> 2008 O/E took OD 2/7 ago treated St Mary's A&E 30 + aspirin att OP at RFH sad ++

Translates to 'overdose 2 days ago treated at St Mary's Hospital accident and emergency department took 30 plus Aspirin is to attend an outpatient appointment at the Royal Free Hospital. Very sad'.

Certainly that sort of entry should be identified, the casualty notes and outpatient attendance notes both from St Mary's and the Royal Free Hospital obtained, the client's instructions on the episode obtained and the nominated expert alerted to the entry. In that way it can be properly dealt with in the evidence.

8.20 Each case is sensitive to its own facts, but consideration should be given to the existence of and gathering in of employment records and these should include records from the occupational health department. These records are particularly helpful when there are issues concerning performance at work. Occupational health records are kept separately from personnel records and require a separate consent for release. School and university records and reports may also be of use. There may be social service records, or prison records and separate prison hospital notes. If there has been an inquest then consideration should be given to gathering in the inquest depositions.

8.21 If there is to be an inquest, then consideration should be given to attending the same and taking note of what the witnesses, if any, say. This could be the first and last time that the defendant is seen giving evidence before any trial and his or her demeanour and attitude will be useful in considering the level of risk in proceeding should there be outstanding issues on liability and contribution. The same goes for a criminal prosecution—whether by the police or the Health & Safety Executive—where, depending on the likely size and value of the claim, a watching brief may need to be taken. All of these records could be helpful in understanding the severity of the incident, and how the claimant behaved during the incident and afterwards.

156 *Practical steps*

8.22 Where the ambulance service has attended, these records should be gathered in. The same goes for any helicopter rescue/evacuation service and/or fire brigade involvement. These records can be extremely helpful in pinpointing the time of the accident, the time of the first call, and often provide excellent information on what has been said to the paramedics and others at the point of first attending on the scene. Ambulance personnel are taught to comment on the patient's state of consciousness and their general behaviour, and what they have been told about the circumstances of the accident. If there is a doubt over whether a head injury was, or was not, suffered, these can help and the instructing expert must be provided with a copy of them. Consideration can be given to interviewing the ambulance personnel if clarification is needed.

8.23 The treating hospital notes should be obtained; in particular the accident and emergency notes including triage notes. These are the records of the initial presentation of the patient, and they too will assist greatly where there are allegations of the extent and nature of the injury and what the client said to the attending doctors and nurses.

8.24 Where there are differences between the various witness accounts of events, then the notes should be read to the client and/or the witnesses and they should be asked if they have any comments on the differences. Counsel will certainly want to know what the witness will say.

8.25 It is extremely rare for hospitals to refuse to release their notes; a GP will generally only refuse do so if it is felt that the information contained in the records could harm their patient. Sometimes psychotherapists do not wish to disclose their records for the same reason or may say that doing so may damage their relationship with their patient. It is not unusual that the client himself may not want some or all of the records to be released (and the practitioner should be alert to the client who asks the GP to redact things from the notes). Where there are pre-existing problems that may affect the handling of the ongoing case, the records are discloseable. If the client wants to maintain a claim then the records, in their entirety, must be released and disclosed and to accept partial discovery is unsafe.

3 Building a team

8.26 The running of a claim of substance needs a team approach. Costs control and proportionality is vital, and it is sensible for the partner at the head of the team in the lawyer's office to be able to delegate suitable tasks to less qualified and cheaper colleagues. That does not mean, however, that all work should be delegated. The partner retains the duty to supervise the team and to ensure that he has considered what tasks are appropriate for him to handle and considered all of the evidence gathered in to ensure that the case is properly prepared. It is the solicitor who directs the case, who over a number of years acting for the client gets to know him, his family and lifestyle, and forms, hopefully, a relationship of trust so that the client will understand, contribute to and accept the advice given. Counsel becomes part of that team but like the instructed experts, while counsel can forensically guess what is missing, he will only see snapshots of the case until any trial and it is the solicitor who retains the responsibility to push the matter forwards.

8.27 The failure of a witness to come up to proof at trial is potentially fatal to a claim. If there is a sensitive witness statement, for example a statement from the only independent witness to a serious accident, to be taken then if the partner themselves is not to take it, a trusted and experienced member of staff should be delegated. That witness can, if necessary, be seen by counsel, but generally only after the witness statement is taken and signed[1].

1   See the Bar Code of Conduct, Section 1, Part VII, para 705 and also Section 3, para 6.

8.28 There is a place in the team for outside agency staff, such as medical record sorting agencies and external staff to take witness statements. Care should be taken, however, to ensure that the people who do this work are forensic in their approach and do not bring their own opinions to bear; for example in the way that they prepare witness statements. Often ex police officers join agencies to take witness statements and it is not unusual for such people to have entrenched views on certain types of accidents. They may not, in fact, really understand the difference between civil proof and criminal proof. They may well feel too much sympathy with the potential defendant or perhaps the claimant. This can affect the manner and scope of their questions. Not every incident may elicit such an approach, so care should be taken in each and every case. If the practitioner uses somebody external to his practice to prepare witness statements then at the very least he should speak with that person and discuss, if not face to face then on the telephone, the attitude and manner of the witnesses. If the witness evidence is crucial, and the witness hostile (perhaps they are giving evidence for the defendant) then person who took the statement should attend a conference with counsel at an appropriate point as the case progresses.

A   Counsel

8.29 In a valuable and/or complex claim it is usual to get counsel on board in the early stages of a claim. There are sound practical reasons for this too, for whilst the solicitor's conditional fee agreement will almost certainly have been signed at the first or second meeting, or even by post, where there is a need to obtain 'after the event insurance' it is usual for counsel's opinion to be required. Counsel should never be left evidentially in the dark. They should be sent a complete, full and indexed bundle of all of the available evidence. It is usual for counsel to enter in to a conditional fee agreement and the terms of that agreement should be understood by the retaining solicitor and abided by.

8.30 Appropriate counsel should be chosen given the circumstances of the case. It is most unwise to send a case with a fractious and difficult client who is suffering from significant psychiatric problems (particularly if there is a psycho-somatic component) to a junior barrister, inexperienced in this type of work who is neither particularly brave nor robust. If counsel refuses to accept the case on a conditional fee basis this could cause an insurer, whether 'before the event' or 'after the event', to withdraw their indemnity in the case. Careful consideration of reported cases with

158 *Practical steps*

similar circumstances can help in choosing counsel who are experienced, as will speaking to the senior clerk in the chosen chambers and then picking up the telephone and speaking with counsel. If counsel is not prepared to discuss whether or not he or she would like to consider instructions in the case, then perhaps they are not the best counsel to make up part of the team. Not all counsel respond well to a team approach but in a difficult case, the solicitor should feel able to occasionally pick up the telephone and speak with counsel about difficult issues, and he or she must be certain that their instructions will be promptly dealt with, paperwork returned within a certain time limit and the client treated courteously and sensitively. If not, then alternative counsel should be chosen.

8.31 The attitude of counsel in dealing with the psychiatrically distressed client is very important. It is pointless retaining the cleverest counsel if they are unable to speak with the client. Social skills are especially important in these types of cases. It is not sensible to keep on the case counsel whom the client does not like or whose attitude the client finds off-putting. Under those circumstances the client will often not respect what counsel says. Most counsel will understand this and welcome an early meeting in a case, before a conditional fee agreement is entered into between solicitor and counsel as the costs of breaking that agreement are incurred if counsel's instructions are withdrawn.

B The client and their family as part of the team

8.32 It is an unusual concept for a solicitor and barrister to look upon the client and others as part of the team. But whilst they may not be part of the 'legal' team they are certainly part of the whole endeavour. Often, at the first conference with the barrister, the barrister will sympathise with the client, and say to the client 'I know that your main concern is how long it will take to resolve your claim and how much you are going to get'. And whilst that may be how clients do view the legal process, the fact is that to obtain proper compensation at the 'right' time—that is when the liability issues are sorted out and the client's condition has settled sufficiently to obtain a prognosis—requires the co-operation of the client, his involvement in the process and the involvement, if possible, of a substantial amount of supportive family and friends, if not for anything more than to take careful quantum witness statements from and to support the client through the difficult times.

8.33 It can be difficult for a solicitor to convey to a client that their conduct can materially affect the progress of the litigation claim. It is very challenging for the solicitor to deal with a client whose psychiatric condition causes them to fail to attend appointments, deal expeditiously with requests to complete paperwork or to participate in the process of allowing access to friends, family and employers or even presenting at medical appointments. At the most extreme end of this spectrum is the client who begins the claim but who, somewhere along the way, becomes so hostile, paranoid or difficult that actually getting instructions to continue with the claim becomes impossible. Often, these clients live alone, and have a history of difficult social relationships. The issue of whether the client has legal capacity must be considered (see Chapter 9). Where there are no family members, or where there are family members who cannot cope with the client, it is essential that the Official Solicitor is approached for guidance.

8.34 It is also important to ensure that family and other potential witnesses are dealt with sensitively. Where there are complicated issues of psychiatric attribution, the client's pre-accident personality and behaviour may well be important and careful witness statements should be taken on issues that may cause the statement-givers some anxiety. It is difficult for a parent to criticise a child or visa versa, or for good friends to comment on difficult personality traits that a client may have had, or may have developed since the accident. The client who has capacity retains the right to look at the file on request and nothing should be written on the file that the writer would not want the client to read.

C Legal expense insurers

8.35 Often the average insurer does not really understand psychiatric injury and finds it difficult to understand the client who is hostile or who fails to turn up to appointments. Insurers find the issues of psycho-somatoform illness puzzling and worry about their risk under their indemnity. Their continued funding may be essential to the progress of the claim and so they fall to be part of the litigation team. Needless to say, the contractual obligations under any before the event (BTE) or after the event (ATE) policy must be adhered to, but where there are complexities arising out of psychiatric problems counsel's greater involvement is often necessary to appease the insurer's concerns. Often the insurer will welcome, where the risk and outlay are great, being invited to a conference with counsel.

4 Choosing and instructing experts

8.36 The expert should be chosen according to the presentation of symptoms. Sometimes it is difficult to identify, out of a multitude of physical and emotional problems, exactly what the symptoms are. That which may seem physical may well turn out to be emotional. By that time, a raft of medical reports may have been gathered in that, with the benefit of hindsight, are neither helpful nor accurate. This can cause a problem for the solicitor acting under an agreement where the client does not, under any circumstance, contribute towards their legal costs. Sometimes, where the case is very undermined by a useless and inaccurate expert report, that report will just have to be abandoned and the costs of the same borne in the case. If the report did, in some way, progress the case (even if it were subsequently ditched) then the defendants can be asked to pay for it at detailed assessment. But sometimes costs are wasted and that should be accepted as part of dealing with complex and valuable work:

— choose the 'right' expert.
— instruct them properly.

8.37 The right expert is not only the correct expert for the presenting symptoms, who has the necessary qualifications and professional authority to gain respect from the client, but who will also gain such respect from the defendants, their experts and the court. The excellent expert is one who is also interested and willing to go the extra mile.

8.38 The well-rounded expert is one who is both good on paper and when giving witness evidence. It is possible to gain an idea of how an expert will stand up to giving evidence (if he has not been seen giving evidence before) when in conference with counsel, and for this reason if the expert's evidence is contentious then he should be seen in conference at least once before trial and certainly before the joint expert meeting.

8.39 The expert who takes instructions but who turns out to be too busy or careless in their consideration of the documentation provided, or who fails to actually provide their report on time, is a material challenge to a solicitor who may be already handling a difficult client and working to a tight court timetable.

8.40 Choosing an unknown and untried expert from a medical reporting agency will rarely do when dealing with a client who has complex psychiatric problems. The solicitor needs to think about the client, the condition and the type of expert needed, especially where it is suspected that there is a significant interplay between psychiatric and physical injuries.

8.41 Clients who are mentally unwell often recover less well from their physical injuries. Most clinical experts dealing with the physical aspect of a claim will acknowledge that, but some will not, and some will blithely confirm that 'he should make a full recovery within nine months' failing to take into account any psychiatric condition. It is essential that reports in complex claims are not disclosed in a piecemeal fashion and that the experts present, as far as possible, a cohesive and considered joint approach. This is not difficult with experts who are willing to co-operate. In fact, most good experts are generally pleased to work with an organised, enthusiastic and prepared solicitor who provides them with clear instructions to prepare an initial report, who updates them before they are asked to see a client again, provides comprehensive and meticulous witness evidence, and does not ask them to enter into expert discussions in an unprepared fashion.

8.42 The development of a major psychiatric condition provides a particular evidential challenge to the solicitor. If the expert is being asked to comment on the interplay between pre-existing problems and the current situation, to distinguish between a period of depression prior to the accident and the current situation then the best way to do this (apart from the full provision of all relevant records both medical and other: see above) is with comprehensive and well-written witness statements.

A Which expert

8.43 Cases of psychiatric injury will require a psychiatric report. Psychiatrists are medical doctors, most psychologists are not. Generally speaking, it is not sensible to counter a psychiatrist against a psychologist, as the court will mostly prefer the evidence from the medically-trained expert. It is usually best to start with the report from a psychiatrist where there is no element of head injury.

8.44 Where there is an element of head injury, then generally speaking a neuropsychological report should be gathered in to evaluate what, if any, cognitive damage there has been, followed by a neurologist who can confirm whether there is any objective physical injury. It is a mistake to think that no findings on an MRI scan of brain injury mean that there is no cognitive injury and just psychiatric sequalae. After that a neuro-psychiatrist could be asked to report. A neuro-psychiatrist is a psychiatrist who has a particular interest in the interplay between neurological damage and psychiatric problems. Such an expert's evidence will be more authoritative than a general psychiatric expert opinion where there is a head injury.

8.45 Ideally the reports should be obtained in sequence; the first expert being given the necessary information to report and the second and subsequent experts being given copies of each other's reports. Prior to disclosure of reports, consideration should be given to having a conference with the experts to iron out any professional differences so that their approach correlates.

8.46 Where the client presents with injuries that are vastly out of proportion to the actual damage and it is suspected that there is a case of somatoform type disorder, then all of the necessary reports to exclude or confirm the nature and extent of a physical injury should be gathered in (they probably will have by that point in any event) and then a psychiatric opinion from an expert who both understands and is able to comment on somatoform disorders should be obtained. At this point the solicitor may well find that their retained psychiatric expert is just not up to that job and they may have to be replaced by somebody who is.

8.47 It is a waste of money and a recipe for a series of complaints from a distraught client to obtain a report from an expert who is neither senior enough or experienced enough to deal with the issues in question. Nor is it sensible to instruct an expert who cannot at least be sympathetic to the client. That does not mean that the expert should be biased; far from it. Instructing experts who are known to be biased for 'one side or the other' is not sensible. A careful, clear and respectable opinion from somebody who is kind to the client, reads and properly considers the documentation put before them and provides a comprehensive and clear account of the issues on paper should be the aim.

5 Handling the client
A Difficult clients

8.48 Dealing with a client who has a significant psychiatric injury can be one of the most challenging aspects of the job of a personal injury lawyer, as he must learn to cope with a client who exhibits a whole gamut of psychiatric problems. It is not unusual for a client to present with an excess of emotion, be it anger or unhappiness. From early in their career the solicitor needs to be prepared, and able, to deal with a client who, for example, presents as depressed, crying, sometimes threatening suicide or is just plain paranoid.

8.49 Serious injury litigation can take years; cases cannot be settled until there is a clear prognosis and the clients' expectations, especially when they are emotionally fragile, have to be handled. There is no substitute for good client care, especially when dealing with people whose view of the world is clouded, temporarily or not, by mental illness.

B Capacity

8.50 Most clients who suffer psychiatric injury have full capacity, are perfectly reasonable people and have temporary problems that are amenable to good treatment. But there are a small minority whose problems are so severe that they throw up very difficult issues of day-to-day management. Sometimes their problems are so severe that the solicitor has to consider whether or not they have the capacity to give instructions to manage the litigation.

C Mental Capacity Act

Protecting the client

8.51 The client who calls the office and in conversation threatens to kill himself, or perhaps harm others, presents with a significant ethical challenge. The new Solicitors Regulation Authority (SRA) Code of Conduct, together with its associated Handbook, both published in 2011, provides a set of expected outcomes and indicative behaviours which go towards achieving those outcomes.

Most importantly though, where the solicitor is in need of ethical guidance (whether urgent or otherwise) the SRA's Professional Ethics helpline (0870 6062577) provides a confidential and supportive service to the solicitor who can talk through a problem and guide the solicitor towards a solution without fear of breaching confidence.

8.52 In practice, the client who threatens suicide or self-harm, or who is exhibiting symptoms of psychiatric injury ought to be asked whether or not they object to their GP being contacted on their behalf. The solicitor needs to be quite careful here to get clear instructions, and only when they do have a clear permission should they contact the GP (or perhaps the treating consultant).

8.53 If clear instructions are not obtained, then there are occasions on which confidentiality can be broken. But the best advice here is to call the Solicitors Regulation Authority Professional Ethics Helpline, take a clear note and follow the guidance given.

8.54 The same applies to the client who threatens to kill somebody; such threats must be taken seriously, a clear note made in the file and action given to how to deal with the threat. Tell the client that you are taking their threat seriously, that you may have to report the matter to the police and call the Ethics helpline for advice. Each case turns on its particular circumstances.

Protecting the staff

8.55 An employer has a duty to protect his staff from occupational stress, and harassment in his employees' workplace. Issues of racial and sexual discrimination can found criminal proceedings.

8.56 The fact that a client's difficult behaviour may arise as a result of mental health issues may be—as far as some staff are concerned—a mitigating factor in dealing with the client. But it does not exculpate the employer from his responsibilities.

8.57 Some clients are demanding per se; their pre-accident personalities may lead them to behave in a manner that creates stress to those around them.

The most difficult group of clients to deal with are those who were—pre accident—paranoid type personalities who lived isolated lives in the community (often living in complete dishabille) or who develop a paranoid illness as a result of the accident, perhaps as a result of organic changes arising out of serious head injury. The client who develops a significant paranoid-type illness after an accident can become difficult, abusive, vicious, occasionally violent and can present with the most difficult problems both to access help for; or to protect staff from. This can be compounded by easy access to email accounts, where it is possible to bombard a large group of recipients with emails.

8.58 Watching a client mentally deteriorate can be a very difficult and stressful process. This is especially true if there is no funding available to access effective psychiatric treatment, or if the client resists psychiatric treatment. The Mental Capacity Act 2005, whilst it reads well, in practice makes it difficult to act for these clients, especially if there are no family members available to assist.

8.59 Some clients present such challenging behaviour that the solicitor must risk-manage the situation (both in terms of their own ability to cope and the abilities of those in the team) and raise questions over whether or not he ought to accept instructions and/or continue acting for them.

D   Coming off the record

8.60 Once instructions are accepted, then there has to be good reason to refuse to continue to accept instructions. The solicitor's retainer (the CFA and client care letter) and the Solicitors Code of Conduct deal with circumstances where a solicitor may stop acting for a client.

8.61 The SRA Code of Conduct, together with its associated Handbook, is, it is suggested, less clear in terms of how to deal with difficult clients (despite it saying it is not) as the old and clear duties set out in the Solicitors Code of Conduct of 2007. Within the new code the solicitor is expected to act 'with regard' to the client's mental incapacity:

> Indicative Behaviour IB(1.6): 'in taking instructions and during the course of the retainer, having proper regard to your client's mental capacity or other vulnerability, such as incapacity or duress;'

The old Code provided clarity in situations where the solicitor must refuse instructions or where appropriate cease acting. These included acting where the client was under a mental incapacity where there was no litigation friend and where continuing to act was against the law. It is suggested that even if the current Codes are less clear, the expected outcomes are the same and the fact that there may be no litigation friend does not mean that the client should be abandoned, far from it. In those circumstances where there is no family member to assist, the solicitor has a positive duty to refer the matter to the Official Solicitor.

8.62 There can be very difficult situations. The client who bombards the solicitor's office with emails clearly alleging racism or sexism in a blatant and 'mad' way may or may not, under the Mental Capacity Act 2005, have capacity to continue to instruct. Urgent advice on capacity should be taken from a psychiatrist who is properly instructed on the difficulties that the solicitor is encountering and who has been sent copies of the relevant witness statements and medical report, if there is doubt over capacity. In all but the clearest cases it is wise to steer clear of the client's GP for this purpose, as he or she may not understand the issues in question and may not have seen the client for a considerable period of time.

8.63 There is no easy answer as to how to deal with such clients in an office environment, especially if they do not have capacity and are patients. Robust, understanding staff will assist but it is generally wisest for the solicitor to deal directly with most aspects of the client in such circumstances. If this cannot be done then the client—either directly (if they have capacity) or through the litigation friend (if they do not)—should be asked to instruct another firm of solicitors.

6 Rehabilitation

8.64 Under the Rehabilitation Code 2007[1] there is the intention to foster a collaborative approach between the parties. It is worth looking at this code in detail as it promotes not only the pro-active role of the claimant solicitor in the rehabilitation process but, in the event that there is an argument about the costs of doing so, provides a counter-argument at detailed assessment.

1   Published by the Bodily Injury Claims Management Association (BICMA).

8.65 The Personal Injury Protocol contained within the CPR places on the claimant solicitor a duty to consider the rehabilitation of the claimant, both at the beginning of a claim and through the life of the claim. It also provides that the claimant solicitor has a duty to consider the needs for practical help as well as medical rehabilitation, to consider the needs for aids and equipment and to consider the effects of disability upon employment (2.3). It provides that the solicitor should have to consider the effects of rehabilitation but does not have the 'responsibility' to decide on the needs without appropriate medical or professional advice.

Through this there is some judicial recognition that personal injury solicitors have responsibilities to their clients beyond just litigating the claim.

The aim is that both parties should think about rehabilitation as soon as possible so that the injured person's needs are assessed and 'addressed as a priority'.

8.66 The use and provisions of the Rehabilitation Code are not mandatory. If the Code's aim can be achieved through different means then that will satisfy the intention of the Code.

Under 2.1:

> 'It should be the duty of every claimant's solicitor to consider, from the earliest practicable stage, and in consultation with the claimant, the claimant's family, and where appropriate the claimant's treating physician(s), whether it is likely or possible that early intervention, rehabilitation or medical treatment would improve their present and/or long term physical and mental well being. This duty is ongoing throughout the life of the case but is of most importance in the early stages'.

The same duty is also applied to the 'compensator' at para 3.1.

8.67 Even where liability is in dispute the Code can apply; but it does not apply where liability is in dispute unless the parties agree that it should apply.

8.68 The process is started by what is called an 'Independent Needs Assessment' (INA) and the parties are expected to agree on the person/organisation nominated to prepare this assessment which will generally be carried out by case management agencies who employ nurses and occupational therapists who are experienced in early intervention.

8.69 There are several organisations that provide INA reports. In practice most insurers have their own INA agencies (they may not wear the insurer's company colours, but with a little delving often can be seen in some way to have connections). By choice, an INA provider who is totally independent of the defendant insurance company should be chosen.

8.70 The INA provider should be properly chosen and instructed. The claimant solicitor should see evidence that the case manager instructed to see the client has experience of dealing with psychiatric injury. There is no point asking an occupational therapist who specialises in back problems or suchlike to see a client with a psychiatric injury. The CV of the proposed case manager should be requested and if they do not have the necessary experience another person should be chosen. In addition, the case manager should be properly instructed. That means they should be sent all of the relevant medical records, for example. The insurer who has agreed to the process is expected to fund treatment for injuries 'caused' by the accident, or 'exacerbated' by the accident.

8.71 Asking the defendant to institute an INA and their willingness to do so can indicate that they are likely to accept a degree of fault in the case. But it can also indicate that they are a pro-active insurance company who sees, in a potentially very valuable claim, the need to do something early on to support the claimant whether or not liability is going to be conceded. Most insurance companies these days have specialist teams who deal with cases of significant and serious injury, and who are conscious of the effect and benefits of early intervention. They will often input several thousand pounds' worth of support before they are in a position to take a positive or negative stance on liability, as this could save them money at the end of the day.

8.72 In practice, the Code can operate very much to the claimant's advantage. If used, at the end of the day the claimant will not have to repay any funds made available for rehabilitation if the claim is successful, or any shortfall incurred if there is an element of contributory negligence found against him. For example, if a period of inpatient treatment in a private psychiatric facility is recommended and a four-week stay costs £20,000, then if the claim fails the insurers cannot ask for their money back, or if the claimant is found 50% responsible for the accident then the insurers cannot ask for the £10,000 to be credited off the overall value of the claim.

8.73 The treatment falls outside of the litigation process and as such information gained in the treatment, the assessment reports, are legally privileged unless the parties agree to waive privilege. Careful consideration needs to be given to this. Often the advising litigation expert will ask to see the INA report and ongoing case management notes and permission must be asked of the INA case manager before these can be disclosed.

8.74 There can be difficulties where there is an argument over the attribution of ongoing psychiatric injuries. The compensator is not expected to pay for treatment that is not attributable, or that is in its view unreasonable or which may be obtained in a 'timely fashion' elsewhere.

A Case management outside of the Rehabilitation Code

8.75 The sourcing and application of services to the damaged client is generally best done by way of case management. If there is no INA or perhaps if the insurers will not fund case management, or where the decision is taken to retain independent case management then the claimant who has complicated treatment and care needs almost certainly needs a case manager.

8.76 In addition, it is nearly always better for the claimant to have independent case management than case management provided and controlled by the insurance company following an INA. There are several reasons for this: the control of the process is put into the claimant and the claimant's solicitor's hands. The bureaucracy of direct funding from the insurance company is removed and the claimant will fund the needs through (hopefully) interim payments made by the insurers to his solicitors. The case manager does not have so many people to deal with, and can concentrate on the claimant and his needs rather than satisfying an insurance company that (for example) all avenues have been explored for cheap or free funding of care and treatment before private therapy is purchased.

B Psychiatric rehabilitation facilities

8.77 In practice, psychiatric treatment within the NHS is difficult to access: the delivery of the same is often dependant upon where the claimant lives and the pressure on local services. Therapy is usually time-limited and unless the claimant has a psychotic condition or is in a situation where his or her life or the lives of others are threatened by their mental condition (and hence they are sectionable under the Mental Health Act) private therapeutic intervention will be needed.

C   Counselling and general psychiatric outpatient sessions

8.78   There are many organisations which provide good and effective therapy for conditions such as post-traumatic stress, depression and anxiety. Reputable counselling services will provide a range of treatment approaches, usually hand-in-hand with qualified psychiatric support.

8.79   Any case manager who has experience in dealing with clients with psychiatric injury will be able to research and access appropriate counselling help. The client's GP will almost certainly know of good local private services. The cost of such treatment should be paid for by the insurers through interim payments where liability is conceded. The advising expert should be asked to comment on the necessity of such treatment, the number of sessions it is thought needed and the likely cost of the same. If the insurers will not pay those costs, then an application for funding should be made to the court.

D   In-patient psychiatric care

8.80   There are also facilities that provide ongoing care for those with serious psychiatric conditions, including those with psychotic or dangerous conditions such as intention to harm themselves or others and who need protection and containment under the Mental Health Act.

8.81   Generally, if there is a need for admission to a private psychiatric facility the treating psychiatrist will know of one, or two, choices for admission. If there is a particular need for speciality, for example if the client has PTSD, a more specialist unit may be needed than for the client who is suffering from a general depressive illness.

8.82   There are a limited number of units which provide support and treatment for those with psychiatric conditions which arise out of head injury and an even more limited number who provide for those with 'difficult' treatment needs arising out of psychiatric conditions following a head injury.

8.83   Not all units are suitable for all clients. As the likely cost of a stay at such a unit is likely to be in excess of £140,000 per annum, careful consideration needs to be given to where the client is placed. Needless to say, no client should be placed where they do not want to be and where they do not feel they will thrive. Pre-admission visits are therefore essential.

7   Attitudes of defendants: malingering, fraud and exaggeration

8.84   It is standard practice nowadays for insurers, in their first letter acknowledging notification of a claim, to confirm that they will check information given on the Association of British Insurers Motor Insurance Anti-Fraud and Theft Register and the Claims and Underwriting Exchange Register. Further, it is not unusual for medical examiners (especially those engaged by the insurance company) to want to check that the person who presents for a medical examination is in fact the person they say that they are. It is of course now standard practice for solicitors—as part of their anti-money laundering duties—to check that their client is, in fact, who they say they are.

8.85 We are told that fraud, malingering and exaggerated claims cost the insurance companies staggeringly large sums of money each year. Nobody wants to act for a client who is lying, but there is often a difficulty in distinguishing the client who is (for want of a better phrase) 'over egging the pudding' to those who are consciously exaggerating for the sake of financial or perhaps other gain. Presenting a solid, evidentially well-supported and truthful claim is essential. Some of the problems arise from increasing client expectations, and from the point of taking instructions it is wise to explain to a client that:

— the insurance company do, and will, check the veracity of the claim;
— they can, and where the claim is contentious, probably will, use surveillance evidence in the case; and
— the court has the power to penalise such claims not only with costs orders, but in the most serious cases with loss of liberty.

8.86 Nobody wants to doubt that their client's claims are genuine, but it is plainly foolhardy to accept what is being said without external evidence, especially where the symptoms appear out of proportion to the incident which caused them.

8.87 The gathering in of external evidence to support a claim is one of the lynchpins of the litigation process. It is important that the solicitor carries out a forensic analysis of such evidence, especially in a claim where the allegations made are somewhat out of proportion with the injury suffered. See paras **8.17–8.20** in respect of actually reading the medical records.

8.88 For example, the client who is involved in a rear-end shunting accident and who suffers a period of post-traumatic stress which is treated with several sessions of therapeutic intervention but who not only fails to recover, but who actively deteriorates over the months following the accident leading to an almost complete meltdown of everyday life. Or the client who, after suffering a minor blow to the head, with no loss of consciousness and no appreciable physical injury, who weeks after the event starts stuttering, on occasion exhibiting word-finding difficulties and intense emotional outbursts. Or the client who fractures a leg, and will not bear weight on it despite being told that the fracture is healed, who takes to a wheelchair and three years after the incident is still substantially disabled. All of the above scenarios are likely to lead to both the claimant and the defendant solicitors' perplexion as to what exactly is going on with that client. The above scenarios, whilst uncommon, do happen relatively regularly enough to warrant serious consideration. One may be exaggeration of 'normal' symptoms, the other malingering and another fraud or a somatisation disorder.

8.89 It is extremely important that good witness evidence is gathered in for all cases, but especially where there is an unusual presentation of symptoms. Often clients who present with 'difficult' problems have difficult lives, maybe few friends or family to support their pre-accident condition. But as far as possible their pre-accident lives should be examined and witness statements taken from such friends, family and work colleagues as will be able to help. Previous work records and claims histories should be obtained. If the client has made a previous claim then it is likely that the insurance company will want the previous solicitor's file (and if that claim is completed then it is discloseable in the current case).

8.90 Whilst costs and criminal sanctions can arise against the fraudulent claimant, it is also possible that a witness who lies can face sanction too. CPR 32.14 provides that proceedings for contempt of court may be brought against a person if he makes, or causes to be made, a false statement in a document verified by a statement of truth without an honest belief in its truth. Proceedings under this rule may be brought only by the Attorney General or with permission of the court. So whilst it is true that a witness who lies in his statement or in court is protected by civil immunity from either prosecution or a costs order against him, he is not under public law proceedings and he may face an order against him for contempt of court[1].

1   *KJM Superbikes Ltd v Anthony James Hinton* [2008] EWCA Civ 1280.

A   Malingering

8.91 In this context, a person malingers when they make up physical or psychological symptoms or illnesses in order to increase the value of their claim. A malingering client may be making up the whole of their claim, or only part of it, the latter being the most common. Malingering is not the same as exaggeration. It is not a separate mental disorder and it is not the same as being a hypochondriac, or having a somatisation disorder or a factitious disorder. Malingering is a fraud on the insurance company and the solicitor acting for the client.

8.92 If the defendants wish to allege malingering, exaggeration or fraud when court proceedings are afoot, there is no 'rule' that they must plead it separately, but CPR 16.5 provides that where the defendant denies an allegation, they must state their reasons for doing so and if they intend to put forward a different version of events from that given by the claimant they must state their own version. Which may in practice be the same thing.

8.93 Malingering is one of a gamut of allegations that can be raised against a client whose honesty of account is in doubt.

Detecting malingering is important. No solicitor wants to act for a client who is intentionally making up a claim.

8.94 If a client is found guilty of fraud, then any conditional fee agreement between the solicitor and barrister and the client will be voided, as will any after the event insurance. This leaves the client having to pay their own legal bill but as the chances of the solicitor being paid in these circumstances is small, in practice it will usually be the solicitor who ends up not only losing their own costs but having to pay any legal disbursements incurred.

B How to detect malingering, fraud and exaggeration

8.95 The most obvious answer here is to support what is being told with external evidence.

The burden is on the claimant to prove his case and this can be difficult where, for example, there is a complex somatoform disorder arising out of what may seem to be a trivial incident. If there is no other explanation for the ongoing symptoms but the accident itself, if all of the witnesses support the claimant's account of ongoing symptoms, if the clinical evidence is supportive for the claimant's ongoing symptoms then the court, in the absence of any external evidence to suggest otherwise, is unlikely to find against the claimant because to do so would be perverse. The defendant's experts may not 'believe' the claimant, but that is not enough without external evidence to support the 'belief' of falsehood or exaggeration. It is for this reason that insurance companies go to great trouble in such cases to delve into a claimant's background history and spend large sums of money engaging in video surveillance. One conviction in adolescence for failing to pay a bus ticket could give their experts grounds for discrediting the claimant Video evidence

8.96 It is good practice to always warn a client, both when taking instructions and strategic times during the life of the claim, that they could be videoed. Video evidence is admissible; it should be disclosed in a timely fashion[1] and it may be disallowed if disclosed late[2]. In that case the evidence was disclosed so late before trial that the experts did not have time to review it. The evidence was available much earlier and the judge was persuaded to disallow it in those circumstances.

1 *Uttley v Uttley* [2002] PIQR P12.
2 *O'Leary v Tunnelcraft Ltd* [2009] EWHC 3438 (QB).

8.97 Video evidence should be carefully reviewed; it is difficult to ascertain 'mood' on a video but the client who states that they are depressed, that they rarely leave the house, and that they get little enjoyment out of life may well find themselves having to explain themselves if videoed going to a rave on a Saturday night.

Symptom Validity Testing (SVT)

8.98 There are a whole variety of tests that doctors have derived to test the validity of a claimant's symptoms, especially in neuropsychological testing for organic brain injury following a head injury. The problem with these tests is that whilst they may well sort out those who have, or do not have, an acquired brain injury, they cannot sort out those who are suffering from psychiatric injury from those who are suffering from cognitive deficits. The solicitor must be careful to question the psychologist administering these tests, as to whether the 'failure' of one of them excludes psychiatric injury.

8 Costs and retainer issues

8.99 The standard issues of costs recovery apply to cases involving psychiatric injury. As the matter presently stands, the client will be advised either with the benefit of legal expense funding, or perhaps trade union funding, and/or a conditional fee agreement provided by the solicitor.

8.100 The problem is that often such clients are extremely demanding of time and attention. Sometimes they fail to answer their letters, or telephone. Sometimes, if they are not already under an incapacity at the time of initially taking instructions, their mental condition deteriorates and a litigation friend has to be appointed. Such issues can cause havoc in their family, or if they have no family, an application to the Official Solicitor must be made. In addition, the solicitor with conduct has to abide by the terms of not only the retainer with the client but the contract with the insurer, and all standard retainers have a clause that states that the client must co-operate, must answer correspondence promptly and must—in essence—be a 'good' client. The solicitor is entitled to break their retainer if the client does not co-operate, and any insurer, who will have regard to their risk, will terminate their agreement with the client in such circumstances. This is obviously a situation of last resort but these problems can creep up upon the instructed solicitor, and the most stressful scenario is that where the client becomes demanding, abusive and complaining within a short period of time, often where they have received a report that they do not like, or whose conclusions they cannot or will not accept. For example, where there is an issue over the aetiology of the injury and a psychiatrist in a report states that the injury is not physical, but psychosomatic. The client may not accept this diagnosis and refuse to accept the contents of the report. What in such circumstances should the solicitor do? Or where the client will not present to medical appointments despite the fact that liability is conceded and the solicitor 'only' has to value the claim.

8.101 Sometimes it is possible to remedy the situation by careful client handling, but in addition to that attention needs to be given to the handling of any legal expense or other insurers. They too will be concerned by the behaviour of the client and in order to keep them on board careful attention needs to be given to reporting the difficulties to them to avoid them pulling the funding map from under the client's feet. There is a wealth of difference between telling the insurers that the client will not respond and explaining carefully why the client will not respond, what the diagnosis is and how the solicitor (and barrister, as invariably by this stage the matter has gone to counsel) intend to try to remedy the situation. Often counsel's opinion will be needed to explain why the costs are escalating, why another medical report needs to be sought or why extra funding needs to be allowed to include a step that may not—on immediate perusal—seem necessary. Sometimes, where the claim is very substantial and the risk seems high, the insurers can be invited to a conference to discuss the difficulties.

8.102 There may well be a very substantial cost investment in the case to date, yet the client who is behaving in a way that is completely contrary to either his or his solicitor's interests causes immense problems to the solicitor. The ability to break a retainer may well get the solicitor out of the ethical minefield of sacking a client they can no longer cope with, but if the client is without means to discharge outstanding legal costs, and the case is being run on a conditional fee basis then substantial fees will be forgone in a case where there is no realistic prospect of recovery even where the case is for all intents and purposes 'won'.

8.103 There are no easy answers to the issue of losing control of a client—because that, in reality, is what has happened. All solicitors who deal with personal injury cases develop, some more successfully than others, the ability to deal with difficult client situations. But some clients cannot be persuaded. If it is not possible to get a client to co-operate, and that client is not a patient (and that area must be explored: see Chapter 9) then after all effort has been made, the client must be asked to find another solicitor and the solicitor must come off the court record. Plenty of notice must be given to the client before this step is taken, and the wise solicitor reminds the non-cooperative client sensitively and carefully both verbally—if possible—and certainly in writing before taken this step. If there is insurance, then notice should be given to the insurers who will certainly wish to withdraw their indemnity. It is a fact though that sometimes the situation is beyond remedy and the client who has capacity, but who will not co-operate, or who in their 'co-operation' causes havoc in the office, causes a series of demands that are totally unreasonable, and who will not accept the reasonable evidence gotten in, must be asked to find help elsewhere.

8.104 What about the client whose case has been settled, but who has been so demanding that the costs of running the case are much more substantial than expected?

The standard basis for assessment of costs is that the winner is allowed such costs that are reasonable and proportionate in the circumstances. In considering whether or not the costs were proportionate, the court must have regard to all the circumstances (CPR 44.5).

8.105 One of the issues when dealing with clients who have a psychiatric illness is that they can be extremely difficult to manage. It is not unusual for the solicitor to have to carry out substantially more work than when dealing with a client who is mentally stable. Is it then the case that those costs will form part of the solicitor and own client element of the bill, or it is possible to ask the defendants to pay 'extra' costs incurred because the client is far more demanding as a result of their condition. If so, is there a difference between when the condition is pre-existing or the condition has been caused by the conduct of the defendants and what happens, if there is a difference, to those costs where it is difficult or impossible to distinguish between that difference?

8.106 The current answer to that question can be found in the case of *Evason v Essex Health Authority*[1]. Although old, it is still the appropriate authority for this principle that the defendants must pay for that which they caused, and if they caused the psychological problems, or caused damage to somebody who already had psychological problems then extra costs incurred should fall at their feet.

1 QB review of taxation by Webster J and Assessors (7 April 1992, QBD, reported in Law Society Gazette, 13 July 1994).

8.107 In *Evason*, a Queen's Bench Review of Taxation by Webster J and Assessors, Mrs Evason was told she had a cancerous condition when she did not. She underwent various surgeries for this and believed she was in a terminal state. She lost her husband and her job and she developed significant psychological problems as a result. In the judgment it was said:

'the Plaintiff had suffered an unusual and appalling wrong and ... it is common ground that as a result of the error and its immediate consequence the Plaintiff developed and has continued to suffer from a serious degree of psychological disturbance and that, in consequence, she required much more attention and reassurance then a Plaintiff would normally need'.

The court found that it should take into account, 'for the purposes of taxation, her special and unusual needs for personal attendance'. As a result of this her legal costs, which had been significantly reduced at first instance, were restored on appeal. On review it was held that the costs judge at first instance should have taken the plaintiff as he found her after the incident and should have taken into account for the purposes of taxation her special and unusual needs for personal attendance.

9 The Mental Capacity Act 2005

9.1 When acting for a client who has suffered a psychiatric injury, the legal adviser must be alert from the outset to identify whether their client lacks capacity to make decisions.

9.2 It is a fundamental principle of the Mental Capacity Act 2005 that a person shall be presumed to have capacity unless it is established that he lacks capacity[1]. The nature of the injury will determine the adviser's approach. A severe head injury causing profound cognitive impairment may leave little room for doubt. A client suffering clinical depression following a life-changing experience may at first seem able to make decisions. However as the case progresses the legal adviser may slowly become aware that his client is unable to instruct him on the issues in the case or to make decisions about his life. A working knowledge of the Mental Capacity Act 2005 is therefore an essential tool for the personal injury practitioner advising in cases of psychiatric injury.

1   Mental Capacity Act 2005, s 1(1).

1 Historical perspective

9.3 There has been legal protection for the assets and financial affairs of those who lack capacity for many centuries. The Court of Protection was constituted as a statutory body by the Mental Health Act 1959, Part VIII, reaffirmed by the Mental Health Act 1983, Part VII. Those who were by reason of mental disorder incapable of managing their property and affairs came under the jurisdiction of the Master of the Court of Protection. He did not have powers in relation to personal welfare and health and medical treatment decisions for those who lacked capacity. These were resolved by judges in the High Court exercising their inherent jurisdiction. Registration of Enduring Power of Attorney and applications in relation to them were added to the Court of Protection's responsibilities by the Enduring Powers of Attorney Act 1985.

9.4 The Court of Protection was, until 1 October 2007, an office of the Supreme Court of Judicature responsible for managing the property and affairs of those subject to the jurisdiction of the court, known as 'Patients'. The court was headed by the Master of the Court of Protection. Administrative support was provided by the Public Guardianship Office. Receivers, usually family members or professionals, were appointed to handle day-to-day finances. The investment strategy for large funds and most major decisions on the spending of the patient's money were referred back to the court. Many receivers disliked what they perceived as intrusive and over-controlling management of the patient's funds. The court also authorised the making of statutory wills, settlement or gift of a patient's property and applications under the Trustee Act 1925 in respect of jointly owned and other trust property.

9.5 Procedure in the court after the making of the First General Order was relatively informal. Receivers, patients and family members were used to writing to or telephoning the court in order to obtain a decision without needing to follow a formal procedure with applications, witness evidence and service on affected parties. The Civil Procedure Rules 1998 did not apply to the Court of Protection.

9.6 Costs were determined at the discretion of the court. Rather than costs following the event, where a party had acted in good faith in making an application to the court and was able to show grounds for the application, it was likely that their costs would be paid out of the funds of the patient even if unsuccessful.

2 The new legislation

9.7 The Mental Capacity Act 2005 came into effect on 1 October 2007. It sets out a comprehensive framework within which to approach the issue of decision-making by a person whose capacity is in doubt (referred to as 'P' throughout the Act). It covers decision-making in property and affairs, personal welfare and health. It incorporates the provisions of the Enduring Powers of Attorney Act 1985 and introduces Lasting Powers of Attorney. It defines the circumstances in which advance decisions on medical treatment may be made. It provides for the appointment of independent mental capacity advocates (IMCAs). It sets out the powers of the Court of Protection and the Public Guardian and the relationship between them.

9.8 The Act is supported by the Court of Protection Rules 2007 which comprehensively define the procedures of the court. The Civil Procedure Rules 1998 and Family Procedure Rules 2010 do not apply to applications in the Court of Protection.

9.9 The Act is also supported by a Code of Practice, which gives helpful guidance including examples of typical scenarios in which questions of capacity may arise. Section 42 of the Act sets out the duty of those carrying out functions under the Act or acting in a professional capacity and/or for remuneration to have regard to the Code. The Court of Protection must take into account a provision of the Code, or failure to have regard to it, if it is relevant to the decision the court has to make.

9.10 The Lasting Powers of Attorney, Enduring Powers of Attorney and Public Guardian Regulations 2007[1] may also be of relevance, should the client have signed a Lasting Power of Attorney or Enduring Power of Attorney.

1   SI 2007/1253.

3 The Court of Protection

9.11 When the Mental Capacity Act 2005 came into force, the Court of Protection underwent a profound change. Until that day the Master of the Court of Protection and the Public Guardian had been in charge of a department with one body of staff and set of files. The Mental Capacity Act 2005 separated out the Court of Protection from the

Public Guardian, who would from then on be a party in proceedings before the court. The informal and inquisitorial nature of the court was replaced by a formal court process with the Senior Judge and District Judges as arbiters and decision-makers. The ambit of the court's jurisdiction was widened to cover not only the property and affairs of the incapacitated person but also decisions about their personal welfare. It is perhaps not surprising that it has taken time for practitioners and indeed the court itself to come to terms with its new role.

9.12 The function of the Court of Protection is to make those decisions for P which he is unable to make for himself. The powers and responsibilities of the Court of Protection are defined in the Mental Capacity Act 2005. It is a court created by statute and has only those powers which are given to it by statute. It does, however, have jurisdiction to deal with arguments raised on behalf of P which rely on breaches of rights under the European Convention on Human Rights and to make declarations of incompatability and grant declaratory relief in respect of them[1]. In exercising its jurisdiction the Court of Protection has the same powers, rights, privileges and authority as the High Court (s 47(1)).

1   Mental Capacity Act 2005, Sch 6, para 43 and *YA(F) v A Local Authority* [2010] EWHC 2770.

9.13 The Court of Protection is unable to determine any issue outside the framework of the Mental Capacity Act 2005. Thus, for example, it cannot determine whether or not P has an interest in a jointly-owned property, although it can take a decision on P's behalf as to whether or not that property should be sold or charged or given away and can appoint a litigation friend to take proceedings about the ownership of the property in another court.

4   The principles of the Mental Capacity Act 2005

9.14   Section 1 of the Act sets out the principles on which the Act is based.

(1) The following principles apply for the purposes of this Act.

(2) A person must be assumed to have capacity unless it is established that he lacks capacity.

(3) A person is not to be treated as unable to make a decision unless all practicable steps to help him to do so have been taken without success.

(4) A person is not to be treated as unable to make a decision merely because he makes an unwise decision.

(5) An act done or decision made under this Act for or on behalf of a person who lacks capacity must be done, or made, in his best interests.

(6) Before the act is done, or the decision is made, regard must be had to whether the purpose for which it is needed can be as effectively achieved in a way that is less restrictive of the person's rights and freedom of action.

A   Presumption of capacity

9.15   This is the starting point for the court's consideration of any issue it is called upon to decide. The court's jurisdiction is not engaged in relation to any decision until there is a finding of incapacity (save in relation to the validity of Lasting Powers of Attorney). Section 48 of the Act allows the court to make interim declarations and orders or give directions. The court may not at that point be able to make a determination as to capacity. However no order can be made under s 48 unless the court has reason to believe that P lacks capacity in relation to the matter. Thus there must be some evidence before the court that P does not have capacity, whether medical or witness evidence, which gives rise to a reasonable belief that P may lack capacity. Until the court makes a declaration as to capacity, whether interim or final, P must be assumed to have capacity and therefore be capable of making decisions about his life. As soon as the court is satisfied that P has regained capacity, its jurisdiction is terminated. Any deputyships must be discharged and any orders of the court affecting P will be of no further effect.

B Practical steps to help P make the decision for himself

9.16 This principle requires those concerned with P to think beyond the immediate appearance of incapacity and consider to what extent P is unable to make a decision because he has been deprived of the tools of communication to enable him to impart a decision. A person who has suffered a stroke or who has cerebral palsy may be unable to speak or read, yet they may be able to make choices and express wishes through responding to yes/no questions by a nod of the head or blink of an eye. A person who cannot read or write may be able to communicate through pictures. All that such people may require is assistance to communicate their decisions.

9.17 Where someone is already struggling with decision making, the constraints imposed by such conditions may be the final obstacle to making complex decisions. However the principle remains that P should be given all practicable help to make the decisions that he is able to make before a finding of incapacity is made. Even if assistance with communication is not sufficient to give P the capacity to make a decision, it may enable him to express his wishes and feelings (see 'Best interests' below). 'Practicable help' allows consideration of the time, expense and feasibility of helping P to make the decision.

C Unwise decisions

9.18 It is tempting when someone makes a decision which we feel is unwise to take that decision as evidence of incapacity to manage property and affairs. Yet many people whose capacity is not in doubt make unwise decisions as to how they spend their money, with whom they have relationships or spend time, who should be their solicitor and on many other matters. This principle is a warning to all decision-makers to follow the framework for deciding on capacity in the Mental Capacity Act 2005 and not to leap to conclusions based on what may seem an ill-advised action.

D Best interests

9.19 This is discussed below.

E Least restrictive option

9.20 This duty requires the decision-maker to consider whether the course of action he proposes is necessary or whether there is an alternative which would give P more control and autonomy on the issue in question. For example, a local authority might seek an order to be appointed a deputy for property and affairs for P so that they could enter into a tenancy agreement on his behalf. P's income and savings are all derived from state benefits, for which he has an appointee. All that is needed is an order from the court giving authority for a nominated officer of the local authority to sign the tenancy agreement. There is no need for a full deputyship order giving total control of P's finances to the local authority.

9.21 However while regard must be had to this principle, it is not determinative. The court has to decide what is in P's best interests and it may decide that the more restrictive alternative is best for P.

5 People who lack capacity

9.22 Section 2(1) of the Act sets out the *diagnostic* test:

> 'a person lacks capacity in relation to a matter if at the material time he is unable to make a decision for himself in relation to the matter because of an impairment of, or a disturbance in the functioning of the mind or brain'.

The words 'at the material time' show that the powers of the court can only be invoked for the period during which P lacks capacity and must be abjured if he regains capacity. Thus any evidence about capacity must address the issue of capacity to do an act or take a decision at the time of the application, not in the past. If the court's order is likely to affect future decisions and actions, then the court must have evidence that P will lack capacity at the time they are to be done or made.

9.23 Impairment or disturbance in the functioning of the mind or brain is a wide definition encompassing mental illnesses, cognitive deficits which may be caused by genetic defects, birth injury or acquired brain injury, organic brain disease and dementia.

Section 2(2) specifically states that it does not matter whether the impairment or disturbance is permanent or temporary.

9.24 Section 2(3) underlines the importance of not jumping to conclusions about a person's capacity but going through the process of the diagnostic and functional tests carefully. It states that a lack of capacity cannot be established merely by:

(a) reference to a person's age or appearance; or
(b) a condition of his or an aspect of his behaviour which might lead others to make unjustified assumptions about his capacity.

6 Inability to make a decision

9.25 Section 3(1) of the Act sets out the *functional* test:

For the purposes of s 2 a person is unable to make a decision for himself if he is unable:

(a) to understand the information relevant to the decision;
(b) to retain that information;
(c) to use or weigh that information as part of the process of making the decision; or
(d) to communicate his decision (whether by talking, using sign language or any other means).

A 'To understand the information relevant to the decision'

9.26 P must be able to understand the facts surrounding the decision, what the decision entails, why it is needed and what the consequences will be. Section 3(4) states that the information relevant to a decision includes the reasonably foreseeable consequences of deciding one way or another or of failing to make a decision.

9.27 Section 3(2) provides that a person is not to be regarded as unable to understand the information relevant to a decision if he is able to understand an explanation of it given to him in a way that is appropriate to his circumstances (using simple language, visual aids or any other means).

B 'To retain that information'

9.28 If P is unable to retain the information relevant to the decision he will be unable to move on to the next arm of the functional test, whether he can use or weigh the information.

9.29 The Act recognises that a degree of short-term memory loss may not impede the decision-making process; s 3(2) states that the fact that a person is able to retain the information relevant to a decision for a short period only does not prevent him from being regarded as able to make the decision. It is a question of fact in each case whether P, with the help of notes or reminders, is able to marshall the information needed for the decision and to use or weigh that information and come to a decision. The complexity of the information and ramifications of the decision will have a bearing on P's ability to do this.

C 'To use or weigh that information as part of the process of making the decision'

9.30 P must be capable of putting together the information required to make the decision, retaining that information and then weighing up the pros and cons of deciding between two alternatives or between acting and not acting.

9.31 In a situation where a client at first appears to have capacity, with no difficulty in remembering or retaining the advice given to him, it is this arm of the functional test that may reveal a lack of capacity. The inability to give proper weight to the risks of taking a particular course of action or failure to appreciate that inaction may result in negative consequences are examples of a failure to use or weigh information.

D 'To communicate his decision (whether by talking, using sign language or any other means'

9.32 In the light of s 1(3) above, this test will not impute lack of capacity to those who have very limited means of communication but can nonetheless communicate decisions even if only with the blink of an eyelid or nod of the head. Where a person is completely unable to communicate in any way, for example a person with locked in syndrome, and thus cannot engage in the decision-making process this part of the functional test brings him within the group of those who lack capacity.

7 Passing the test for incapacity

9.33 In order for the jurisdiction of the Court of Protection to be engaged P must pass both the diagnostic and the functional test. If a person suffers from learning disability but is able to make and hold to a decision if presented with the information in a way he can understand, he will have passed the diagnostic but not the functional test. If P appears to be unable or unwilling to understand what is said to him or to engage in a decision-making process but does not suffer from any form of mental illness or cognitive impairment then (even though his affairs may be suffering as a result of his failure to decide) he has not passed the diagnostic test and the court has no jurisdiction.

9.34 Any question whether a person lacks capacity within the meaning of the Act must be made on the balance of probabilities (s 2(4)).

9.35 The tests must be applied in relation to a particular decision. A person who is unable to manage his property and affairs may still have testamentary capacity. A person who can make decisions about contact with his family may not be able to make a decision about where he should live.

9.36 If P passes the diagnostic and the functional test then the decision-maker (for example the doctor in charge of P's medical treatment court or a deputy appointed to make decisions about property and affairs or the court) can make the decision in question. Any decision made by the court must be made in the best interests of P.

8 Best interests checklist

9.37 There is no definition of 'best interests' in the Mental Capacity Act 2005. The decision-maker is simply required to consider all the relevant circumstances in relation to the specific decision which must be taken for P by taking the steps set out in the best interests checklist. The Code of Practice says:

> 'It is important that the best interests principle and the statutory checklist are flexible. Without flexibility it would be impossible to prioritise factors in different cases, and it would be difficult to ensure that the outcome is the best possible for the person who lacks capacity ... Some cases will be straightforward. Others will require decision-makers to balance the pros and cons of all relevant factors'[1].

---

1 At para 5.62.

9.38 The best interests checklist is set out in the Mental Capacity Act 2005, s 4:

'(1) In determining for the purposes of this Act what is in a person's best interests, the person making the determination must not make it merely on the basis of—
(a) the person's age or appearance, or
(b) a condition of his, or an aspect of his behaviour, which might lead others to make unjustified assumptions about what might be in his best interests.

(2) The person making the determination must consider all the relevant circumstances and, in particular, take the following steps.

(3) He must consider—
(a) whether it is likely that the person will at some time have capacity in relation to the matter in question, and
(b) if it appears likely that he will, when that is likely to be.

(4) He must, so far as reasonably practicable, permit and encourage the person to participate, or to improve his ability to participate, as fully as possible in any act done for him and any decision affecting him.

(5) Where the determination relates to life-sustaining treatment he must not, in considering whether the treatment is in the best interests of the person concerned, be motivated by a desire to bring about his death.

(6) He must consider, so far as is reasonably ascertainable—
(a) the person's past and present wishes and feelings (and, in particular, any relevant written statement made by him when he had capacity),
(b) the beliefs and values that would be likely to influence his decision if he had capacity, and
(c) the other factors that he would be likely to consider if he were able to do so.

(7) He must take into account, if it is practicable and appropriate to consult them, the views of—
(a) anyone named by the person as someone to be consulted on the matter in question or on matters of that kind,
(b) anyone engaged in caring for the person or interested in his welfare,
(c) any donee of a lasting power of attorney granted by the person, and
(d) any deputy appointed for the person by the court,
as to what would be in the person's best interests and, in particular, as to the matters mentioned in subsection (6).

(8) The duties imposed by subsections (1) to (7) also apply in relation to the exercise of any powers which—
(a) are exercisable under a lasting power of attorney, or
(b) are exercisable by a person under this Act where he reasonably believes that another person lacks capacity.

(9) In the case of an act done, or a decision made, by a person other than the court, there is sufficient compliance with this section if (having complied with the requirements of subsections (1) to (7)) he reasonably believes that what he does or decides is in the best interests of the person concerned.

(10) 'Life-sustaining treatment' means treatment which in the view of a person providing health care for the person concerned is necessary to sustain life.

(11) 'Relevant circumstances' are those—
(a) of which the person making the determination is aware, and
(b) which it would be reasonable to regard as relevant'.

9.39 Section 4(1) and 4(3) require the court or decision-maker to avoid assumptions based on a person's attributes, appearance or behaviour and to facilitate the active engagement of P in the decision-making process so far as is possible. They mirror ss 2(3) and 3(2) discussed above, but in the context of establishing best interests for P who lacks capacity rather than deciding whether or not he has capacity in the first place. The decision-maker must consider all the relevant circumstances (s 4(2) and 4(11)) and must take the steps set out in s 4(3)–(7).

9.40 Section 4(6) requires the decision-maker to consider what P would have wanted or would have done. If P has made a written statement (for example a will or Enduring Power of Attorney or Lasting Power of Attorney) that may provide useful indications about the person he wanted to look after his affairs or what he wanted done with them. P may be able to express some wishes or feelings about the decision now. There may be evidence as to what he said about the decision in the past when he still had capacity.

9.41 The decision-maker also has to consider the beliefs and values of P. Even if there is no specific evidence of his wishes and feelings, his past decisions or statements may reveal principles of great importance to him: greater or lesser attachment to family and friends, religious beliefs or attitudes towards money which may be relevant.

9.42 However the Mental Capacity Act 2005 does not require the decision-maker to make the decision on the basis of what P would have done if he had had capacity. That could result in the decision-maker making a decision for P which is not in his best interests, for example an unwise decision. When P is able to express wishes and feelings about a decision they will be a very important element in the best interests consideration but they are not conclusive. The decision-maker can still make a different decision if in his view all the relevant circumstances lead him to the conclusion that it is in P's best interests. There is some conflicting case law on this point. The primacy of P's wishes and feelings have been discussed in a number of recent cases[1].

1   *Re S and S (Protected Persons), In the matter of P* [2009] EWHC 163 (Ch); *ITW v Z* [2009] EWHC 2525 (Fam).

9.43 Section 4(7) identifies the people who must be consulted by the decision-maker if it is practical and appropriate. There is no specific requirement to consult family members but only those engaged in caring for P or interested in his welfare. That may well include family but allows for the situation in which those most concerned for P are his friends rather than family from whom he is estranged. It may be very expensive or likely to cause considerable delay to consult certain family or friends. It may create a difficult situation if there has been a breakdown in relationships. In those circumstances it may be not practical or appropriate to do so.

9.44 Section 4(8) provides for a decision made by the court or another decision-maker for someone who retains capacity. The court has a power to make decisions about the validity of a Lasting Power of Attorney which may be registered by a donor while they still have capacity. The person for whom the decision is made may turn out to have capacity after all, although that was not known at the time. The best interests checklist must also be applied for those decisions.

9.45 Section 4(9) sets out that a decision-maker other than the court must reasonably believe that the decision he has made is in the best interests of P. This is an objective test. The decision maker must be able to establish, by showing how he reached his decision employing the criteria in the best interests checklist, why he reached the view that his decision was a reasonable one.

9.46 In making a decision for P the decision-maker must take the steps required by the best interests checklist and having done so weigh up what act or decision is in the best interests of P. Some of the steps may not be relevant but they should be considered if only to be discarded. There is no one factor which is more important than the others per se. In some cases the decision may be finely balanced. In others there may be a factor of 'magnetic importance', for example P's wishes and feelings. However the decision-maker still has to weigh up all the factors before making the decision or taking the action in question.

9   Children who lack capacity

9.47 The Mental Capacity Act 2005 does not apply to any person under 16 (s 2(5)). Until the age of 18 the family courts have jurisdiction in relation to incapacitated minors. Between 16 and 18 there is an overlap in jurisdiction. The family court may decide to transfer to the Court of Protection the case of a person lacking the capacity to make a decision in relation to residence or contact who is approaching his 18th birthday, because the decision which is to be taken is likely to affect his life well beyond his 18th birthday. The Court of Protection may decide to refer a decision regarding contact with family members for a 17-year-old to the family court dealing with other members of the family.

9.48 There is one exception to this provision, which is found in the Mental Capacity Act 2005, s 18(3) (and see s 2(6)). The powers under s 16 to make decisions and appoint deputies in relation to property and affairs can be exercised even though P has not yet reached 16 if the court considers it likely that P will still lack capacity to make decisions in respect of that matter when he reaches 18. This applies to all the powers listed in s 18(1) except the power to make a statutory will which cannot be done until P reaches the age of 18 (s 18(2)). This allows the court to appoint deputies for children who have suffered brain injury at an early stage. The medical evidence in support of the application has to address the issue of whether it is likely P will be unable to make decisions about his property and affairs once he reaches the age of 18.

10   Acts in connection with care or treatment

9.49 Given the comprehensive scope of the Mental Capacity Act 2005, the protection previously provided by the common law doctrine of necessity for those caring for a person lacking capacity needed to be defined. Sections 5 and 6 deal with this issue.

9.50 A person caring or providing treatment for P (described as 'D') must first establish that P lacks capacity and when doing the act must reasonably believe that P lacks capacity in relation to the matter and that it will be in P's best interests for the act to be done. If those conditions are fulfilled then D will not incur any liability for the act that he would not have incurred if P had had capacity to consent and had consented to that act being done (s 5(1) and (2)).

Nothing in the section excludes D's civil liability for loss or damage or his criminal liability, resulting from his negligence in doing the act (s 5(3)).

9.51 Section 6 sets out limitations on s 5 acts. Section 6(1)–(4) deals with limitations on s 5 acts in relation to the use of restraint. Section 6(6) prevents D from doing an act which conflicts with a proper decision made by a donee of a Lasting Power of Attorney or deputy. Section 6(7) provides protection for a D providing life sustaining treatment or treatment to prevent serious deterioration in P's condition while a decision of the court is sought.

A Powers of the court

9.52 By s 15 the court may make declarations as to:

(a) whether a person has or lacks capacity to make a decision specified in the declaration;
(b) whether a person has or lacks capacity to make decisions on such matters as are described in the declaration;
(c) the lawfulness of any act done or yet to be done in relation to that person.

9.53 By s 16(2) when a person lacks capacity in relation to a matter or matters concerning P's personal welfare or P's property and affairs, the court can make the decision for them or can appoint a deputy to make the decision or do the act.

9.54 When considering whether to make the decision itself or to appoint a deputy the court must have regard to the principle that:

(a) a decision by the court is to be preferred to the appointment of a deputy to make a decision; and
(b) the powers conferred on a deputy should be as limited in scope and duration as is reasonably practicable in the circumstances (s 16(4)).

9.55 This principle reiterates the importance of limiting as far as possible the interference with P's control over his own affairs. A decision by the court is focused and made with the input of all relevant parties. Appointment of a deputy hands over control of all decision-making in a particular sphere.

Deputies can be appointed to act alone, jointly or jointly and severally.

9.56 If a deputy is appointed the order may be for a limited period of time if, for example, recovery is expected. The order may limit the authorisation given to the deputy, for example to decisions about contact and social activities but not decisions about residence.

9.57 Chapter 8 of the Code of Practice provides some helpful guidance on this issue. In practice the Court of Protection will generally be ready to appoint a deputy to manage P's property and affairs but will be reluctant to appoint a personal welfare deputy unless there really is justification for it.

B Litigation capacity

9.58 In civil proceedings a person who lacks capacity must have a litigation friend to conduct proceedings on his behalf. Part 21 of the Civil Proceedure Rules 1998 is the relevant rule. In the past capacity to litigate has been assessed according to the test set out in the Mental Health Act 1983, Part VII. The landmark case of *Masterman Lister v Brutton & Co*[1] was an important stepping stone towards the institution of the issue specific approach to capacity embodied in the Mental Capacity Act 2005.

1   [2002] EWCA Civ 1889.

9.59 The Civil Procedure (Amendment) Rules 2007 created a new Part 21 of the CPR 1998 to give effect to the changes made by the Mental Capacity Act 2005. They created new terminology: a person who lacks capacity to litigate is a protected party and a person who receives an award of damages is a protected beneficiary. The case of *Saulle v Nouvet*[1] made it clear that the civil courts were required to adopt the new definition of capacity set out in the Mental Capacity Act 2005. However the Mental Capacity Act 2005 does not itself give the Court of Protection any jurisdiction over civil proceedings.

1   [2007] EWHC 2902 (QB).

9.60 The test set out in the case of *Masterman Lister* was 'whether the party to legal proceedings is capable of understanding with the assistance of such proper explanation from legal advisers and experts in other disciplines as the case may require, the issues on which his consent or decision is likely to be necessary in the course of those proceedings'. That test can be applied using the approach required by the Mental Capacity Act 2005 to determine whether or not the litigant has capacity.

9.61 Capacity to litigate is issue-specific, in line with the general approach of the Mental Capacity Act 2005. A litigant may have capacity to litigate in respect of one claim yet lack the capacity to litigate in another. The test for capacity set out in the Mental Capacity Act 2005, ss 1–3 must be applied in each claim.

9.62 The Court of Protection can take evidence and make a declaration as to capacity to litigate pursuant to the Mental Capacity Act 2005, s 15. It has power under s 16 and s 18(1)(k) of the Act to make decisions about the conduct of legal proceedings in P's name or on P's behalf and to appoint a person to act as litigation friend. It may appoint a litigation friend for P in proceedings within the Court of Protection. An order of the Court of Protection appointing a litigation friend for proceedings in another court enables the litigation friend to institute proceedings without filing a certificate of suitability[1].

1   CPR 1998, r 21.5.

9.63 However there is no authority for the proposition that those powers allow the decision of Court of Protection on capacity to litigate to preempt or replace the decision of the court seised of the matter. An application to the Court of Protection to overturn a decision made in a personal injury claim in the QBD as to whether the claimant lacks capacity to litigate or to manage his property and affairs is likely to be unsuccessful. Expert evidence in the personal injury claim will include evidence from neurologists, neuropsychologists or neuropsychiatrists as to litigation capacity and capacity to manage property and affairs. This may be a hotly-contested issue, with a significant impact on the size of the final award of damages. The judge in the QBD is best placed to understand the nature of the issues at stake and to determine from the conduct of the action by P whether or not he has capacity to litigate. Litigation capacity may fluctuate. The litigation friend may be appointed and discharged, perhaps more than once. It is submitted that it would not be appropriate or proportionate in relation to costs for a separate application to be made to the Court of Protection to determine litigation capacity in an action which is outside its jurisdiction or for the Court of Protection to seek to bind another court by a declaration as to litigation capacity. CPR 1998, r 21.6 provides that the court can appoint a litigation friend. CPR 1998, r 21.7 empowers the court to change the litigation friend. If the court has appointed a litigation friend then a deputy appointed by an order of the Court of Protection is not entitled to be the litigation friend[1].

1   CPR 1998, r 21.4(1).

9.64 An application for appointment of a litigation friend should be supported by medical evidence as to capacity in relation to the particular issues in the claim. Practitioners should also consider filing a witness statement setting out their experience of taking instructions and giving advice to P, which will frequently be of equal weight to the medical evidence in determining whether P is 'capable of understanding with the assistance of such proper explanation from legal advisers and experts in other disciplines as the case may require, the issues on which his consent or decision is likely to be necessary'.

11 Managing property and affairs

9.65 Once liability issues are resolved in favour of the claimant so that an award of damages is likely to be made, the legal adviser needs to consider whether his client is able to manage that award. Compensation to cover a lifetime of need has to be carefully managed to provide income and capital over the whole period of loss. Psychiatric injury may interfere with the claimant's ability to do this.

9.66 Before an application for appointment of a deputy for property and affairs is made, the legal adviser should establish whether the claimant has signed an Enduring Power of Attorney or a Lasting Power of Attorney (Property and Affairs) appointing someone to manage their property and affairs in the event that they lose capacity to do so. Older clients are more likely to have done this. The Enduring Power of Attorney or Lasting Power of Attorney sets out P's choice and wishes in relation to management of his affairs. Generally the Court of Protection will seek to give effect to those wishes rather than appointing a deputy for property and affairs. If not already registered, an application must be made to the Public Guardian for registration of the instrument. If the Attorney does not feel up to the task of managing a substantial award of damages he may disclaim the appointment by written notice to the Public Guardian in the case of an Enduring Power of Attorney or by completing and filing the appropriate form in the case of a Lasting Power of Attorney. Alternatively an order revoking the appointment can be made by the court with the consent of the Attorney.

9.67 The court will generally not make an order appointing a deputy for property and affairs if P's income and savings are derived only from state benefits. The appropriate course is then for the Department of Work and Pensions to appoint an appointee; the Court of Protection has no role in this. Once P's savings are substantial, the range of powers and costs of a deputy may be justifiable. Where P is expected to receive a personal injury award, the court may appoint a deputy in anticipation of an interim or final award, while P's estate is still minimal. As noted above the court will appoint a deputy for property and affairs for a P under 16 years of age pursuant to s 18(3) if the court considers it likely that P will still lack capacity to make decisions in respect of property and affairs when he reaches 18.

9.68 Section 18 sets out particular powers in relation to P's property and affairs which may be exercised by the court or the deputy. These are not exhaustive. The general authority given to the deputy by the standard wording of the deputyship order allows the deputy to 'take possession or control of the property and affairs of P and to exercise the same powers of management and investment as he has as beneficial owner, subject to the terms and conditions set out in the order'.

9.69 The particular powers identified in the section are:
(a) the control and management of P's property;
(b) the sale, exchange, charging, gift or other disposition of P's property;
(c) the acquisition of property in P's name or on P's behalf;
(d) the carrying on, on P's behalf of any profession trade or business;
(e) the taking of a decision which will have the effect of dissolving a partnership of which P is a member;
(f) the carrying out of any contract entered into by P;
(g) the discharge of P's debts and of any of P's obligations, whether legally enforceable or not;
(h) the settlement of any of P's property, whether for P's benefit or for the benefit of others;
(i) the execution for P of a will;
(j) the exercise of any power (including a power to consent) vested in P whether beneficially or as trustee or otherwise;
(k) the conduct of legal proceedings in P's name or on P's behalf.

9.70 Schedule 2 to the Act sets out some supplementary provisions with regard to the making of statutory wills, which must be approved by the Court of Protection on a separate application, and with regard to settlements and other interests in property.

Claimants in personal injury cases have been advised that a personal injury trust should be set up to receive damages awards. Where the claimant is a protected party the approval of the Court of Protection must be obtained to the formation of such a trust. An application must be issued and the Official Solicitor is generally appointed to represent the interests of P in the application. A recent judgment by HHJ Marshall[1] sets out the matters that the court is likely to consider in coming to a decision as to whether a trust or a deputyship is in the best interests of P.

1   *SM v HM by the Official Solicitor* (COP case no 11875043).

9.71   Section 19 sets out provisions in relation to the appointment of deputies. Deputies may be lay deputies, usually a member of the family or a close friend. They may be professional deputies. The Public Guardian maintains a panel of professional deputies who may be invited to act by the court if a deputyship or attorneyship has been revoked or P is otherwise in need of someone to manage their property and affairs. A trust corporation may be deputy for property and affairs (but not for personal welfare)[1]. Where P's estate is substantial the court will need to be satisfied that a lay deputy has the experience and skills to manage that estate; involvement of a professional deputy whether sole or acting jointly with a family member may be preferred.

1   Mental Capacity Act 2005, s 19(1)(b).

9.72   Section 19(9) gives the court power to require a deputy to give to the Public Guardian such security as the court thinks fit for the due discharge of his function and to submit to the Public Guardian such reports at such times or at such intervals as the court may direct.

9.73   The court will invariably require the deputy to give security as protection for P against fraudulent or negligent default. While the court does have power to approve other security, the vast majority of deputyships are bonded through a deputyship bond scheme currently administered by Marsh Brokers Ltd. This scheme provides two unique protections for P: payment is made on the bond within 14 days without enquiry in the event of default, thus ensuring that P's needs will continue to be met, and security cannot be cancelled without order of the court. Any application to provide alternative security will have to address those protections to persuade the court that it is in P's best interests.

9.74   The setting and amount of the security can be controversial. They were the subject of a detailed judgment by HHJ Marshall in the matter of H[1]. Considerations as to security affect the wording of the deputyship order and extent of the unfettered authority given to deputies. Inevitably because of the much greater control and independence that deputies now have in the management of P's financial affairs, the level of security is higher than it was before the Mental Capacity Act 2005 came into effect.

1   *Baker v H and the Official Solicitor as amicus curiae* COP11461874.

12   Making an application to the Court of Protection

9.75   An application to the Court of Protection must be made on Form COP1 accompanied by the relevant supporting documentation.

9.76 For an application to be appointed property and affairs deputy, the forms required are COP1 (Application form), COP1A (Annex A supporting information for property and affairs applications), COP3 (Assessment of capacity) and COP4 (Deputy's declaration). These forms are also required for an application to be appointed litigation friend for P.

9.77 For an application to be appointed personal welfare deputy the forms required are COP1 (Application form), COP1B (Annex B supporting information for personal welfare applications), COP2 (Permission form), COP3 (Assessment of capacity) and COP4 (Deputy's declaration).

A Application for property and affairs deputyship

COP1 Application form

9.78 In this form the applicant must set out the order he wants the court to make. He is also required to identify the parties to be served or notified of the application.

9.79 It is essential that P is notified of the application. Notification of P is covered by the Court of Protection Rules 2007, Part 7. The Rules set out what information must be given to P. Rule 46 states that the person effecting notification must provide P with the required information in a way that is appropriate to P's circumstances. Rule 49 deals with an application to dispense with notification. The Court of Protection will only rarely agree to dispense with notification of P. Practice Direction 7A9 states that an application to dispense with notification of P:

> 'would be appropriate where for example P is in a permanent vegetative state or a minimally conscious state; or where notification by the applicant is likely to cause significant and disproportionate distress to P'.

Even if P cannot understand or retain information about his property and affairs, he is entitled to know that someone is dealing with his affairs for him and to know who that person is.

9.80 The Court of Protection also expects that other interested parties will be made aware of the application, whether through service or notification. Notification of parties is dealt with in Court of Protection Rules Part 9 PD9B. The practice direction identifies people who must be notified (para 10) and sets out the approach to notification of family and friends. Service of documents is dealt with in Part 6 of the Rules. If a person is to be joined as a party to the application then he must be served rather than notified.

9.81 Those notified and served have 21 days in which to file Acknowledgment of Service and object to the application if they wish. The Rules set out what forms must be handed to those who are served or notified. When the application is issued the court provides copies of the relevant forms and instructions for the applicant. The applicant must file certificates of service with the court.

COP1A Supporting information for property and affairs deputyships

9.82 This form requires the applicant to provide some information about P's personal circumstances and living arrangements. The applicant must provide full details of the income, expenditure, assets and liabilities of P, giving valuations in respect of all assets. If the applicant is unable to obtain this information the court will issue an interim order to give him authority to obtain it. The purpose of the COP1A is to enable the court to issue a deputyship with the appropriate powers and authorities and to set security at the right level.

9.83 If P is likely to receive an award of damages or compensation, the court will want to have an estimate of the value of the claim and an indication of when a final order is likely to be made. A deputyship order will be issued taking account of interim payments which have been or are likely to be made and the terms of the order will be revised on the making of the final order.

COP3 Assessment of capacity

9.84 It is essential that the court is satisfied that P lacks capacity in relation to the particular issue at stake, here the capacity to manage property and affairs. A general statement in a condition and prognosis report that P is unable to manage his property and affairs or needs to be under the jurisdiction of the Court of Protection will not suffice. The court will need to see an assessment which addresses the diagnostic and functional tests; form COP3 will allow the practitioner to do this. Reports are generally provided by medical practitioners. However the court may also accept reports by psychologists, psychiatric nurses, speech therapists, social workers or other professionals who are suitably qualified and experienced in the assessment of capacity.

9.85 The evidence of incapacity needs to be current. An old report may not be accepted. Form COP3 requires the practitioner to set out the views of P on the issue. It also requires the practitioner to indicate whether P is likely to recover. If so, the court will probably make a time-limited order to ensure that the matter is brought back before the court and P's capacity reconsidered at the point when recovery may have taken place.

COP 4 Deputy's undertaking

9.86 This must be completed by all proposed deputies apart from local authorities. It requires the deputy to confirm his suitability for the role, posing questions about his solvency and financial reliability, also his criminal record. The deputy is required to give a series of undertakings to ensure that he is fully committed to his obligations: to take due care, avoid conflict of interest, maintain confidentiality, report to the Public Guardian, keep P's finances separate from his personal finances and to maintain security.

B Application for personal welfare deputyship

COP1, COP4

9.87 As above.

COP1B Annex B information for personal welfare deputyships

9.88 This form requires the provision of personal information in a truncated form.

COP2 Permission form

9.89 By the Mental Capacity Act 2005, s 50(1), permission is not required if the application is made by P, or anyone with parental responsibility for P if he is under 18, the donor or donee of a Lasting Power of Attorney, a deputy appointed by the court or a person named in an existing order of the court if the application relates to the order.

9.90 Rule 51 of the Court of Protection Rules 2007 sets out that permission is not required where the application is made by the Official Solicitor or the Public Guardian. It is not required when the application concerns P's property and affairs (with exceptions listed in r 52), or a Lasting Power of Attorney or Enduring Power of Attorney. It is not required when applications are made within proceedings.

9.91 Therefore permission is required for an applicant to proceed with an application to be appointed personal welfare deputy (unless any of the above exceptions apply). Before permission is granted the court must be satisfied of the matters set out in s 50(3). The applicant may be asked by the court to file a witness statement setting out the reasons why he says it is in P's best interests for a deputy for personal welfare to be appointed, rather than allowing those concerned with his well-being to make a co-operative decision or the issues being resolved by a decision of the court. If the court does give permission they may require service of the application and witness statement on other interested parties, including the health and local authorities responsible for providing services for P, to give them an opportunity to object.

COP3 Assessment of capacity

9.92 See above. The COP3 must address the specific issues on which welfare decisions need to be made and confirm that P lacks the capacity to make them.

C Personal welfare decisions

9.93 The court has power to make personal welfare decisions for P particularly in relation to residence, contact, care and medical treatment. By amendments to the Mental Capacity Act 2005 introduced by the Mental Health Act 2007 the court may also make orders and declarations in relation to deprivation of liberty. Such applications are less likely to be made than applications relating to property and affairs in cases involving personal injury damages and are not dealt with in this chapter.

D Contested applications

9.94 If an acknowledgment of service in COP5 is filed objecting to the application, for example, for appointment of a deputy for property and affairs, the court will serve a copy of the form COP 5 on the applicant. Directions will be given for the filing of witness evidence and medical evidence if appropriate. This will usually be done without a hearing.

9.95 If any party is unhappy with an order of the Court of Protection made without a hearing, r 89 of the Court of Protection Rules 2007 allows him to apply for reconsideration within 21 days of service of the order on him. The application should be made on COP9 supported by a witness statement in COP24 if necessary. The judge who made the order or the senior judge will reconsider the order and may confirm, set aside or vary the order. He may reconsider without directing a hearing or arrange for the application to be listed for a hearing.

9.96 Once the evidence is filed and served, directions for trial will be given. The application will be listed for hearing at the Court of Protection in Archway or in one of the Regional Court Centres where there are judges nominated as Court of Protection judges, if that is most convenient for the parties.

9.97 Personal welfare applications seeking a decision of the court will usually be listed for an early attended directions hearing whether at Archway or the Regional Court Centres.

13 Costs

9.98 Part 19 of the Court of Protection Rules deals with costs. The general rule as to costs differs depending on whether the application concerns property and affairs or personal welfare.

9.99 Rule 156 sets out the general rule for property and affairs applications:

> 'Where the proceedings concern P's property and affairs the general rule is that the costs of the proceedings or of that part of the proceedings that concerns P's property and affairs, shall be paid by P or charged to his estate'.

9.100 Rule 157 sets out the general rule for personal welfare applications:

> 'where the proceedings concern P's personal welfare the general rule is that there will be no order as to the costs of the proceedings or of that part of the proceedings that concerns P's personal welfare'.

9.101 Rule 158 provides for apportionment of costs where an application covers personal welfare and property and affairs issues.

9.102 Rule 159 sets out the criteria for departing from the general rule:

> '(1) The court may depart from rules 156 to 158 of the circumstances so justify, and in deciding whether departure is justified the court will have regard to all the circumstances including:

(a) the conduct of the parties;
(b) whether a party has succeeded on part of his case, even if he has not been wholly successful; and
(c) the role of any public body involved in the proceedings.

(2) The conduct of the parties includes:

(a) conduct before as well as during proceedings;
(b) whether it was reasonable for a party to raise, pursue or contest a particular issue;
(c) the manner in which a party has made or responded to an application or a particular issue; and
(d) whether a party who has succeeded in his application or response to any application, in whole or in part, exaggerated any matter contained in his application or response.

(3) Without prejudice to rules 156 to 158 and the foregoing provisions of this rule the court may permit a party to recover their fixed costs in accordance with the relevant practice directions'.

9.103 Judges in the Court of Protection will make decisions as to costs at the conclusion of the case but do not carry out costs assessments, which will be done by the Senior Courts Costs Office.

10 The future

1 The Law Commission report

10.1 The preceding chapters describe how the common law has developed in its treatment of psychiatric injury during the 20th century. The courts have wrestled with resolving the tensions between the improving medical understanding of psychiatric conditions, the fear of opening the floodgates to claims and yet staying abreast with public opinion. At the end of the last century in *Frost v Chief Constable of South Yorkshire Police/White v Chief Constable of South Yorkshire Police*[1] the House of Lords came to a despairing conclusion. The common law had gone as far as it could go in resolving these tensions. It would be a matter for Parliament to take matters further. This was perhaps a reasonable assumption to make, as the Law Commission, the statutory body created by Parliament to advise on law reform, had reported the previous year[2] at great length on psychiatric injury. It had recommended changes to the law which Parliament should take forward. The Law Commission had argued that whilst a complete codification was unnecessary, Parliament needed to take a lead, particularly in respect of 'secondary victims':

> 'Moreover, we believe that in such a turbulent area—where medical knowledge and society's understanding are growing apace—there is much to be said for allowing the common law to develop by incremental judicial decision. On the other hand, we firmly believe—and this was strongly supported on consultation—that in some respects, and most notably in the decision of the House of Lords in *Alcock v Chief Constable of South Yorkshire Police*[3], the common law has taken a wrong turn. Legislation can cure the defects in the common law at a stroke and with certainty. To wait for the House of Lords to reverse *Alcock* may be to wait for a very long time indeed. Our policy may therefore be described as one of recommending minimal legislative intervention curing serious defects in the present law but otherwise leaving the common law to develop.
>
> We therefore recommend that at this stage, legislative codification of the whole of the law on negligently inflicted psychiatric illness would not be appropriate. On the contrary, we recommend that, while legislation curing serious defects in the present law is appropriate, the law should otherwise be allowed to develop by judicial decision-making'.

1 [1999] 2 AC 455.
2 *Liability for Psychiatric Illness* Law Com no 249.
3 [1992] 1 AC 310.

10.2 However, Parliament did not rise to the challenge. The Law Commission report, along with most of the others commissioned in respect of compensation for personal injury in the 1990s, remained at the Ministry of Justice and its predecessor departments for more than a decade before any work was undertaken on its recommendations. And when the department did get round to looking at it, its conclusion was that the common law was working perfectly well and that there was no need for statutory intervention. In May 2007 the then Department of Constitutional Affairs in the consultation paper[1] rejected the Law Commission's recommendation for statutory intervention on the grounds that:

> 'It is difficult at this stage to see how legislation could successfully assimilate the differing perspectives and arguments in this complex area into a simple and coherent system which would improve upon the current principles established by the courts, without running the risk of imposing rigid requirements which are not readily able to accommodate developments in medical knowledge and jurisprudence, and without opening the way to speculative and inappropriate claims',

concluding that it was:

> '... preferable to allow the courts to continue to develop the law on liability for psychiatric illness rather than attempt to impose a statutory solution'.

1   *The Law on Damages* CP 09/07.

10.3   The response to consultation[1] was published on 1 July 2009 (two years later). The government concluded:

> 'The consultation paper did not ask any specific questions in this area, but indicated that the Government would welcome any views that consultees wished to express. Responses on this issue were mixed, with a small majority disagreeing with the Government's position that it is preferable to leave development of the law in this area to the courts. Widely differing views were expressed on particular aspects of the current common law framework, such as the "shock" requirement and the range of people who should be eligible to claim. The arguments in this complex and sensitive area are finely balanced. On balance the Government continues to take the view that it is preferable for the courts to have the flexibility to continue to develop the law rather than attempt to impose a statutory solution'.

1   *The Law on Damages* CP(R) 9/07.

10.4   The previous (Labour) government put forward a Civil Justice Bill. This dealt with some other recommendations of the Law Commission relating to personal injury damages, but fell at the general election in 2010. Notably, this did not include any of the recommendations of the Law Commission relating to psychiatric injury. The new coalition government has already indicated that it does not propose to revive the limited proposals in this Civil Justice Bill.

10.5   The prospects for any statutory intervention therefore now seem minimal. It might be argued that this is the correct course of action. The courts have been prepared to use the common law as a flexible tool for the development of law in this field in the past. The fact that it is a politically sensitive arena does not mean that the courts should not tread in it.

2 The Australian experience

10.6 The treatment of psychiatric injury claims for primary and secondary victims in England and Wales resulting from the House of Lords decisions in *Page v Smith*, *Alcock v Chief Constable of South Yorkshire Police* and *Frost v Chief Constable of South Yorkshire Police/White v Chief Constable of South Yorkshire Police* have not been without criticism. Elsewhere in common law jurisdictions the courts have followed a different path.

10.7 In particular, the High Court of Australia in the conjoined appeals of *Tame v NSW; Annetts v Australian Stations Pty*[1] rejected the English approach of special rules to restrict psychiatric injury claims. Instead it went back to basic principles of negligence: direct perception, sudden shock and foreseeable harm were factors that might assist in determining liability, but were not essential ingredients before liability can be established.

1   (2003) 211 CLR 317 HCA.

10.8 In *Tame*, Mrs Tame had been involved in a minor road traffic accident in which she suffered slight physical injuries for which she was compensated by the insurers of the driver. However, the police officer had incorrectly recorded that she had been found to have alcohol in her bloodstream after the accident. The shock of reading this in the police report had led to her developing a psychiatric condition.

10.9 In *Annetts* a 16-year-old had been employed as a 'jackeroo'. His parents had been assured by the employer that he would be supervised, but he had been placed at a remote post in the outback 100km from the station. The parents were told that their son was missing and his father collapsed (the son was later found dead of dehydration).

10.10 The Australian Supreme Court rejected the requirements of 'shock' and 'direct perception' (unlike the House of Lords in *Alcock v Chief Constable of South Yorkshire Police*[1]). The majority also required the claimant to establish both that he had suffered a 'recognised psychiatric condition' and that a person of 'reasonable fortitude' would have suffered injury.

1   [1992] 1 AC 310.

10.11 As a result, the appeal in *Tame* was rejected as the police officer making the error could not have contemplated the particular vulnerability of Mrs Tame, but the appeal in *Annetts* was allowed as it was reasonable to expect a person of normal fortitude to have reacted in the same way to the news of their son's disappearance.

10.12 However, this departure from the position under English law was overtaken by the alleged insurance crisis in Australia. This followed the collapse of the general insurer HIH which led to some knee-jerk and arguably excessive tort reform to restrict claims and limit cost. The much clearer formulation of the law in *Tame and Annets* had been hailed by many commentators as a great improvement on the English position. But this was hurriedly amended by statutory intervention in many states greatly limiting the extent of liability for psychiatric injury[1].

1   See Harvey Teff *Causing Psychiatric and Emotional Harm* (Hart Publishing, 2009).

3 The insurers

10.13 In *Liability for Psychiatric Illness*[1] the Law Commission accepted that their proposal would lead to an increase in claims and therefore also in claim costs:

> 'We recognise that, in practice, the cost of the recommendations which we have made in this Report is likely to be borne by a large section of the public through higher insurance premiums. In order to assess how great that impact might be, we asked the Association of British Insurers (ABI) if they could provide us with an estimate of the increase in premiums that our proposals would have in one particular sector, the motor insurance market. We are most grateful for the help that the ABI has given us on this issue. It is clear that any estimate must be a very speculative one. In particular, whatever methodology is used, it is necessary to predict the increase in the number of personal injury claims that would be brought as a result of our proposals. Since there is no existing data on which to base this prediction, any figure chosen must be based on insurers' general "feel" and understanding of the market. Our discussions with the ABI suggested that a reasonable assumption seems to be that our proposals would give rise to a ten per cent increase in the number of personal injury claims'.

1 Law Com no 249.

10.14 It is interesting to note that in their 2007 consultation paper the government accompanied their proposal to reject the Law Commission recommendations with an impact assessment. This contained information from insurers and the National Health Service Litigation Authority, but with no data from any claimant group at all:

> 'The NHSLA has informed us that the NHS would be particularly susceptible to claims not induced by shock or proximity in space and time to the accident or its aftermath. Removing this restriction would allow, for example, close relatives of a patient in hospital following an incident of clinical negligence, who subsequently suffer a psychiatric illness, to claim for damages. Thus, instead of one patient claiming damages following an incident of clinical negligence, there could potentially be several claims over an extended period of time.
>
> The NHSLA consider that these changes would increase the numbers of individuals able to recover damages by approximately 450 claims per year. It has provisionally estimated that the increased cost to the NHS in England alone could be £35m per annum, plus the need for increases in reserves of over £300m. As any additional money paid out in damages would result in reduced resources being available for other NHS expenditure, there could be very substantial disbenefits to patients and other NHS users generally.
>
> The ABI estimated in 2001 that the increased costs to the insurance industry of implementing the Commission's recommendations would be approximately £235m per annum... the majority of these costs would fall to motor insurance. No costs are anticipated in respect of employers' liability, as the Commission did not recommend reform to the law as it applies to employees. There would also potentially be costs of around £468m if any change were to be made retrospective'[1].

1 *The Law on Damages* CP 09/07.

10.15 The anticipated increase of some 5%–10% in the total number of clinical negligence claims simply as a result of the relaxation for psychiatric injury proposed by the Law Commission seems very high. Average damages of £80,000 per such new psychiatric injury claim is implausible. No detail of the ABI's estimate was produced at all. However, the Law Commission had said[1] in their 1998 report:

> 'Using this assumption [ie a 10% increase in the number of claims], one might then calculate that an insurance company which currently spends £100 million on personal injury claims out of a total £500 million spent on motor claims altogether would see an increase in claims of £10 million if our proposals were to be implemented, representing a two per cent rise overall. Premiums would therefore have to be increased by at least two per cent to cover this rise. These figures, however, are based on two further assumptions that will not always be borne out. The first assumption is that the average cost of a claim made under our proposals would be the same as the average cost of a personal injury claim made today. If the average cost of a psychiatric illness claim under our proposals were in fact higher, then the percentage increase in cost would be greater. The second assumption relates to the ratio of spending on personal injury claims as opposed to vehicle damage claims. The proportion of a motor insurance premium which covers personal injury as opposed to vehicle damage is greater in a third party policy than in a comprehensive policy. So, if, in the example above, the insurance company held a larger proportion of third party policies and spent £100 million on personal injury claims out of a total of only £200 million on motor claims altogether, then the £10 million increase would represent a five per cent rise overall. It is because of the various assumptions that must be made in attempting to pinpoint any figure, that it is very difficult to reach any firm estimate. However, we understand from our discussions with the ABI, using the sort of methodology we have here set out, that it is reasonable to estimate that our proposals would give rise to an increase in motor insurance premiums in the range of two to five per cent'.

1   Law Com no 249.

10.16   All these figures are obviously highly speculative. However, the insurance and indemnity providers are obviously nervous about any relaxation of the rules relating to psychiatric injury. Any significant change by the courts or through proposed statutory intervention in the United Kingdom would no doubt produce a 'tort reform' lobby response similar to the one in Australia.

4   Alternatives proposed for the United Kingdom

10.17   *Atiyah's Accidents, Compensation and the Law*[1], more recently edited by P Cane, has over the years seen the solution to the vagaries and perceived inequity of tortious liability (perhaps seen in the sharpest focus in psychiatric injury) in a no-fault scheme. The state would compensate all victims of accidents, as has been implemented in New Zealand. However, this is a 1970s-style, big state solution and would either be hugely expensive to the state or disappointingly meagre to accident victims. It would certainly not meet the expectation of the clients that if wrong is done to them the wrongdoer should pay to put this right. There is still a strong public sense of corrective justice which the tort system can to an extent meet, notwithstanding the contrary compensation culture clamour (often expressed, in a supreme example of 'double-think', by the very same individuals and media organisations).

1   Cambridge University Press, 2006.

10.18 In *Causing Psychiatric and Emotional Harm*[1], Harvey Teff puts forward a proposal for legislative reform. This would remove the artificial distinctions between primary and secondary victims and remove the distinction between psychiatric and other personal injury claims (by removing the requirement to show a 'recognised psychiatric injury'). But he would also place a minimum value on the award for non-pecuniary loss for all personal injury claims (not just psychiatric injury) which must be achieved for a claim to be litigated. This is a rational proposal, although it would be deeply controversial with practitioners, in particular, outside the field of psychiatric injury.

[1] Hart Publishing, 2009.

10.19 Most current personal injury claims are relatively low value. Therefore any imposition of a minimum threshold of value for personal injury claims would be likely to significantly reduce the number of litigated personal injury claims overall. In practice, the imposition of this kind of threshold has been achieved by the small claims track limit. If a claim falls into the small claims track, then only very limited legal expenses can be awarded on top of any compensation. This means that most such cases are not in fact litigated, as the cost of doing so is likely to exceed any benefit. However, even proposals to increase the small claims track limit have been controversial. This has remained at £1,000 for pain, suffering and loss of amenity in personal injury cases since the late 1990s. This is despite the effect of inflation over the period and despite numerous government consultations on raising the limit.

5 Possible future developments

10.20 Given that statutory intervention is extremely unlikely, the courts will in due course in appropriate cases have to resolve the problems with the current common law position. Indeed, it might well be argued that the House of Lords only got themselves into the current mess in respect of 'secondary victims' by declining the claims by the Hillsborough relatives in *Alcock v Chief Constable of South Yorkshire Police*. They then imposed overly-restrictive proximity tests, and then feeling that politically they could not subsequently allow claims by police officer rescuers in *Frost/White*. Almost simultaneously, however, they abolished the body/mind dichotomy, but only for primary victims in shock cases in *Page v Smith*.

10.21 Since Hillsborough, most other mass disasters in the United Kingdom have arisen from crimes (for example, the 7/7 London bombings). The position in negligence under the common law has not really been tested further. However, the reaction to the harrowing stories given to the inquest into 7/7 London bombings of the long-term psychological effect of being caught up in the incident (even if some would struggle to fall into category of 'direct participant' as they were not on the bombed trains or rescuers at any real personal risk of injury) suggests that in a similar transport disaster caused by negligence rather than criminal actions, public opinion would not accept that such victims are prevented from claiming compensation. Similarly, if a dumping of chemical waste in *Trafigura*-type incident occurred in the United Kingdom with immediate fear of physical illness for self or loved ones, but ultimately the fear was more disabling than the actuality, would public opinion accept that the victims of the psychiatric injury could not claim because of the *Alcock* proximity tests?

10.22 The Supreme Court is more than capable of addressing these policy issues. Indeed, the Law Commission always anticipated that once Parliament had sorted out its wrong turn in *Alcock v Chief Constable of South Yorkshire Police* the common law would be left to develop—a complete codification was never in contemplation:

> 'We should emphasise the novelty of the method of legislative reform which we have adopted. Rather than laying down all the requirements of liability, we have provided for one, albeit central, component of liability: the existence of a duty of care. We intend that all other aspects of the tort of negligence, for example the rules relating to the standard of care, causation, remoteness and contributory negligence, are to apply in the normal way. Although one might draw comparisons with the Occupiers' Liability Acts 1957 and 1984, which have been described as simply "applied negligence", our proposals are not directly analogous. We do not propose to set up a new statutory tort relating to liability for psychiatric illness, but rather to lay down one segment of a finding of liability under the tort of negligence, the duty of care, but otherwise to leave the common law rules in play'.

The most problematic current issues are set out below.

A 'Recognised psychiatric injury'

10.23 The requirement to show a recognised psychiatric injury to obtain compensation for negligence is not easy to justify in the light of wider redress which is available for breach of contract and under the statutory torts created by Parliament. However, the use of diagnostic tools and the greater credence given to expert psychiatric evidence means that this is rarely a significant difficulty for deserving cases in practice. And in cases where the claimant is a primary victim and has suffered physical injury, even if a recognised psychiatric injury cannot be established, there is no tariff system of damages. The judge can, if he or she so chooses, include in the award for pain and suffering and loss of amenity the impact of the injury on this particular claimant.

10.24 So it is only in the case of primary victims of shock cases where there is no physical injury, primary victims in non-shock cases or secondary victims where the distinction may be particularly relevant. It is extremely difficult to calculate the numbers of additional claims that would be involved in such a change. However, it must be accepted that such a change to the law would increase the number of potential claimants. Members of families, who suffer natural grief and emotional disturbance as a result of a serious injury to a loved one, provided that they are present at the scene or the aftermath, would be able to claim in the proceedings. The amount of damages awarded as compensation for emotional harm short of a recognised psychiatric injury might be very limited, but the costs incurred in litigating the additional claims would be significant.

10.25 It might also be argued that many of the concerns about claims for psychiatric injury fall away when claims are limited to recognised psychiatric conditions, as the injury is seen to be grounded in professional medical opinion rather than as a result merely of judicial perception. It seems unlikely, therefore, that the courts will take lightly the step of abandoning the restriction of the need to establish a recognised psychiatric injury resulting from negligence. What is perhaps more likely is, as psychiatric medicine continues to develop, that more conditions will fall within the definition of psychiatric injury and thus the courts will allow compensation for them.

B   The Page v Smith controversy

10.26   Even the position of accident victims who suffer psychiatric injury, but no physical injury, in a shocking event is not entirely secure, as can be seen from the examination in Chapter 2 of the decision in *Page v Smith*[1] in subsequent decisions House of Lords and Supreme Court.

1   [1996] 1 AC 155.

10.27   However, notwithstanding the obvious concern of some of the Supreme Court justices, it would be a massively retrograde step to depart from *Page*. This would mean reverting to the mind/body dualism which regards injuries to the mind as entirely separate from injuries to the body. That cannot really be justified in the 21st century. And in practice *Page* seems to work well and has not unleashed a flood of unmeritorious or spurious claims.

Whilst a retrenchment cannot be entirely ruled out, as the years go by since the *Page* decision, departure from its basic principles seems more and more unlikely.

C   Rescuers

10.28   As can be seen in Chapter 2, the decision in *Frost/White*[1] has entrenched some rather arbitrary and harsh rules for involuntary participants and rescuers who are employees of the wrongdoer. If they are sufficiently close to the scene (standing next to a man who electrocutes himself with a pole) they are primary victims who need merely to establish they have a recognised psychiatric injury. If, however, they are in or following a van from which a colleague falls to his death they are mere bystanders.

1   [1999] 2 AC 455.

10.29   And even with regard to non-employee rescuers, is it right that a rescuer should only be able to recover for psychiatric injury if he is in danger of physical injury? Surely the law should encourage selfless acts assisting victims of accidents and thus be prepared to compensate the rescuers if they develop a recognised psychiatric injury in consequence? It has been seen that it is doubtful whether Mr Chadwick ever was in physical danger, or that the trial judge considered this was a pre-requisite for recovery, notwithstanding the subsequent gloss provided by the Lords in *Frost/White*. The experiences of the 7/7 London bombings rescuers given to the inquest show how traumatic and shocking the aftermath of a disaster can be, how valuable to the relatives of the bereaved and to survivors it was that someone was with the victims providing emotional support. It might be argued that in the context of 7/7 the 'rescuers' were in potential physical danger as it was not certain there be no other attacks or that infrastructure might collapse, but it seems totally artificial that the right to recover compensation for psychiatric injury as a result of 'doing the right thing' in a disaster is entirely dependant upon a hypothetical risk of personal danger.

10.30 In addition, there seems little doubt that *Frost/White* would have been decided differently but for the earlier Hillsborough decision in *Alcock v Chief Constable of South Yorkshire Police*. It therefore seems possible that a future 'rescuer' or involuntary participant test would be decided differently by the Supreme Court. Applying the test of reasonable foreseeability of psychiatric injury in such cases would lead to fewer unjust distinctions, whilst allowing a barrier to remain to claims by mere onlookers, save in a case where it could be established that the event witnessed was so shocking that it was reasonably foreseeable that even onlookers would develop a recognised psychiatric injury.

D The requirement of foreseeability of psychiatric injury in stress at work cases

10.31 The primary victims of non-shock cases who are employed (mainly stress at work claimants) are not able to take advantage of *Page v Smith* because there is usually no shocking event whereby the wrongdoer could foresee some form of physical injury to the claimant. Thus in *Hatton*, whilst firmly stating that such victims are primary victims, the Court of Appeal held (largely upheld by the House of Lords in *Barber v Somerset County Council*[1]) that to succeed it was necessary for the claimant to show that the likelihood of psychiatric injury was foreseeable to the employer.

1   [2004] ICR 457.

10.32 This can create odd situations. For example, if a claim can also be brought under the Protection from Harassment Act 1997 or for statutory discrimination under the equalities legislation in the employment tribunal there is no need to prove foreseeability of psychiatric harm. And in bullying cases it is in practice much easier to establish foreseeability through the route of vicarious liability of the employer for the individual bully's actions[1], whereas this is much more difficult to establish in overwork cases which tend to be based upon systemic problems in the workplace. In overwork claims 'second breakdown' cases are therefore much more likely to succeed, even though the most serious psychiatric damage was usually done in the first breakdown. There is some evidence that the Court of Appeal is dealing with this by way of a growing intolerance for the failure of big employers to effectively follow their own procedures and consequently accepting relatively minor signs of distress as evidence to establish foreseebility[2]. The High Court has, however, consistently rejected claims based on strict liability for breach of the Management of Health and Safety at Work Regulations 1999[3].

1   For example, *Green v DB Group Services (UK) Ltd* [2006] EWHC 1898 (QB).
2   See *Intel Corpn (UK) Ltd v Daw* [2007] EWCA Civ 70 and *Dickins v O2 plc* [2008] EWCA Civ 1144, dealt with in Chapter 3.
3   SI 1999/3242. See, for example, *Paterson v Surrey Police Authority* [2008] EWHC 2693 (QB) and *Mullen v Accenture Services Ltd* [2010] EWHC 2336 (QB).

10.33 Removing entirely the requirement for foreseeability of psychiatric injury in stress cases seems to be an unlikely step. The volume of sickness absence related to workplace stress now exceeds even musculoskeletal injury. So even if the requirement to show a recognised psychiatric injury is maintained, the courts will be wary of opening floodgates to stress at work claims.

E Secondary victims' proximity: close ties of love and affection

10.34 The test of requiring a close tie of love and affection is becoming harder to justify as time passes. The specific relationships mentioned in *Alcock v Chief Constable of South Yorkshire Police* as raising a presumption (eg spouses, parents/children) would have to be restated in a subsequent case to avoid discriminatory outcome (for example, civil partners and adopted children). The comments about the nature of brotherly love in the case seemed insensitive to many even at the time.

10.35 However, the Lords in *Alcock* did not rule out any particular tie of 'love and affection' as being incapable of founding a claim by a secondary victim in principle and some felt that in an appropriately shocking case even a bystander might still recover.

10.36 The effect of seriously traumatic events on close friends (as opposed to blood relatives and partners) of victims can be seen from the press coverage of the Norwegian massacre carried out by Anders Behring Breivik in July 2011. That this can also be the case in respect of injuries to strangers can be seen from the effect of the 7/7 and 9/11 atrocities on bystanders.

10.37 Mass tort actions in respect of such shocking events are thankfully rare. A relaxation of this aspect of the law in an appropriate case is unlikely to open floodgates.

F Secondary victims' proximity: 'shock' and space and time

10.38 As can be seen from Chapter 4, although the House of Lords in *Alcock v Chief Constable of South Yorkshire Police* reaffirmed the requirement of a secondary victim to be proximate in space and time, in *McLoughlin v O'Brian*[1] they had already extended this to the 'aftermath' and subsequent case law has stretched the aftermath even further.

1   [1983] 1 AC 410.

10.39 One reason for this particular control mechanism would seem to be that in *Alcock* secondary victims were required to show that the psychiatric injury arose from a 'shocking event'. This is a quaint throwback to the mid-20th century and old-fashioned notion of 'nervous shock'. As we have seen, the medical opinion of consultees to the Law Commission felt that this was unhelpful and much of the 21st century case law has related to stress at work cases which very rarely results from a shocking event. There seems no compelling reason of principle why only a secondary victim should be required to prove shock and this, together with the artificiality of the 'aftermath' definition, suggests that the requirement for a 'shock' perceived close to the time and at the scene or its aftermath might be abandoned in an appropriate case before the Supreme Court.

G Secondary victims' proximity: means of perception

10.40 The proximity test set out in *Alcock v Chief Constable of South Yorkshire Police*, requiring direct perception by sight or sound of the shocking event, simply does not bear scrutiny in the 21st century. The world has moved on since the Hillsborough disaster of 15 April 1989. Even if the proximity tests set out in *Alcock* were justifiable then, they cannot be justified today because of changes in media and technology.

10.41 Despite the comments of the House of Lords in *Alcock*, we have seen that, notwithstanding the broadcasting code, shocking events will in fact be shown live on television in this era of rolling 24-hour news (for example, the collapse of the World Trade Centre towers on 9/11 or the explosion after launch of the Space Shuttle Columbia). Primary victims were able to talk to friends and family on mobile phones before they died in the 9/11 attacks. In the Norwegian massacre victims were texting friends and family from the scene of the shooting. Events can be followed almost in real time on the internet or via social media sites such as Twitter.

10.42 In these circumstances the proximity tests relating to media established by the House of Lords in *Alcock* are archaic. It seems inevitable in the case of a mass tort in the United Kingdom that the issue of proximity for secondary victims would be revisited by the Supreme Court.

H Divisible/indivisible injury

10.43 A rather more technical point that remains for final determination by the courts is whether psychiatric injury (which is often multi-factorial in nature) should be treated as a divisible injury (like, for example, industrial deafness) or as an indivisible illness (like mesothelioma, where it is not possible to say which exposure caused the medical condition to occur). The distinction is critical as if the illness is 'divisible' in nature it is possible to apportion liability to the various proximate causes, meaning that the wrongdoer is only responsible for the part of the psychiatric condition the court finds is as a result of the tort. The wrongdoer can, however, still argue that the psychiatric injury would have occurred in any event at some point in the future by reason of vulnerability, so that compensation is limited to the period of 'acceleration'.

10.44 As set out in Chapter 7, the Court of Appeal in *Hatton v Sutherland*[1] and *Dickins v O2 plc*[2] reached different conclusions, obiter. In *Thaine v London School of Economics*[3], the EAT backed 'apportionment' of a 'divisible' injury in the context of a discrimination claim over a period of time, but it is doubtful whether this can apply in the case of PTSD following a single shocking event. It is argued that the 'indivisible' but 'acceleration' approach is to be preferred logically, but that the courts may prefer to leave judges with both apportionment and acceleration as tools in psychiatric injury.

1   [2002] ICR 613.
2   [2008] EWCA Civ 1144.
3   [2010] ICR 1422.

6 Conclusion

10.45 Psychiatric injury claims remain at the cutting edge of personal injury law. The aim of this work is to set out practical guidance for practitioners as to what constitutes an actionable claim under the current law, and how to litigate it.

10.46 However, although statutory intervention now seems unlikely, and the 'tort reform' lobby will continually demand 'floodgates', the common law has developed the law over the last century broadly in tandem with advances in medical understanding of psychiatric injury, so that in appropriate cases there will always be an opportunity for practitioners to test and further develop the common law when litigating psychiatric injury claims.

10.47 The funding reforms following implementation of Jackson LJ's recommendations may impact adversely on the development of law in this context. It seems inevitable that with success fees not being recoverable from wrongdoers (and capped when taken from claimant's damages), lawyers will be far more cautious in litigating cutting edge claims where the law may have to be changed to enable recovery. The *Alcock* and *Page* cases were funded by legal aid (unavailable for personal injury cases since 1 April 2000) and *Frost/White* by the rescuers' 'trade union' (the Police Federation, which in this context at least acted as a trade union) as was *Simmons v British Steel*. Trade unions may be prepared to continue to back exceptional claims on behalf of their members, but the future seems uncertain in an environment of no recovery of success fees. Even if clients sign up at the outset to the idea of paying a proportion of any compensation eventually awarded, settlement remorse often sets in at the end when they have to write out a cheque to the lawyers. This can be seen in areas where costs are not presently awarded. According to the Birmingham Post[1], after the Japanese Labour Camp Survivors' Association sent letters to ex-servicemen and their widows inviting them to contribute £500 to legal costs out of the compensation payments made by the government, Steve McCabe MP said 'I question the morality of this effort to pocket part of the Government's payment to these brave people' even though the association had said 'it was simply trying to get a fair deal for the lawyers who had worked for more than a decade on a no-win-no-fee basis to get the compensation'.

1   Article by Jonathan Walker (2001) Birmingham Post, 16 April.

10.48 Proportionality is also likely to be an issue for psychiatric injury claims. Because of the likelihood of some form of recovery from the injury in the long term, compensation is usually far more limited than for catastrophic physical injuries. Proportionality was argued even in its pre-Jackson form in *Trafigura*, by any stretch of the imagination a risky case for, as it transpired, relatively low individual compensation, against an obdurate and well-resourced multi-national defendant. There must, therefore, be a significant risk that the Jackson costs reforms and the permanent loss of public funding for such cases will stultify development of the common law in this field.

10.49 However, provided that such practical obstacles can be overcome, the rational future for psychiatric injury claims must be to follow the path set out by Lord Griffiths in his minority judgment in *Frost v Chief Constable of South Yorkshire Police/White v Chief Constable of South Yorkshire Police*:

> 'The House of Lords by a majority [in *Page v Smith*] held that in circumstances such as a road accident in which a defendant owes a duty of care not to cause personal injury it mattered not whether the injury suffered as a result of the defendant's negligence was physical injury or psychiatric injury and liability would be established without the necessity to prove as an independent part of the cause of action that psychiatric injury, in the absence of physical injury, was foreseeable.
>
> For my part I regard this as a sensible development of the law and I note from the Law Commission Report on Liability for Psychiatric Illness (1998) (Law Com No 249) that it has been supported by the majority of practitioners. If some very minor physical injury is suffered and this triggers a far more serious psychiatric disorder no one questions that damages are recoverable for the psychiatric disorder. If the victim of the negligence escapes minor physical injury but the shock or fear of the peril in which he is placed by the defendant's negligent conduct causes psychiatric injury I can see no sensible reason why he should not recover for that psychiatric damage.
>
> As medical science advances we realise how difficult it is to separate out the physical and psychiatric consequences of trauma, and I believe the law would do better to regard both as personal injury as *Page v Smith* requires in the case of primary victims, that is victims who are imperilled or reasonably believe themselves to be imperilled by the defendant's negligence. Insofar as secondary victims are concerned, that is those who are bystanders, we can still ask the question was personal injury reasonably foreseeable if we regard psychiatric damage as personal injury. For as I have pointed out no question of physical injury arises in the case of the bystander'[1].

So that in future:

- psychiatric injury and physical injury should be both treated as personal injury; and
- 'reasonable foreseeability' of any injury, in the case of primary victims, and of psychiatric injury, in the case of secondary victims (where physical injury cannot have been in contemplation), should be the determinant of liability.

1   [1999] 2 AC 455, [1999] 1 All ER 1 at 5e.

Index

[all references are to paragraph number]

Acceleration
causation of damage, and, 7.94–7.96
Acts in connection with care or treatment
generally, 9.49–9.51
litigation capacity, 9.58–9.64
powers of the court, 9.52–9.57
Adjustment disorders
generally, 6.44–6.45
meaning of 'psychiatric injury', and, 1.12
Aftermath
generally, 4.39–4.43
summary, 4.72
Agoraphobia
generally, 6.27
Alcohol misuse
generally, 6.68–6.73
Anxieties and phobias
agoraphobia, 6.27
depression, and, 6.42–6.43
'flight or fight' mechanisms, 6.23
generally, 6.23
meaning of 'psychiatric injury', and, 1.12
obsessive compulsive disorder, 6.30–6.32
panic attacks, 6.28–6.29
phobic avoidance, 6.23
social phobia, 6.33
travel anxiety, 6.24–6.25
Apportionment
future developments, 10.43–10.44
generally, 7.86–7.93
Assault
generally, 5.4–5.7
overview, 5.1
Attention deficit and hyperactivity disorder (ADHD)
generally, 6.96
Australia
case decisions, 10.6–10.12
Autistic disorders
generally, 6.94–6.95

Battery
generally, 5.2–5.3
overview, 5.1

Best interests
mental capacity, and, 9.37–9.46
BIMCA Rehabilitation Code 2007
generally, 8.64–8.74
Bipolar affective disorder
generally, 6.67
Brain injuries
generally, 6.74–6.76
primary victims, and, 2.7–2.9
Broadcasters
secondary victims, and, 4.65–4.67
Bystanders
causes of action, and, 1.44

Capacity of clients
generally, 8.50
Mental Capacity Act
protection of client, 8.51–8.54
protection of staff, 8.55–8.59
Case management
claim process, and, 8.75–8.76
Case managers, carers and buddies
special damages, and, 7.56–7.63
Causation of damage
acceleration, 7.94–7.96
apportionment, 7.86–7.93
introduction, 7.83
material contribution, 7.84–7.85
summary, 7.97
Causes of action
contractual claims, 1.47–1.49
criminal injuries compensation, 1.55
holiday cases, 1.48
introduction, 1.35
negligence, 1.36–1.46
statutory discrimination, 1.50–1.54
Children
mental capacity, and, 9.47–9.48
types of psychiatric injury, and, 6.92–6.97
Chronic fatigue syndrome
generally, 6.48–6.50
meaning of 'psychiatric injury', and, 1.9
Chronic pain
generally, 6.52–6.60

207

CICA tariff scheme
  damages, and, 7.50–7.54
Clinical depression
  meaning of 'psychiatric injury', and, 1.12
Clinical opinion
  types of psychiatric injury, and, 6.2
Close ties of love and affection
  future developments, 10.34–10.37
  generally, 4.32–4.38
  summary, 4.72
Code of Practice
  Mental Capacity Act 2005, and, 9.9
Cognitive behavioural psychotherapy
  generally, 6.85–6.89
Coming off the record
  handling clients, and, 8.60–8.63
Compensation
  acceleration, and, 7.94–7.96
  apportionment, and, 7.86–7.93
  background, 7.1–7.12
  case managers, carers and buddies, 7.56–7.63
  causation of damage
    acceleration, 7.94–7.96
    apportionment, 7.86–7.93
    introduction, 7.83
    material contribution, 7.84–7.85
    summary, 7.97
  CICA tariff scheme, 7.50–7.54
  counselling, 7.64–7.65
  DSM-IV, and, 7.10
  general damages
    general psychiatric damage, 7.21–7.34
    generally, 7.13–7.20
    post-traumatic stress disorder, 7.35–7.40
    problematic medical/psychological conditions, 7.41–7.49
  general psychiatric damage
    introduction, 7.21
    minor, 7.31–7.34
    moderate, 7.28–7.30
    moderately severe, 7.26–7.27
    severe, 7.22–7.25
  ICD 10, and, 7.10
  individual needs assessments, 7.55
  inpatient psychological assessment and rehabilitation, 7.67–7.69
  JSB Guidelines, 7.14–7.19
  material contribution, and, 7.84–7.85
  mitigation, and, 7.70–7.77
  outpatient facilities, 7.66
  pain, suffering and loss of amenity, 7.13–7.20
  post-traumatic stress disorder
    introduction, 7.35
    minor, 7.40

Compensation – *contd*
  post-traumatic stress disorder – *contd*
    moderate, 7.39
    moderately severe, 7.38
    severe, 7.36–7.37
  primary victims, and, 7.5
  problematic medical/psychological conditions, 7.41–7.49
  provisional damages, 7.78–7.82
  recognised psychiatric illness, and, 7.10
  secondary victims, and, 7.6
  short term treatment interventions
    counselling, 7.64–7.65
    inpatient psychological assessment and rehabilitation, 7.67–7.69
    outpatient facilities, 7.66
    therapy, 7.64–7.65
  special damages
    case managers, carers and buddies, 7.56–7.63
    counselling and therapy, 7.64–7.65
    generally, 7.55
    inpatient psychological assessment and rehabilitation, 7.67–7.69
    outpatient facilities, 7.66
    short term treatment interventions, 7.64–7.69
    therapy, 7.64–7.65
Complex regional pain syndromes
  generally, 6.59
Contractual claims
  causes of action, and, 1.47–1.49
  generally, 5.20–5.22
Costs
  dealings with client, and, 8.99–8.107
  deputyship applications, and, 9.98–9.103
Counsel
  dealings with client, and, 8.29–8.31
Counselling
  dealings with client, and, 8.78–8.79
  special damages, and, 7.64–7.65
Court of Protection
  background, 9.4–9.5
  generally, 9.11–9.13
Criminal injuries compensation claims
  causes of action, and, 1.55
  damages, and, 7.50–7.54
  generally, 5.12–5.19
'Customary phlegm'
  secondary victims, and, 4.22–4.23

Damages
  acceleration, and, 7.94–7.96
  apportionment, and, 7.86–7.93
  background, 7.1–7.12
  case managers, carers and buddies, 7.56–7.63

Damages – *contd*
  causation of damage
    acceleration, 7.94–7.96
    apportionment, 7.86–7.93
    introduction, 7.83
    material contribution, 7.84–7.85
    summary, 7.97
  CICA tariff scheme, 7.50–7.54
  counselling, 7.64–7.65
  DSM-IV, and, 7.10
  general damages
    general psychiatric damage, 7.21–7.34
    generally, 7.13–7.20
    post-traumatic stress disorder, 7.35–7.40
    problematic medical/psychological conditions, 7.41–7.49
  general psychiatric damage
    introduction, 7.21
    minor, 7.31–7.34
    moderate, 7.28–7.30
    moderately severe, 7.26–7.27
    severe, 7.22–7.25
  ICD 10, and, 7.10
  individual needs assessments, 7.55
  inpatient psychological assessment and rehabilitation, 7.67–7.69
  JSB Guidelines, 7.14–7.19
  material contribution, and, 7.84–7.85
  mitigation, and, 7.70–7.77
  outpatient facilities, 7.66
  pain, suffering and loss of amenity, 7.13–7.20
  post-traumatic stress disorder
    introduction, 7.35
    minor, 7.40
    moderate, 7.39
    moderately severe, 7.38
    severe, 7.36–7.37
  primary victims, and, 7.5
  problematic medical/psychological conditions, 7.41–7.49
  provisional damages, 7.78–7.82
  recognised psychiatric illness, and, 7.10
  secondary victims, and, 7.6
  short term treatment interventions
    counselling, 7.64–7.65
    inpatient psychological assessment and rehabilitation, 7.67–7.69
    outpatient facilities, 7.66
    therapy, 7.64–7.65
  special damages
    case managers, carers and buddies, 7.56–7.63
    counselling and therapy, 7.64–7.65

Damages – *contd*
  special damages – *contd*
    generally, 7.55
    inpatient psychological assessment and rehabilitation, 7.67–7.69
    outpatient facilities, 7.66
    short term treatment interventions, 7.64–7.69
    therapy, 7.64–7.65
Delayed onset of serious psychiatric injury accompanying physical injury
  primary victims, and, 2.12–2.13
Depression
  anxiety, and, 6.42–6.43
  generally, 6.34–6.41
Deputyship applications
  personal welfare
    assessment of capacity, 9.92
    contested applications, 9.94–9.97
    COP 1 form, 9.87
    COP 1B form, 9.88
    COP 2 form, 9.89–9.91
    COP 3 form. 9.92
    COP 4 form, 9.87
    costs, 9.98–9.103
    personal welfare decisions, 9.93
    supporting information, 9.88
  property and affairs
    assessment of capacity, 9.84–9.85
    contested applications, 9.94–9.97
    COP 1 form, 9.78–9.81
    COP 1A form, 9.82
    COP 3 form. 9.84–9.85
    COP 4 form, 9.86
    costs, 9.98–9.103
    supporting information, 9.82–9.83
    undertakings by deputy, 9.86
Diagnosis
  types of psychiatric injury, and, 6.1–6.5
Direct participants in events
  brain injury, 2.7–2.9
  delayed onset of serious psychiatric injury accompanying physical injury, 2.12–2.13
  introduction, 2.3
  'personality change', 2.7–2.9
  psychiatric injury associated with significant physical injury, 2.4
  serious psychiatric injury associated with minor physical injury, 2.10–2.11
  soft-tissue injury and depression, 2.5–2.6
Disability discrimination
  'arising from a disability', 5.54
  association discrimination, 5.55–5.57
  causes of action, and, 1.50–1.54
  damages, 5.64–5.68
  direct discrimination, 5.49–5.51

Disability dscrimination – *contd*
generally, 5.44–5.45
indirect discrimination, 5.52–5.53
injury to feelings, 5.65–5.67
introduction, 5.43
meaning, 5.44
perceived discrimination, 5.55–5.57
practical considerations in claim, 5.58–5.63
protected characteristics, 5.44–5.45
psychiatric injury, and, 5.46–5.48
Discrimination
See also **Disability discrimination**
causes of action, and, 1.50–1.54
introduction, 5.43
primary victims, and, 3.14–3.15
protected characteristics, 5.44–5.45
Divisible injury
future developments, 10.43–10.44
generally, 7.86–7.93
DSM-IV
damages, and, 7.10
types of psychiatric injury, and, 6.3–6.5

'Eggshell personality'
secondary victims, and, 4.24
Eggshell skull rule
primary victims, and, 2.19
Employer's liability
breach of duty, 3.5–3.
development of case law, 3.5–3.8
harassment, 3.12–3.13
Hatton guidelines, 3.9–3.11
pleural plaques, 3.16–3.18
unfair dismissal, 3.14–3.15
Enduring powers of attorney
mental capacity, and, 9.7
Exacerbation of existing conditions
generally, 6.61–6.64
Exaggeration by client
dealings with client, and, 8.84–8.90
Experts
choice, 8.36–8.47
difficulties with obtaining reports, 6.110–6.114
introduction, 6.98
medical notes and reports, 6.104–6.109
psychiatrists, 6.99
psychologists, 6.100
psychometric tests, 6.102–6.103
psychotherapists, 6.101

Factitious disorder
generally, 6.58
Family of client
handling clients, and, 8.32–8.34

'Fireman's rule'
primary victims, and, 2.46
'Flight or fight' mechanisms
types of psychiatric injury, and, 6.23
Foreseeability
causes of action, and, 1.39–1.40
Fraud by client
dealings with client, and, 8.84–8.90
Funding issues
See also **Costs**
future developments, 10.47–10.48

General damages
general psychiatric damage
introduction, 7.21
minor, 7.31–7.34
moderate, 7.28–7.30
moderately severe, 7.26–7.27
severe, 7.22–7.25
generally, 7.13–7.20
JSB Guidelines, 7.14–7.19
post-traumatic stress disorder
introduction, 7.35
minor, 7.40
moderate, 7.39
moderately severe, 7.38
severe, 7.36–7.37
problematic medical/psychological conditions, 7.41–7.49
General psychiatric damage
introduction, 7.21
minor, 7.31–7.34
moderate, 7.28–7.30
moderately severe, 7.26–7.27
severe, 7.22–7.25
GP notes and records
claim process, and, 8.15–8.25
Grief
distinction from psychiatric injury, and, 1.31

Handling clients
capacity, 8.50–8.59
coming off the record, 8.60–8.63
difficult clients, 8.48–8.49
Harassment claims
checklist, 5.42
defendants, 5.25–5.26
generally, 5.23–5.24
meaning, 5.27–5.36
outside the workplace, 5.37–5.41
primary victims, and, 3.12–3.13
Head injuries
generally, 6.74–6.76
Hillsborough disaster
secondary victims, and, 4.3–4.7

'Hindsight'
secondary victims, and, 4.25–4.27
Holiday cases
causes of action, and, 1.48
Hysterical conversion disorder
generally, 6.47
meaning of 'psychiatric injury', and, 1.9

ICD 10
damages, and, 7.10
types of psychiatric injury, and, 6.3–6.4
Inability to make a decision
'communicate his decision', 9.32
introduction, 9.25
'part of process of making the decision', 9.30–9.31
'retain that information', 9.28–9.29
'understand the information relevant to the decision', 9.26–9.27
'use or weigh that information', 9.30–9.31
Individual needs assessments
special damages, and, 7.55
Infliction of harm
generally, 5.8–5.11
Injury to feelings
discrimination, and, 1.17
Inpatient psychiatric care
dealings with client, and, 8.80–8.83
Inpatient psychological assessment and rehabilitation
special damages, and, 7.67–7.69
Intentional acts
assault
generally, 5.4–5.7
overview, 5.1
battery
generally, 5.2–5.3
overview, 5.1
contractual liability, 5.20–5.22
criminal injuries compensation scheme, 5.12–5.19
disability discrimination
'arising from a disability', 5.54
association discrimination, 5.55–5.57
damages, 5.64–5.68
direct discrimination, 5.49–5.51
generally, 5.44–5.45
indirect discrimination, 5.52–5.53
injury to feelings, 5.65–5.67
introduction, 5.43
meaning, 5.44
perceived discrimination, 5.55–5.57
practical considerations in claim, 5.58–5.63
protected characteristics, 5.44–5.45
psychiatric injury, and, 5.46–5.48

Intentional acts – *contd*
harassment
claims checklist, 5.42
defendants, 5.25–5.26
generally, 5.23–5.24
meaning, 5.27–5.36
outside the workplace, 5.37–5.41
infliction of harm, 5.8–5.11
'Involuntary participants'
primary victims, and, 2.55–2.64

JSB Guidelines
general damages, and, 7.14–7.19

Lasting powers of attorney
mental capacity, and, 9.7
Law Commission papers and reports
'Law on Damages' (LCCP No 9, 2007), 10.2–10.5
'Liability for Psychiatric Illness' (LCCP No 137, 1995), 1.1
'Liability for Psychiatric Illness' (Law Com No 249)
generally, 10.1
insurers, and, 10.13–10.16
Legal expense insurers dealings with client, and, 8.35
Litigation
mental capacity, and, 9.58–9.64

Malingering
background, 8.84–8.90
detection, 8.95–8.98
generally, 8.91–8.94
symptom validity testing, 8.98
video evidence, 8.96–8.97
Managing property and affairs
deputyship applications
assessment of capacity, 9.84–9.85
contested applications, 9.94–9.97
COP 1 form, 9.78–9.81
COP 1A form, 9.82
COP 3 form, 9.84–9.85
COP 4 form, 9.86
costs, 9.98–9.103
supporting information, 9.82–9.83
undertakings by deputy, 9.86
generally, 9.65–9.74
Material contribution
causation of damage, and, 7.84–7.85
Means by which events are perceived
secondary victims, and, 4.44–4.48
Means of perception
future developments, 10.40–10.42
generally, 4.65–4.67

Medical notes and records
claim process, and, 8.15–8.25
types of psychiatric injury, and, 6.104–6.109
Medication
types of psychiatric injury, and, 6.84
Mental Capacity Act 2005
acts in connection with care or treatment
generally, 9.49–9.51
litigation capacity, 9.58–9.64
powers of the court, 9.52–9.57
background, 9.3–9.6
best interests, 9.37–9.46
children lacking capacity, 9.47–9.48
Code of Practice, 9.9
Court of Protection
background, 9.4–9.5
generally, 9.11–9.13
enduring powers of attorney, 9.7
fundamental basis, 9.2
general principles, 9.14–9.21
generally, 9.7–9.10
historical perspective, 9.3–9.6
inability to make a decision
'communicate his decision', 9.32
introduction, 9.25
'part of process of making the decision', 9.30–9.31
'retain that information', 9.28–9.29
'understand the information relevant to the decision', 9.26–9.27
'use or weigh that information', 9.30–9.31
introduction, 9.1–9.2
lasting powers of attorney, 9.7
litigation capacity, 9.58–9.64
managing property and affairs, 9.65–9.74
personal welfare
applications, 9.87–9.92
decisions, 9.93
generally, 9.75–9.77
personal welfare decisions, 9.93
personal welfare deputyship
applications
assessment of capacity, 9.92
contested applications, 9.94–9.97
COP 1 form, 9.87
COP 1B form, 9.88
COP 2 form, 9.89–9.91
COP 3 form. 9.92
COP 4 form, 9.87
costs, 9.98–9.103
personal welfare decisions, 9.93
supporting information, 9.88
persons lacking capacity, 9.22–9.24
presumption of capacity, 9.2
principles, 9.14–9.21

Mental Capacity Act 2005 – *contd*
property and affairs
applications, 9.78–9.86
generally, 9.65–9.74
property and affairs deputyship
applications
assessment of capacity, 9.84–9.85
contested applications, 9.94–9.97
COP 1 form, 9.78–9.81
COP 1A form, 9.82
COP 3 form. 9.84–9.85
COP 4 form, 9.86
costs, 9.98–9.103
supporting information, 9.82–9.83
undertakings by deputy, 9.86
protection of client, 8.51–8.54
protection of staff, 8.55–8.59
Public Guardianship Office, 9.4
test for incapacity, 9.33–9.36
Mitigation
damages, and, 7.70–7.77
Munchausen's syndrome
generally, 6.58
Myalgic encephalopathy (ME)
generally, 6.48
Myofascial painsyndrome
generally, 6.60

Negligence
causes of action, 1.36–1.46
primary victims
See also **Primary victims**
non-shock cases, in, 3.1–3.23
shock cases, in, 2.1–2.66
secondary victims
See also **Secondary victims**
excluded categories, 4.49–4.55
Hillsborough disaster, 4.3–4.7
introduction, 4.1–4.2
Law Commission proposals, 4.56–4.59
meaning, 4.8–4.15
reasonable foreseeability, 4.16–4.48
subsequent case law, 4.60–4.69
summary, 4.70–4.73
Neighbour principle
secondary victims, and, 4.19
Nervous shock
meaning of 'psychiatric injury', and, 1.24
No fault liability scheme
generally, 10.17–10.19
'Normal phlegm'
secondary victims, and, 4.22–4.23

Obsessive compulsive disorder (OCD)
generally, 6.30–6.32

Occupational stress
discrimination claims, 3.14–3.15
employer's liability, 3.5–3.11
employment law, 3.14–3.15
future developments, 10.31–10.33
harassment, 3.12–3.13
pleural plaques, 3.16–3.18
OPCRIT
types of psychiatric injury, and, 6.2
Outpatient facilities
special damages, and, 7.66
Outpatient sessions
dealings with client, and, 8.78–8.79

Pain, suffering and loss of amenity
general damages, and, 7.13–7.20
Panic attacks
generally, 6.28–6.29
Pathological grief disorder
meaning of 'psychiatric injury', and, 1.9
Personal injury claims
meaning of 'psychiatric injury', and, 1.2
Personal welfare
decisions, 9.93
deputyship applications
assessment of capacity, 9.92
contested applications, 9.94–9.97
COP 1 form, 9.87
COP 1B form, 9.88
COP 2 form, 9.89–9.91
COP 3 form. 9.92
COP 4 form, 9.87
costs, 9.98–9.103
supporting information, 9.88
generally, 9.75–9.77
'Personality change'
primary victims, and, 2.7–2.9
Personality disorder
generally, 6.63–6.64
Phobias and anxieties
agoraphobia, 6.27
'flight or fight' mechanisms, 6.23
generally, 6.23
obsessive compulsive disorder, 6.30–6.32
panic attacks, 6.28–6.29
phobic avoidance, 6.23
social phobia, 6.33
travel anxiety, 6.24–6.25
Physical injury
types of psychiatric injury, and, 6.77
Pleural plaques
non-shock cases, in, 3.16–3.18
shock cases, in, 2.35
Post-traumatic stress disorder (PTSD)
avoidance, 6.13
criteria A, 6.9–6.11
criteria B, 6.12

Post-traumatic stress disorder (PTSD) – *contd*
criteria C, 6.13
criteria D, 6.14–6.22
general damages, and
introduction, 7.35
minor, 7.40
moderate, 7.39
moderately severe, 7.38
severe, 7.36–7.37
generally, 6.6–6.7
hyper-arousal, 6.14–6.22
meaning of 'psychiatric injury', and, 1.11
numbing, 6.13
primary victims, and, 2.4
re-experiencing symptoms, 6.12
secondary victims, and, 4.64
Pre-existing vulnerability
generally, 6.78–6.82
Primary victims
attending interviews with mass murderer, 3.23
brain injury, 2.7–2.9
causes of action, and, 1.44
damages, and, 7.5
delayed onset of serious psychiatric injury accompanying physical injury, 2.12–2.13
direct participants in events
brain injury, 2.7–2.9
delayed onset of serious psychiatric injury accompanying physical injury, 2.12–2.13
introduction, 2.3
'personality change', 2.7–2.9
psychiatric injury associated with significant physical injury, 2.4
serious psychiatric injury associated with minor physical injury, 2.10–2.11
soft-tissue injury and depression, 2.5–2.6
discrimination claims, 3.14–3.15
employer's liability
breach of duty, 3.5–3.
development of case law, 3.5–3.8
harassment, 3.12–3.13
Hatton guidelines, 3.9–3.11
pleural plaques, 3.16–3.18
unfair dismissal, 3.14–3.15
harassment claims, 3.12–3.13
introduction, 2.1–2.2
no physical injury and no shocking event, with, 2.41
non-shock cases, in
employer's liability, 3.5–3.11
harassment, 3.12–3.13

Primary victims – *contd*
  non-shock cases, in – *contd*
    introduction, 3.1–3.4
    non-employer's liability, 3.19–3.23
    pleural plaques, 3.16–3.18
    stress at work, 3.5–3.18
    unfair dismissal, 3.14–3.15
  occupational stress
    discrimination claims, 3.14–3.15
    employer's liability, 3.5–3.11
    employment law, 3.14–3.15
    harassment, 3.12–3.13
    pleural plaques, 3.16–3.18
  other 'involuntary participants', 2.55–2.64
  'personality change', 2.7–2.9
  physical injury to claimant was foreseeable, where, 2.14–2.40
  pleural plaques, 3.16–3.18
  psychiatric injury associated with significant physical injury, 2.4
  'pure' psychiatric injury arising from accident
    no physical injury and no shocking event, with, 2.41
    physical injury to claimant was foreseeable, where, 2.14–2.40
  rescuers, 2.42–2.54
  secondary victims, and, 4.68–4.69
  serious psychiatric injury associated with minor physical injury, 2.10–2.11
  'shock cases', in
    direct participants in events, 2.3–2.13
    introduction, 2.1–2.2
    other 'involuntary participants', 2.55–2.64
    'pure' psychiatric injury arising from accident, 2.14–2.41
    summary, 2.65–2.66
  soft-tissue injury and depression, 2.5–2.6
  stress at work
    discrimination claims, 3.14–3.15
    employer's liability, 3.5–3.11
    employment law, 3.14–3.15
    harassment, 3.12–3.13
    pleural plaques, 3.16–3.18
  unfair dismissal, 3.14–3.15
  witnessing destruction of property, 3.19–3.21
Problematic medical/psychological conditions
  general damages, and, 7.41–7.49
Property and affairs
  deputyship applications
    assessment of capacity, 9.84–9.85
    contested applications, 9.94–9.97
    COP 1 form, 9.78–9.81
    COP 1A form, 9.82

Property and affairs – *contd*
  deputyship applications – *contd*
    COP 3 form. 9.84–9.85
    COP 4 form, 9.86
    costs, 9.98–9.103
    supporting information, 9.82–9.83
    undertakings by deputy, 9.86
  generally, 9.65–9.74
Proportionality
  future developments, 10.48
Provisional damages
  generally, 7.78–7.82
Proximity
  causes of action, and, 1.40–1.41
Proximity in time and space
  generally, 4.39–4.43
  interpretation, 4.61–4.62
  summary, 4.72
Psychiatric injury
  adjustment disorders, 6.44–6.45
  agoraphobia, 6.27
  alcohol misuse, 6.68–6.73
  anxieties and phobias
    agoraphobia, 6.27
    depression, and, 6.42–6.43
    'flight or fight' mechanisms, 6.23
    generally, 6.23
    obsessive compulsive disorder, 6.30–6.32
    panic attacks, 6.28–6.29
    phobic avoidance, 6.23
    social phobia, 6.33
    travel anxiety, 6.24–6.25
  attention deficit and hyperactivity disorder, 6.96
  autistic disorders, 6.94–6.95
  bipolar affective disorder, 6.67
  brain injuries, 6.74–6.76
  children, 6.92–6.97
  chronic fatigue syndrome, 6.48–6.50
  chronic pain, 6.52–6.60
  classification systems, 6.3
  clinical opinion, and, 6.2
  cognitive behavioural psychotherapy, 6.85–6.89
  complex regional pain syndromes, 6.59
  depression
    anxiety, and, 6.42–6.43
    generally, 6.34–6.41
  diagnosis, 6.1–6.5
  DSM-IV-TR, 6.3–6.5
  exacerbation of existing conditions, 6.61–6.64
  experts
    difficulties with obtaining reports, 6.110–6.114
    introduction, 6.98

Psychiatric injury – *contd*
　experts – *contd*
　　medical notes and reports, 6.104–6.109
　　psychiatrists, 6.99
　　psychologists, 6.100
　　psychometric tests, 6.102–6.103
　　psychotherapists, 6.101
　factitious disorder, 6.58
　'flight or fight' mechanisms, 6.23
　head injuries, 6.74–6.76
　hysterical conversion disorder, 6.47
　ICD 10, 6.3–6.4
　meaning, 1.1–1.18
　medical notes and reports, 6.104–6.109
　medication, and, 6.84
　Munchausen's syndrome, 6.58
　myalgic encephalopathy (ME), 6.48
　myofascial painsyndrome, 6.60
　obsessive compulsive disorder, 6.30–6.32
　OPCRIT, 6.2
　panic attacks, 6.28–6.29
　personality disorder, 6.63–6.64
　phobias and anxieties
　　agoraphobia, 6.27
　　'flight or fight' mechanisms, 6.23
　　generally, 6.23
　　obsessive compulsive disorder, 6.30–6.32
　　panic attacks, 6.28–6.29
　　phobic avoidance, 6.23
　　social phobia, 6.33
　　travel anxiety, 6.24–6.25
　physical injury, and, 6.77
　post-traumatic stress disorder
　　avoidance, 6.13
　　criteria A, 6.9–6.11
　　criteria B, 6.12
　　criteria C, 6.13
　　criteria D, 6.14–6.22
　　generally, 6.6–6.7
　　hyper-arousal, 6.14–6.22
　　numbing, 6.13
　　re-experiencing symptoms, 6.12
　pre-existing vulnerability, 6.78–6.82
　psychometric instruments, 6.2
　psychometric tests, 6.102–6.103
　psychosis, 6.65
　psychotic disorders, 6.65–6.67
　recognised psychiatric conditions, 6.1–6.5
　schizophrenia, 6.66
　SCID-R, 6.2
　'signs' observed, 6.2
　sleep disturbance, 6.35
　social phobia, 6.33
　somatisation, 6.46–6.51
　structural brain injuries, 6.74–6.76
　substance misuse, 6.68–6.73

Psychiatric injury – *contd*
　'symptoms' described, 6.2
　travel anxiety, 6.24–6.25
　treatments, 6.83–6.91
　types, 6.6–6.73
　whiplash, and, 6.77
Psychiatric injury associated with significant physical injury
　primary victims, and, 2.4
Psychiatric injury claims
　areas of concern, 1.27–1.34
　attitudes of defendants
　　exaggeration, 8.84–8.90
　　fraud, 8.84–8.90
　　generally, 8.84–8.90
　　malingering, 8.91–8.98
　BIMCA Rehabilitation Code 2007, and, 8.64–8.74
　building a team approach
　　client, 8.32–8.34
　　counsel, 8.29–8.31
　　family of client, 8.32–8.34
　　introduction, 8.26–8.28
　　legal expense insurers, 8.35
　capacity of clients
　　generally, 8.50
　　Mental Capacity Act, 8.51–8.59
　case management, 8.75–8.76
　causes of action
　　contractual claims, 1.47–1.49
　　criminal injuries compensation, 1.55
　　holiday cases, 1.48
　　introduction, 1.35
　　negligence, 1.36–1.46
　　statutory discrimination, 1.50–1.54
　choice of experts, 8.36–8.47
　coming off the record, 8.60–8.63
　costs, 8.99–8.107
　counselling, 8.78–8.79
　counsel's role, 8.29–8.31
　difficult clients, 8.48–8.49
　exaggeration by client, 8.84–8.90
　family of client, 8.32–8.34
　fraud by client, 8.84–8.90
　GP notes and records, 8.15–8.25
　handling clients
　　capacity, 8.50–8.59
　　coming off the record, 8.60–8.63
　　difficult clients, 8.48–8.49
　history, 1.19–1.26
　identification of potential injury, 8.1–8.9
　in-patient psychiatric care, 8.80–8.83
　legal expense insurers' role, 8.35
　malingering
　　background, 8.84–8.90
　　detection, 8.95–8.98
　　generally, 8.91–8.94

Psychiatric injury claims – *contd*
  malingering – *contd*
    symptom validity testing, 8.98
    video evidence, 8.96–8.97
    medical records, 8.15–8.25
    Mental Capacity Act, and
      protection of client, 8.51–8.54
      protection of staff, 8.55–8.59
    psychiatric outpatient sessions, 8.78–8.79
    psychiatric rehabilitation facilities, 8.77
    rehabilitation approach, 8.64–8.74
    retainer, and, 8.99–8.107
    review of past medical history, 8.10–8.25
    symptom validity testing, 8.98
    team approach, 8.26–8.28
    video evidence, 8.96–8.97
Psychiatric outpatient sessions
  dealings with client, and, 8.78–8.79
Psychiatric rehabilitation facilities
  dealings with client, and, 8.77
Psychometric instruments
  generally, 6.2
Psychometric tests
  generally, 6.102–6.103
Psychosis
  generally, 6.65
Psychotic disorders
  generally, 6.65–6.67
Public Guardianship Office
  generally, 9.4
Public policy
  secondary victims, and, 4.18
'Pure' psychiatric injury arising from accident
  no physical injury and no shocking event, with, 2.41
  physical injury to claimant was foreseeable, where, 2.14–2.40

Reasonable foreseeability
  close ties of love and affection, 4.32–4.38
  'customary phlegm', 4.22–4.23
  'eggshell personality', 4.24
  generally, 4.16–4.21
  'hindsight', 4.25–4.27
  means by which events are perceived, 4.44–4.48
  neighbour principle, and, 4.19
  'normal phlegm', 4.22–4.23
  proximity in time and space, 4.39–4.43
  public policy, and, 4.18
  'shock', 4.28–4.31
  summary, 4.71
Recipients of news
  secondary victims, and, 4.54–4.55
Recognised psychiatric illness
  damages, and, 7.10

'Recognised psychiatric injury'
  future developments, 10.23–10.25
  generally, 6.1–6.5
  meaning, 1.10
Rehabilitation approach
  claim process, and, 8.64–8.74
Rescuers
  future developments, 10.28–10.30
  primary victims, and, 2.42–2.54
  secondary victims, and, 4.11
Retainer
  claim process, and, 8.99–8.107
Review of past medical history
  claim process, and, 8.10–8.25

Schizophrenia
  generally, 6.66
SCID-R
  types of psychiatric injury, and, 6.2
Secondary victims
  aftermath
    generally, 4.39–4.43
    summary, 4.72
  broadcasters, and, 4.65–4.67
  case law
    Alcock v South Yorkshire Police, 4.3–4.15
    background, 4.2
    Page v Smith, 4.12–4.15
    post-*Alcock*, 4.60–4.69
  causes of action, and, 1.44
  close ties of love and affection
    future developments, 10.34–10.37
    generally, 4.32–4.38
    summary, 4.72
  'customary phlegm', 4.22–4.23
  damages, and, 7.6
  distinction from primary victims
    generally, 4.70
    introduction, 4.9
  'eggshell personality', 4.24
  excluded categories
    introduction, 4.49
    recipients of news, 4.54–4.55
    self-harm be defendant, 4.50–4.53
  Hillsborough disaster, 4.3–4.7
  'hindsight', 4.25–4.27
  history of claims, and, 1.26
  introduction, 4.1–4.2
  Law Commission proposals, 4.56–4.59
  meaning, 4.8–4.15
  means by which events are perceived, 4.44–4.48
  means of perception
    future developments, 10.40–10.42
    generally, 4.65–4.67
  neighbour principle, and, 4.19

Secondary victims – *contd*
  'normal phlegm', 4.22–4.23
  post-traumatic stress disorder, 4.64
  primary victims' liability, and, 4.68–4.69
  proximity in time and space
    future developments, 10.38–10.39
    generally, 4.39–4.43
    interpretation, 4.61–4.62
    summary, 4.72
  public policy, and, 4.18
  reasonable foreseeability
    close ties of love and affection, 4.32–4.38
    'customary phlegm', 4.22–4.23
    'eggshell personality', 4.24
    generally, 4.16–4.21
    'hindsight', 4.25–4.27
    means by which events are perceived, 4.44–4.48
    neighbour principle, and, 4.19
    'normal phlegm', 4.22–4.23
    proximity in time and space, 4.39–4.43
    public policy, and, 4.18
    'shock', 4.28–4.31
    summary, 4.71
  recipients of news, 4.54–4.55
  rescuers, and, 4.11
  self-harm be defendant, 4.50–4.53
  'shock'
    generally, 4.28–4.31
    summary, 4.72
  subsequent case law
    broadcasters, 4.65–4.67
    interpretation of proximity, 4.61–4.62
    introduction, 4.60
    means of perception, 4.65–4.67
    sudden, shocking event, 4.63–4.64
    summary, 4.70–4.73
  time and space
    future developments, 10.38–10.39
    generally, 4.39–4.43
    interpretation of proximity, 4.61–4.62
    summary, 4.72
Self-harm by defendant
  secondary victims, and, 4.50–4.53
Serious psychiatric injury associated with minor physical injury
  primary victims, and, 2.10–2.11
'Shock'
  primary victims, and
    direct participants in events, 2.3–2.13
    introduction, 2.1–2.2
    other 'involuntary participants', 2.55–2.64
    'pure' psychiatric injury arising from accident, 2.14–2.41
    summary, 2.65–2.66

'Shock' – *contd*
  secondary victims, and
    generally, 4.28–4.31
    summary, 4.72
Short term treatment interventions
  counselling, 7.64–7.65
  inpatient psychological assessment and rehabilitation, 7.67–7.69
  outpatient facilities, 7.66
  therapy, 7.64–7.65
Significant physical injury associated with psychiatric injury
  primary victims, and, 2.4
Sleep disturbance
  generally, 6.35
Social phobia
  generally, 6.33
Soft-tissue injury and depression
  primary victims, and, 2.5–2.6
Somatisation
  choice of expert, and, 8.46
  chronic pain, and, 6.53–6.54
  damages, and
    problematic medical/psychological conditions, 7.41–7.49
    PSLA, 7.19
  depression, and, 6.41
  generally, 6.46–6.51
  malingering, and, 8.91
  medical notes and records, and, 6.105
  psychiatric experts, and, 6.99
  whiplash, and, 6.77
Special damages
  case managers, carers and buddies, 7.56–7.63
  counselling, 7.64–7.65
  generally, 7.55
  inpatient psychological assessment and rehabilitation, 7.67–7.69
  outpatient facilities, 7.66
  short term treatment interventions
    counselling and therapy, 7.64–7.65
    inpatient psychological assessment and rehabilitation, 7.67–7.69
    outpatient facilities, 7.66
    therapy, 7.64–7.65
Statutory discrimination
  causes of action, and, 1.50–1.54
  'arising from a disability', 5.54
  association discrimination, 5.55–5.57
  causes of action, and, 1.50–1.54
  damages, 5.64–5.68
  direct discrimination, 5.49–5.51
  generally, 5.44–5.45
  indirect discrimination, 5.52–5.53
  injury to feelings, 5.65–5.67

Statutory discrimination – *contd*
  introduction, 5.43
  meaning, 5.44
  perceived discrimination, 5.55–5.57
  practical considerations in claim, 5.58–5.63
  protected characteristics, 5.44–5.45
  psychiatric injury, and, 5.46–5.48
Statutory harassment
  claims checklist, 5.42
  defendants, 5.25–5.26
  generally, 5.23–5.24
  meaning, 5.27–5.36
  outside the workplace, 5.37–5.41
Stress at work
  discrimination claims, 3.14–3.15
  employer's liability, 3.5–3.11
  employment law, 3.14–3.15
  harassment, 3.12–3.13
  future developments, 10.31–10.33
  pleural plaques, 3.16–3.18
Structural brain injuries
  generally, 6.74–6.76
Substance misuse
  generally, 6.68–6.73
Sudden, shocking event
  secondary victims, and, 4.63–4.64
Symptom validity testing
  malingering, and, 8.98

Therapy
  special damages, and, 7.64–7.65
Time and space, proximity of
  generally, 4.39–4.43
  interpretation of proximity, 4.61–4.62
  summary, 4.72
Travel anxiety
  generally, 6.24–6.25
Treatments
  types of psychiatric injury, and, 6.83–6.91

Unfair dismissal
  primary victims, and, 3.14–3.15

Video evidence
  malingering, and, 8.96–8.97

'Whiplash' injury
  primary victims, and, 2.5–2.6
  types of psychiatric injury, and, 6.77
Witnessing destruction of property
  primary victims, and, 3.19–3.21
Workplace stress
  discrimination claims, 3.14–3.15
  employer's liability, 3.5–3.11
  employment law, 3.14–3.15
  harassment, 3.12–3.13
  future developments, 10.31–10.33
  pleural plaques, 3.16–3.18